EVERYDAY BUSINESS
SPEECH

EVERYDAY BUSINESS
SPEECH

By

ALFRED D. HUSTON

Formerly of the Division of Speech,
University of Illinois

And

ROBERT A. SANDBERG

Formerly of the Division of Speech,
University of Illinois

PRENTICE-HALL, INC.

New York

First Printing.....................March, 1943
Second Printing................December, 1945
Third Printing....................August, 1946
Fourth Printing.....................July, 1947
Fifth Printing....................March, 1948
Sixth Printing...................August, 1948
Seventh Printing.................January, 1949
Eighth Printing......................July, 1949
Ninth Printing.....................April, 1950

PRINTED IN THE UNITED STATES OF AMERICA

Preface

E*veryday Business Speech* is the outgrowth of the authors' efforts to supply a practical course in speech to those whose business or professional career will make demands upon their ability to speak effectively. Recognizing that the average person in business does more conference speaking than public speaking, we chose to begin our work at that point. An investigation was made of the most common types of speech situations engaged in by business and professional people. In this study we were aided by the personnel and training departments of numerous large organizations which generously offered their time and advice and supplied us with quantities of material for study. We gratefully acknowledge the valuable contributions to our work made by the following organizations: Procter and Gamble Co., The Armstrong Cork Co., General Motors Corporation, The Firestone Rubber Co., The Chamber of Commerce of the United States, The Metropolitan Life Insurance Co., The National Association of Credit Men, The National Dry Goods Association, Pepsodent, Kiwanis International, and the American Farm Bureau Federation.

It was found that students who gained some effectiveness as conference speakers invariably could prepare and deliver effective public speeches with a minimum of instruction, the chief problem being one of adaptation to a larger audience. Our job then was, first, to offer training in the common types of conference speaking, giving the student speaker an insight into the importance of having complete mastery of his subject material, organizing it for efficient and effective use, and presenting it in an interesting manner; and second, to show how the techniques of the conference may be modified for use on the platform.

The book was first prepared in mimeographed form for use in the Business and Professional Speaking courses at the University of Illinois. The experimental period was passed, and the merits of the methods used were firmly established. Students were eager to engage in the realistic speaking assignments in which they could see a practical application. Their suggestions and criticisms aided the authors in the final revision.

We are indebted to our friends and associates who have read the manuscript and who have given valuable criticism and encouragement, especially Professors J. H. McBurney and Irving J. Lee of Northwestern University; our colleagues, Professors W. M. Parrish and S. J. Crandell of the University of Illinois; Professor Maynard Lee Daggy of the State College of Washington; and Howard Chenery of Central High School, Kalamazoo, Michigan. For invaluable aid with the chapter on application interviews we are indebted to Professor C. R. Anderson of the University of Illinois; for suggestions on the chapter on sales we are indebted to Professors Frederic A. Russell and Frank H. Beach of the University of Illinois and Bernard Mosier, District Manager of Country Life Insurance Co. To these kind critics and friends we owe much of whatever is good in this volume, though they are in no wise responsible for its defects.

For generous permission to quote their speeches we are indebted to the following: Edwin A. Boss, President of the Boss Hotels, Paul G. Hoffman, President of the Studebaker Corporation, Franklin Bliss Snyder, President of Northwestern University, Col. John H. Jouett, President of the Aeronautical Chamber of Commerce of America, Bruce Barton, President of Batten, Barton, Durstine and Osborn, and Dr. Ernest Freemont Tittle, pastor of the First Methodist Church of Evanston, Illinois.

A. D. H.
R. A. S.

Contents

PART I

Introduction

PART II

The Business Conference

PART III

Public Speaking

Foreword to the Instructor

IN THIS BOOK it is our purpose to supply a course of study which provides realistic assignments in the types of speech situations most common in business and professional employment. The modern student, ever conscious of the practical application of his work, enters wholeheartedly into the speaking assignments of such a course. When he is given opportunity to speak in situations likely to be encountered after graduation, he makes better preparation and attacks his problem with more enthusiasm.

In several years' experience teaching business and professional speaking we have been convinced of the wisdom of giving instruction in the business conference, not only because conference speaking has been a rather neglected field of speech training, but also because it is a valuable aid to the art of public speaking.

We have found that the teaching of conference speaking is wholly practical and effective. Nervousness and stagefright become almost negligible problems after the first two or three conferences. The method is disarming to the student and enables him to concentrate on presentation of material. We insist on adequate preparation and organization in all assignments. Even though the course of presentation may be altered by questions and objections from the conferee, it has been shown that the student who has a well-prepared plan is the most likely to achieve his specific purpose. A conference can be organized and outlined in a way similar to that used for a public speech.

The transition from conference speaking to public speaking has been found to be highly successful. The informality and directness fostered in the conference is carried over into the public speech. After several weeks' work on conference speaking, students go to the platform and maintain their directness and conversational spirit.

The ABLE MAN Theory. If nothing more, the study of the ABLE MAN emphasizes that effective speaking requires something in addition to preparation of material and delivery technique. It will be obvious that our ABLE MAN is an imaginary and utopian figure. Students will say that, according to the definition, "no one could ever be an ABLE MAN." That is probably right, but it will be readily admitted that the closer one can approach the definition, the greater will be his chances of securing respect and attention from his audiences, other things being equal. The idea is introduced to the class during the first week, and thereafter private criticism may be given from time to time—criticism which will show the student the relationship between pure technique and personal characteristics. Such comment keeps the ABLE MAN idea alive without making a fetish of it.

In the original concept of the ABLE MAN, from Aristotle and Quintillian, the name has been taken to signify the "good" in a man, identifying the individual as honest, sincere, and possessing capabilities which set him "out from the crowd." If, in our writing, the idea of success and material attainment predominates the original definition, it results more from our effort to make the idea palatable than from a desire to misconstrue the meaning.

The Conference in Class. The assignment of business conferences for classroom recitation does not constitute a problem for the instructor, and it has a definite advantage in that it doubles the amount of speaking time allowed each student. Students act as conferees and as conferrers, and are graded on their work in both capacities.

If a large platform is available in the front of the room, one may set an office scene by using a desk and two or three chairs, or it may be set on the floor in front of the class. It may be helpful to provide other office property such as a typewriter, telephone, and desk equipment. These are not necessary, but they add to the feeling of realism.

The Public Speeches. After students become acquainted with the conference technique some time should be spent in studying Chapter XI and in pointing out in discussion the ways in which conference and public speech differ. Selected readings on delivery in other speech books may be helpful at this time. Study of the samples of public speeches in Chapter XIII prove a valuable aid. One or two of these should be outlined to point up matters of organization and style.

When the public speeches begin, it is wise to stress the fact that the only essential difference to be considered is the adaptation to a number of people. Show how this fact must affect the choice of material and the presentation of it.

On the first one or two speeches the transition from conference speaking may be made easier by allowing a few minutes for questions after each speech, or even by interrupting the speaker during his talk to ask a question or to seek clarification of a point. Questions will not disturb the speaker nor will interruptions upset his plan.

On occasion we have found it helpful to urge the class to show their approval of a speaker by giving him generous applause. Indications of disapproval are not encouraged but they are often indicated rather obviously. In this way the speakers may be made aware of their progress, and, as is true of most speakers, may feed on the fruits of their rhetoric. Furthermore, members of the audience feel a greater sense of participation and thus become more attentive.

The Course of Study. The following suggested schedule for the business and professional speaking course is outlined for a class which meets thirty-two times. However, it may be altered freely to serve in classes which meet more or less often. Furthermore, it may be advisable to revise the content of the assignments to meet the needs of the particular type of students enrolled. Thus, if the class is primarily interested in salesmanship and promotion, additional assignments in the sales conference and the promotional type of speech may be used. If a large number of engineers and professional students are enrolled, the emphasis may be placed on the expositional conferences, the oral report, and the question of policy.

In certain situations, where the class is composed of men and women who have had experience in conference speaking, it may be felt that greater emphasis should be placed on public speaking. This would be particularly useful in adult businessmen's classes.

In our classes we have attempted to hold our recitations in several different rooms from time to time. Here again there is a tedious problem of administration, but speakers learn to adapt themselves to a variety of physical surroundings. It is advisable to use large rooms for the public speeches.

When time has permitted we have held a dinner for the classes toward the end of the term.   Students have been made responsible for all arrangements.   The purpose of the dinner is to provide a realistic after-dinner speaking situation during which time each student presents a short speech on a subject of his own choosing.   It has been said that the only requirement for an after-dinner speech is that it come after dinner.   We have learned to respect the definition.   Again, the aim is to break down the unreality of the classroom atmosphere and to encourage spontaneity.

*Suggested Schedule for Business and
Professional Speaking Course*

*Class
Meeting*

1. Lecture: Organization of course and orientation
   Assign: Chapters I and II for discussion
2. Discussion: Chapters I and II
   Assign: Self-analysis paper and arrange conference with instructor
3. Lecture: Conversation as the basic speech situation
   Assign: Chapters III and IV
4. Discussion: Chapters III and IV
   Assign: Four-minute conferences demonstrating rhetorical techniques
5. Demonstrations: (Assign: Chapter V)
6. Demonstrations continued
7. Discussion: Chapter V
   Assign: Chapter VI
8. Discussion: Chapter VI
   Assign: Six-minute expositional conferences
9. Expositional conferences
   Assign: Chapter VII
10. Expositional conferences continued
11. Expositional conferences continued
12. Discussion: Chapter VII
    Assign: Chapter VIII
13. Discussion: Chapter VIII
    Assign: Question of policy conferences (policy-determining conferences) 20-50–minute conferences depending on the number of conferees participating
14. Question of policy conferences
    Assign: Chapter IX
15. Question of policy conferences continued
16. Question of policy conferences continued
17. Discussion: Chapter IX
    Assign: Six-eight–minute sales demonstration conferences

18. Sales demonstration conferences
19. Sales demonstration conferences continued
    Assign: Chapter X
    Prepare schedule for application interviews to be held outside of
    class. Assign due dates for company, job, and conferee analysis
    and application letter
20. Sales demonstration conferences continued
    Assign: Chapters XI and XII
    Memorize 3-minute selection for delivery practice
21. Discussion: Chapters XI and XII
22. Delivery practice. (Hold class in an auditorium or large lecture
    hall if possible.) During the time in which the class is having
    delivery practice, the application interviews will be held outside
    of class. Appointments are made with persons acting as the
    employers.
23. Delivery practice continued
24. Delivery practice continued
    Assign: Chapter XIII
25. Discussion: Chapter XIII
    Assign: Five-minute goodwill speeches
26. Goodwill speeches continued
27. Goodwill speeches continued
    Assign: Six-eight–minute policy-confirming speeches
28. Policy-confirming speeches
29. Policy-confirming speeches continued
30. Policy-confirming speeches continued
31. Final examination

Students are required to hand in outlines for all speeches at least
two class periods before the speech is due. These outlines are
graded by the instructor and returned to each student one class
period before the speech is due. The student then hands in his
final draft of the outline on the same day that he presents his
speech. The instructor then writes his final comments on the
outline and the speech as delivered, and returns the outline and
the comments to the student the following period.

Part I

INTRODUCTION

A Point of View

I. THE VALUE OF SPEECH IN A DEMOCRACY
    Patriotism kindled by speech
    Courage to speak
II. THE VALUE OF SPEECH IN BUSINESS
    Spokesman in business
    Business success dependent on salesmanship
III. THE VALUE OF SPEECH TO THE INDIVIDUAL
    Speech as part of personality
    Speech necessary to all business activity
        Speaking an everyday job
IV. THE PLAN OF STUDY
    Progressive steps to follow
        Conversation
        Conference speaking
        Public speaking
    The triad of effective speaking
        Speaker must be an ABLE MAN
        He must have something to say
        He must know how to say it

A Point of View

NOTICE

to

Citizens of the United States

You are hereby warned that from this date forward no person within the boundaries of this country or its territorial possessions shall be allowed the privilege of FREE SPEECH.

CAN YOU imagine what such a law would mean? Besides limiting your right to speak and write what you wished it would indirectly deprive you of your right to THINK as you wished! All means of human communication would be subjected to the strictest kind of regulation and censorship. Public gatherings would be outlawed, the radio and the press would be controlled by those in power, your business and personal correspondence would be carefully read by government-trained censors—in short, it would be impossible for you to express a single thought without permission.

Any encroachment upon the right of free speech constitutes a strangle hold on democracy. Among the diverse definitions of a democratic form of government the one which is most widely used and accepted is "the rule of the people." Such a definition presupposes that the people rule by their right to *speak* what is in their hearts and minds. One is not facetious in saying that "democracy is government by talk."

The Value of Speech in a Democracy

The greatest heritage of man is freedom but that heritage, by its very nature, implies responsibility in its exercise, if it is to be

3

protected and preserved.   Since freedom of speech is the only medium through which we can peacefully secure and hold all other
freedoms, the people of a democracy must learn to use speech with
effectiveness.

Patriotism kindled by speech

During the last twenty years people in this country have become apathetic in their demonstrations of patriotism.   A patriotic
population is a homogeneously active and united people striving
to preserve common ideals.   In it there is little room for the
selfish bickering of embittered factions or the quarreling, dissatis-
fied atmosphere that tends only to divert attention from the broad
principles of human freedom.

Patriotic feeling will continue in our democracy so long as our
people, united in a common cause, continue to express the pre-
vailing feelings of their hearts.   In the nineteenth century even
the youngest child had a chance on Friday afternoon to declaim
his fragment of a nationally known oration, some lines of patriotic
poetry, or some bit of sound political philosophy.   Americans felt
that this nation was the greatest thing that had ever happened to
mankind.   Not a Fourth of July passed without the Declaration
of Independence being read at home or at the village square.
Citizens were invited to express their thoughts concerning the
privilege of living in America, but they usually needed no invitation.   In small groups and large, patriotism lived through the
spoken word.   In the dawn of the twentieth century great scientific progress gave us the moving picture, the radio, and increased
opportunities for reading.   Certainly these things brought much
that was patriotic, but it was of a different sort.   It was not par-
ticipatory.   Citizens watched, listened, and read silently as the
common voice became stilled and a limited few increased their
control over the many.

Courage to speak

It is not necessary to limit the public utterance of any person.
It is paramount that every person exercise his right to think and
give voice to what he thinks.   Hitler's Germany tied the tongues
of its people to the everlasting shame of that government, but
even there private thoughts surge for expression.   The courage

that prompted Pastor Niemoeller to say, "Not you, Herr Hitler, but GOD is my Führer," defies dictatorship and glorifies the freedom of democracy. It is the essence of that freedom that requires all of us to exemplify the actions of our Niemoellers, Patrick Henrys, Jeffersons, Whitmans, and all like them. If a democracy is worth *fighting* for, it is worth *speaking* for. If democracy lives, it must be an operating democracy. The "rule of the people" must be heard in the home, on the street, in the factory, in the classroom, and in the halls and chambers of our government.

The Value of Speech in Business

Just as speech is essential to the life of democracy, it is also indispensable to business and professional activity. Speech is the most commonly used tool of communication; it is, indeed, the medium through which a large portion of business is conducted. It can no more be dispensed with in the day's work than can the wheels in the operation of a factory. One is dependent upon the other.

Spokesman in business

Any person experienced in business recognizes the necessity for making his ideas clear to the world. Men in the shop must work together, *not only with tools and machines, but with words as well*. Competition must be met in a battle of words and ideas, and these are the salesman's tools. Business interests must have a voice in the government. In fact, in any enterprise the tongue usually means the difference between success and failure. If two identical businesses operate on an equal technical basis, the one with the most effective voice will prevail. All business and professional people, those whose problem is purely technical and those directly involved in public relations, come sooner or later to the realization that only through effective use of speech can successful operation of their business be maintained.

Some few years ago business and industry suffered the reputation of being "hard and cruel" and lacking in regard for individual interests. The circumstances of depression and the increased influence of organized labor forced "big business" to pay more attention to the individual. Out of this *change of attitude* has grown a deliberate effort to "humanize" the whole of business and industry. The day of the "soulless corporation" is gone. The fact has been recognized that workers possess mind and initiative that can be made to operate effectively in the interests of the organization. A real emphasis on collective bargaining and employer-employee co-operation has emerged. This means that, more than ever, speech plays a vital part in business progress. Every person has a voice, and the opportunity to be heard is free for the asking.

Business success dependent on salesmanship

Surveys of opinion among persons engaged in all types of work show by an overwhelming majority that success is largely dependent upon the individual's ability to sell himself and his idea to his market. The history of scientific progress bolsters this opinion even more strikingly. Pasteur and Edison and all men of creative nature and accomplishment found it necessary to gain the acceptance of the people for whom they worked before attaining success in their field of work. Charles M. Schwab once made the statement that "We are all salesmen every day of our lives. We are selling our ideas, our plans, our knowledges and enthusiasms to those with whom we come in contact."

The Value of Speech to the Individual

The broader values and implications of speech in society and in business have their basis within the individual, and since speaking must be a personal problem, we are compelled to begin our study of *Everyday Business Speech* with the individual.

Speech as part of personality

You were introduced to a stranger yesterday. You exchanged a few words with him, and you made up your mind either that he was likable, intelligent, and friendly or that he was dull, sullen, and stupid. What did you think of him? Or, more important, what did he think of you? Or were you so ineffective as a person and as a speaker that he has already forgotten you? Will he say something complimentary about you when he speaks to mutual friends? Your success in creating a favorable impression and opinion stems directly from your ability as a speaker. It is impossible to separate your personality from your speech.

It has been estimated that the average person uses 30,000 words a day—30,000 words used and spoken effectively or 30,000 words working against the speaker. Can any person afford to live on day by day without giving the most careful attention to his speech? Each time a person speaks ineffectively, in conversation, in business conference, or on the platform, he is contributing to his own bankruptcy. He is increasing his personal liabilities.

Speech necessary to all business activity

Tomorrow countless sales will be lost because salesmen will be ineffective. They may say, "Business is bad," but it is not business! Salesmanagers will attempt to stimulate their salesmen to greater effort. Executives will meet to determine matters of policy vital to their organizations. Statesmen and politicians will be attempting to gain support for their proposals. Lawyers will argue cases. Architects will explain plans. Doctors will give instructions. Business associations will attempt large-scale promotional schemes. Civic organizations will solicit contributions. Hundreds of teachers will face thousands of students in the classroom. In all of these instances the ability to speak effectively will mean the difference between success and failure.

Daniel Webster once said, "If all my possessions and powers were taken from me with one exception, I would choose to keep the power of speech, for by it I could soon recover all the rest." Consider the possibilities! Thomas A. Edison's inventive genius, with all its universal benefits, might never have been brought to fruition had he not been able to convince his parents that he be allowed to experiment in the house. On March 4, 1933, President Roosevelt spoke to the entire nation and overnight aroused the people from deepest despair to a feeling of confidence and hope. His words were heard in millions of homes, words which were sincere and vigorous. Numerous examples could be cited to show the effect words have had in the accomplishment of important objectives. Furthermore, the case for speech is not weakened by the fact that unscrupulous persons have misused this power to gain ends opposed to the common good. The tremendous power achieved by Hitler and Mussolini in their respective countries was due in part to the effectiveness of their speaking ability in arousing the emotions of their people. Whether the motive is good or bad is beside the point. In fact, a higher degree of knowledge concerning the techniques of speech might have prevented the majority of people from succumbing to the irrational rhetoric of the dictator orators.

Speaking an everyday job. Few persons recognize that speech ability must be a constant factor in one's life. It is not like a dress suit, which can be put on when the occasion arises. Most people wait for the moment of the *test* before they take pains to improve. There are college students who never give a thought to their speech, until, upon graduation, they are confronted with the necessity of interviewing a prospective employer for a position. Then they cringe! Salesmen with many years of selling experience have been known to seek expert advice in utter desperation when scheduled to appear before more than the usual audience of one prospect. Businessmen go along blithefully unaware of the inadequacies of their speaking ability until a formal speech situation confronts them and they find themselves hopelessly unprepared. A prominent dentist in a small community confessed that he declined the nomination to the presidency of a civic organization, a post which he had secretly coveted, simply because he felt that he could not handle the speaking assignments that would be necessary. Had his everyday speech been more effective, he would not have needed to forego the honor.

Such poor judgment can be explained only by the queer quirk in human nature that causes us to pay the least attention to those things that are the most common. Speech is as common to us as walking. Have you ever watched an amateur style show? Young people who never thought it necessary to give attention to physical poise and carriage are called upon to move gracefully across a stage to show the latest style in gowns or suits. What happens? They feel the pressure of walking correctly, and, being unaccustomed to the niceties of graceful movement, they are forced into stiff and awkward posturing with the result that such style shows draw more attention to the affectations of the models than to the clothes being modeled. So it is with speech. Being unskilled in daily speech situations may force you into harmful affectations when speaking under circumstances where the premium is higher than usual.

If you are to make the most of your career, contribute to the prestige of your business or profession, and liquidate your debt to democratic society, you will be wise to begin your study of speech by analyzing your potentialities as a speaker.   Your present effectiveness in everyday speech should constitute the level from which you begin improvement.

The Plan of Study

The authors of this book do not mean to concentrate their efforts on "public" speaking; that is only one phase of speech.   A person cannot be an effective "public" speaker and at the same time an ineffective conference speaker or conversationalist.   And don't be misled into believing that great speakers are "born that way."   Successful "public" speakers are usually men of simple, plain virtues who have learned to use their heads and the elements of speech effectively in the give-and-take of conversation and who are able to adapt their talents to the larger platform situation. Business and professional men and women bear out the contention that in the shop, across the counter, and in the office they speak to one another with the purpose of influencing conduct in commercial, industrial, civic, and personal matters quite as much as from the public rostrum.

Progressive steps to follow

The plan of study we recommend is one of achieving ease and proficiency in meeting the daily exchange of thought in face-to-face conversation so that when the occasion presents itself you will be prepared to approach and conquer the more formal situation in which the audience is made up of many persons instead of one. Public speaking is best when it retains the finest qualities of conversation.   One reason why many of us do not give good public speeches is because we cannot give good private ones.

Our plan of study then is to study conversation first; apply what we can learn there to the more formal business conference; and finally to learn how to carry over the best qualities of conversation and conference speaking to the public speech situation.

Conversation.   As the basis from which springs any development as an effective business speaker we must consider conversation.   Our interest does not lie in the type of conversation that we all recognize as being merely time-consuming chatter.   Such talk may be delightful and highly enjoyable and certainly skill in this type of conversation is much sought after by all who enjoy "smoker" sociability, but this we shall relegate to the Emily Posts. We shall, on the other hand, consider conversation that makes some contribution to worth-while living. In this sense then, *conversation is the unpremeditated and lively exchange of ideas between two or more persons.* Such speaking is spontaneous, yet you will seek by your participation to gain personal prestige, acceptance of an idea, support for a policy or belief, or some other more or less definite response. A student, for example, may meet his instructor on the street corner while both are waiting for a bus. Their conversation may concern almost any subject, yet the student will attempt by his participation to make his instructor believe him to be a bright fellow. The student feels that such an opinion held by the instructor will serve as an advantage when the grades are made out, and he is probably right. Speech situations of this type must be studied because certain basic qualities of conversation must be retained in good conference speaking.

Conference speaking. Conference speaking is a conversation which is arranged and prepared for the accomplishment of a single specific purpose. Conferences are subject to the limitations of place, time, and order. Into this category will fall the speaking of the salesman, the applicant, the reporter, and that of any other person who enters into an arranged speech situation to accomplish a specific purpose. These conferences, since they are the core of business speech and the direct lead into public speaking, will receive major emphasis in this book.

Public speaking. Public speaking is essentially a monologue in which the speaker seeks a response from an audience of several people. The specific purposes of the speaker will be similar to those sought in the conference. He may be attempting to persuade, explain, or entertain. But only one person does the speaking. The elements and techniques of public speaking are similar to those of conference speaking. There must be a lively sense of communication, a well-organized presentation of material, and a delivery that will catch and hold attention. The chief difference lies only in the fact that a public speaker speaks without interruption to an audience of several persons. He must anticipate the questions and objections that might be asked if his speech were a conference and make provision for them in his organization. His analysis of the audience will consider their average knowledges and interests. Finally, his delivery will need enlargement and amplification in order for him to reach every member of the audience.

The triad of effective speaking

Our approach to business speech is predicated on the thesis that the best speaking is done by (1) an ABLE MAN, (2) with something to say, and (3) the ability to say it effectively. We believe that proficiency in these three attributes is best achieved through a progressive study and application of the principles of conversation, conference speaking, and public speaking.

The speaker must be an ABLE MAN. Mere glibness and rhetoric does not constitute effective speech. Audiences are quick to sense the intrinsic values in personality and character. If a speaker reveals essential weaknesses or inadequacies of person the audience will be inclined to reject him as one upon whom reliance and faith cannot be placed.

He must have something to say. A speaker who presumes to influence others must be an "expert" or an "authority" on the subject he handles. His contributions must be the result of general and specific information crystallized by sufficient thought and preparation. Speeches that are mere summaries or repetitions of the thoughts of others do not carry the conviction and sincerity adequate for acceptance.

He must know how to say it. The ABLE MAN speaker, besides having something to say, must possess a knowledge of speech construction and the vocal and physical skill necessary to express his ideas effectively to an audience. The speech teacher must of necessity confine the emphasis of his job to the development of material and expression. However, ABLE MAN criteria cannot be passed without notice. The least that can be done is to set up rather arbitrary qualifications for our ABLE MAN and insist that anyone who desires to be a speaker put himself to the test by self-analysis. Failure to do this can result only in the most superficial and useless expenditure of time by anyone who wishes to become an effective speaker.

QUESTIONS

1. What is the value of speech in a democracy?
2. Does a citizen in a democracy have a responsibility to speak?
3. To what extent does a successful businessman depend on effective speaking?
4. Can you name any business in which speech makes no contribution toward success?
5. Does the average businessman speak more in conference situations or public platform situations?
6. Can one best learn to become a good conference speaker by first becoming a good platform speaker or vice versa?
7. Does mastery of the ability to speak improve one's personality?
8. Can one afford not to practice effective speaking until the actual speech situation occurs?
9. What are the three progressive steps to follow in studying effective speaking?
10. In what order should they be studied?   Why?
11. What is the triad of effective speaking?

CHAPTER II

ABLE MAN Analysis

I. A START IN THE RIGHT DIRECTION
II. INTRODUCTION TO THE ABLE MAN
 ABLE MAN idea not new
 Self-analysis necessary
III. ABLE MAN QUALIFICATIONS
 Impressiveness
 Observation
 Initiative
 Thoroughness
 Decision
 Adaptation
 Organizing ability
 Concentration
 Constructive imagination
IV. A PLAN FOR SELF-ANALYSIS
 Speech triad as a basis
  ABLE MAN
  Something to say
  Ability to say it effectively
 Sample balance sheet
V. COMPENSATING FOR LIABILITIES

ABLE MAN Analysis

A Start in the Right Direction

THERE IS a great misconception about the ability to speak that most people either consciously ignore or of which they are blissfully unaware. The interesting conversationalist, the successful salesman, the star radio announcer, and the capable public speaker seem to achieve results with such little effort. It looks and sounds so easy and simple, and it is—IF! If a man has the essential moral, personal, and mental qualifications, if he has the expert's knowledge of the specific subject to be talked about, and if he has the ability to express his ideas effectively in terms of his audience, speaking will be easy.

Teachers of speech are often forced to conduct their classes with the cards stacked against them. Often they are faced with students who have no real motivating interest in learning to speak. This is particularly true in colleges and universities where students elect a course in speech to fill out a schedule or because they think they have discovered a "snap" course. This attitude is the worst possible one with which to begin the learning of effective speech. Professional schools and "night classes," on the other hand, seldom encounter this type of beginner. They find individuals who have made some sacrifice of time and money to achieve a skill that they have already recognized as being indispensable for success in business.

There is also a class of students, for the most part sincere and earnest, who approach their training in speech with great enthusiasm and then lose all interest when they discover that effective speaking requires an infinite amount of application and hard work. Some may have expected that a secret formula would be administered to them in the short duration of the course—a formula, so to speak, that could be taken out of the pocket and used whenever a speech situation appeared.   Prescriptions of this sort, however, have not yet been prepared.   You will find no easy rules that will enable you to "win audiences after six week's study," and surely few persons are naive enough to be taken in by advertisements beginning, "They all laughed when I got up to speak. *But . . .*"   The beginner must realize that speaking requires attention to the *whole* person—your ability as an ABLE MAN to say something effectively.   This is where our study must begin.

Introduction to the ABLE MAN

Let us examine the fundamental qualities of the individual that make for his success as a speaker or, indeed, success in his business or profession.   We know that there are some people whom we will listen to and believe simply because we sense in them a strength of intellect and character that inspires confidence.   Wendell L. Willkie, although he lost the 1940 presidential election, won a large following of friends and supporters primarily because his appearance and manner as a man inspired confidence.   Certainly he could not be classified as a great orator or even as an effective speaker.   But during the final days of his campaign, when his voice was raucous and worn-out through misuse, his spirit and vitality as an ABLE MAN continued to win him votes. William Knudsen and Cordell Hull, neither of whom could be considered model speakers, nevertheless cause audiences to listen and react through sheer respect and confidence in their integrity and ableness as men.   Although it is true that the influence of such persons on us may be partially the result of their fame and reputation, yet we sense things in these men that would set them out from the crowd under any circumstances.

There are also persons whose very presence causes us to doubt or draw away.   An intuition, or "sixth sense," tells us this man is bluffing, that he cannot be trusted, or that his tongue is quicker than his mind.   Some clues to his intrinsic worth are discernible— raucous voice, sloppy posture, shifty eye contact, or insinuating vocal inflections.   There are other "feelings," arising from a number of imperceptible causes, which crystallize a complete impression.   In the same manner in which reflected radio waves give the radar operator a complete image of the enemy ship on the radar 'scope, so do a multitude of minute perceptions give us our impression of a speaker's ableness as a man. We cannot always put our finger on the things that cause our distrust, but we seldom fail to sense them, if they are there.

No amount of speaking technique is enough to cover up deficiencies in intrinsic worth. However, any person who is willing to evaluate his qualities and begin a constructive program of self-improvement may ultimately profit by training in the art of effective speaking. On the other hand, a person unwilling to make a thoughtful and honest analysis of himself is doomed as a speaker; and this is as it should be, for otherwise he cannot justify respect from his audience. This may be illustrated by the story of a young woman who enrolled in a business speaking course. She had for a few years previous to this been employed as a stenographer by a number of firms. From each job she had been dismissed after only a short period of employment. She was sour on the world, careless about her appearance, and so unstable mentally and emotionally that the personnel bureau of the school gave up completely in the attempt to conduct her through its tests. One needed only a momentary glance at her to conclude that she was a misfit in a college class. Whether such a conclusion is fair or not is beside the point; the impression was there, and that is what we are talking about. She lost her jobs not because she lacked ability, for she was highly skilled as a stenographer, but because her personality revealed many weaknesses in the intrinsic worth of her character. If one were to help this woman acquire proficiency in meeting everyday speech situations, he would have to solicit the aid of numerous psychologists, psychiatrists, and "Ph.D.s of Common Horse Sense," all on indefinite tenure. There must be a basically sound individual as the first requirement if skill in speech is to be acquired.

ABLE MAN *idea not new*

Sarett and Foster include in their six basic principles of speech the statement that "Speech is effective, other things being equal, in proportion to the intrinsic worth of the speaker." The idea stems from Aristotle who expounded this simple truth some 300 years before the birth of Christ. Sarett and Foster continue their argument by saying,

> Speech is a form of self-expression. Obviously, there are two aspects of self-expression: one is the "self"; the other is the expression. Consciously a speaker expresses his ideas; unconsciously he reveals his character, his personality, his emotional state at the moment, and his attitude toward himself and his audience. In short, a speaker cannot *express* himself without sooner or later *revealing* himself.[1]

Emerson said, "WHAT YOU ARE THUNDERS SO LOUD I CAN'T HEAR WHAT YOU SAY." That is a statement worth remembering.

Self-analysis necessary

As a mariner takes his bearings, charts his course, surveys the condition of his ship, its engines, and supplies before starting on a voyage, so you should study your equipment and potentialities before beginning the study of speech. This statement is made because too many persons have been observed studying and practising speech "behind the eight-ball." You will be wise to stop any effort toward speaking until you discover your assets and liabilities and make a constructive attempt to "balance your books." That is where self-analysis comes in.

ABLE MAN Qualifications

Through self-analysis you may find out *what* you are and thereby determine your present and potential attributes for learning to speak. In order to insure effectiveness there are some necessary qualifications that every speaker must have in varying degree. These qualifications may also be considered as essentials to success in any business or professional career. They are the things that an audience *senses* in a speaker, the things that cause an audience to react favorably or unfavorably, the things that a speaker unconsciously reveals and that he cannot dissemble. They may be called *ABLE MAN qualifications.*[2]

---

[1] Sarett, Lew, and Foster, W. T., *Basic Principles of Speech,* Houghton Mifflin Company, New York, 1936, p. 19.

[2] The basis for the ABLE MAN qualifications is found in Hoopingarner, Newman L., *Personality and Business Ability Analysis,* A. W. Shaw Company, New York, 1927.

A. Is your appearance satisfactorily IMPRESSIVE?

B. Are your powers of OBSERVATION well developed?

C. Do you possess the INITIATIVE to tackle a job without being prodded?

D. Are you THOROUGH in your work?

E. Do you make DECISIONS easily and have enough faith to stick by them?

F. Are you able to ADAPT yourself to new situations?

G. Do you have ORGANIZING ABILITY?

H. Are you able to CONCENTRATE on a problem to the exclusion of all else?

I. Do you have a CONSTRUCTIVE IMAGINATION that is constantly seeking and finding new and better ways of doing the job?

Read the following discussions on each of these qualifications carefully. Attempt to find illustrations within your own experience that might be used as guides in determining to what degree you possess each of the qualifications.

Impressiveness

Impressiveness embodies those outward manifestations of personality and appearance that attract favorable attention. It consists of physical attractiveness, well-being, and dress. Basic to this quality is the posture, carriage, and poise with which a person deports himself. It also includes the person's physical condition and emotional attitude which reveals him as being energetic, radiant, enthusiastic and lively, or lethargic, dour, indifferent, and dull. The quality of impressiveness is seen in the neatness and appropriateness of dress, as distinguished from attire which is gaudy, dirty, unpressed, ill-cut, or extreme. The quality of impressiveness sets a man out favorably above the crowd. For our purposes it can be considered as that evaluation which is made in the first few moments of meeting.

Observation

Observation involves keen perception and the ability to retain what is observed. You may classify yourself as high in observation if you are constantly on the alert to factual material, ideas, and emotional stimulations about you. This is the quality that motivates a study of and interest in everything. There is no more revealing statement made by the typical undergraduate or, for that matter, by many adult citizens than, "Oh, I'm not interested in that stuff." To the *uninteresting person* all things are uninteresting.

Memory must also be included under this quality, for without it observation becomes only open-eyed stupidity. "Memory is the treasure house of oratory," and memory works only on things observed. A man with a poor memory is like a chap who takes pictures without proper light and focus—his album is full of blurred impressions.

Few people can truthfully claim a high rating in observation. Witness the inability of the average person to remember names, telephone numbers, addresses, the license number of his car or to observe the color of the eyes of his best girl friend or the new dress she is wearing for his approval. Perhaps the best illustration of a low degree of observation is the story of the old farmer's horse that was continually running into fences, barns, and trees. When asked if the horse was blind, the farmer replied, "Oh no, he just doesn't give a darn!"

Initiative

Initiative is a combination of determination, originality, and enthusiasm. It is the quality that propels a person toward accomplishment. It is the difference between the self-starter and the old, out-moded crank that was formerly used to start the engine of an automobile. Initiative is one thing executives look for when selecting men for promotion. The lack of it causes people to talk of "the same old grind," students to reach the end of the semester loaded with work that they should have done weeks before, and persons who want to be able to speak effectively to do nothing about it.

You need a tenacious will and an energetic stick-to-itiveness to advance beyond the crowd. Initiative is what carried the "message to Garcia." Initiative was back of our Constitution and Declaration of Independence. The whole world sits in wait for the men who will "make the first move in the right direction." Yet is it not curious that some individuals when faced with a momentous decision or an important job can find a hundred things that have to be done first?

Thoroughness

The thorough man is a *checker*. He doesn't accept things that are merely hearsay nor is he satisfied with only half-done jobs. He is the sort of person who takes pride in doing a good job and derives satisfaction from knowing that it is right. Thoroughness involves accuracy and dependability in performing any task. When a man retires he will probably regret not the fact that he did not do more work, but that he did not do BETTER work.

Do you make it a rule to study other phases of work besides your own in order to continually broaden your knowledge? Do you make it a point to do your work better than others? Are you satisfied with being able to *get by?* (There are millions of people "just getting by.") Do you rely on preparation or good luck to carry you through?

Decision

Decision is that quickness of thought and comprehension that enables a person to arrive at a conclusion without undue hedging and hesitation. It includes the important quality of confidence in one's self, without which few people are able to live up to their aspirations. Decision manifests itself in the ability to separate the "wheat from the chaff," to select the pertinent aspects of a problem and proceed confidently to a solution. Most persons in responsible key positions are called upon daily to exercise good judgment, often in split-second timing. Anyone with the ability to do this accurately can command a five-figure salary.

William M. Marston, a prominent psychologist, believes that hard work and the ability to make impulsive decisions are the two prime factors in successful living. So many of us are faced daily with inner flashes of impulse and idea that, if we acted upon them, might very likely change the whole course of our lives. Impulses born in moments of sober judgment should be obeyed. William James said, "Every time a resolve or a fine glow of feeling evaporates without bearing fruit, it is worse than a chance lost; it works to hinder future emotions from taking the normal path of discharge." This is warning that indecision in the small daily problems may lead to a habit of indecision that will prevent achievement of satisfactory action on more important tasks to come. One's habit of indecision may find one some day carrying the mattress and throwing the china out the window while his house burns behind him.

The executive of a famous Chicago department store made the startling estimate that if women could only make up their minds about their purchases, the retail price of everything in the store could be cut thirty per cent. The indecision suggested by such common phrases as, "I'm just shopping," "I'm just looking," "Guess I'll look around a little more," and "Send that out on approval," costs the average retailer several dollars each year. Money is lost in delivery charges, wasteful bookkeeping, salaries to clerks who must bear with the customer regardless of her inability to decide, and new merchandise that must be marked down or put on sale because it is "slightly soiled."

Adaptation

Adaptation is the quality of mental alertness, speed of thinking, and facility in changing mental set. A successful salesman must possess this quality to a high degree, for it will provide him with the right answer for any question or objection that may be offered by any type of person. "Canned" sales speeches seldom have much effectiveness because they offer little chance for adaptation to unforeseen situations. They are only the "better than nothing" technique when good salesmen cannot be found.

It is perhaps trite to point out that any business venture that would succeed in these days must be amenable to change. The priority rulings and rationing laws introduced during World War II have forced many businessmen into bankruptcy because they were unwilling to adapt their facilities to other types of work. Their one-track minds saw no opportunity in anything but the slogan, "Business as usual."

In any kind of speech situation the ability to adapt speech to the audience is of vital concern. In conversation or in a business conference this quality is still more necessary because of the active EXCHANGE of ideas. Questions may be asked or unforeseen plans and distracting opinions may arise to confuse the speaker if he is unable to adapt his knowledge and manner to take care of the situation.

Organizing ability

Organizing ability manifests itself in the mental capacity tc analyze and synthesize problems working toward the most efficient solution.   It involves placing the elements of a problem in their proper relationship and proceeding according to a plan.

In this day of mass production and complicated organization there is a premium on the ability to act as the "brains" behind a great concerted effort; and to act as the "brains" means little more than that one individual has the unique ability to organize. Labor, business, and professions of all kinds keep highly paid executives for this very purpose.   They achieve a successful result primarily because they are able to map out plans and to work according to a method.   The world is full of businessmen whose only method is an alarm clock that rings every morning, heralding a new day at the office.   From there on it is only "come-what-may" and "the devil-take-the-hindmost."   Effort of this kind is seldom described in business magazines or success stories.

The most effective speakers are the ones who can combine a fine sense of communication and delivery with a well-organized and purposeful speech.   That is probably the reason why there are today so many who speak so beautifully and so long without saying anything.   Take a lesson from the driver on a delivery wagon.   He arranges his delivery tickets to cover all the territory without having to backtrack.   His loadings are then planned to conform to the ticket arrangement, making his problem of delivery relatively simple.

Concentration

Concentration is necessary to real constructive thinking.   The "scatterbrain" never gains respect for his efforts and seldom progresses to a position where respect is necessary, unless he marries the boss' daughter.   Even inspiration, which many try to substitute for thought, comes only as a tardy reaction to previous concentration.

Concentration requires the complete submission of distractions and a total attention to the matter at hand.   If you can maintain strict attention on a thing for a length of time it becomes sharp for you. Your concentration lends a degree of emphasis to the thing you study and the result of your thinking becomes a permanent possession for you. Only through deep concentration can reason be given power in human affairs. Intensive thinking about a subject causes it to come to life and motivates decisions, resulting in great satisfaction.

Constructive imagination

Constructive imagination is a combination of mental and emotional traits, each stimulating and acting on the other. It must not be confused with mental meandering and idle daydreaming, for the inherent aspect of instructive imagination is that it ARRIVES. This is not the product of the ne'er-do-well but of the doer. It is the difference between the genius who "might have been" and the genius who is. Edison, Marconi, Shakespeare, and Beethoven all possessed it to a high degree.

Imagination is a quality that we must guard jealously. So much of what is about us tends constantly to destroy it. Our jobs are cut out for us and put on a schedule; our books are digested and summarized; pictures are substituted for description; and the large majority of motion pictures leave absolutely nothing to the imagination. Such a diet cuts at the very heart of our innate desire to go beyond what is on the surface.

A Plan for Self-Analysis

Any efficient businessman with a job to do first takes time to survey all the angles and possibilities with which he may be concerned. He knows that only through careful study and analysis will he be able to save himself unnecessary effort and costly mistakes. Therefore, as a student of speech you may insure an efficient use of your time by immediately determining your assets and liabilities.

A businessman plans his future operations in terms of capital, personnel, equipment, production, and market. These facts and statistics are carefully entered in business ledgers and reports which may be consulted from time to time in order to maintain perspective. You will be wise to follow a similar procedure

Prepare a balance sheet showing your assets and liabilities and make use of the analysis as you continue your effort to improve your speaking ability.

Speech triad as a basis

Three things determine your potentialities as a speaker: (1) your ABLE MAN qualifications, (2) your knowledge of something to say, and (3) your ability to say it effectively. This triad must be the basis of your self-analysis and your progress. Each is important, for without one, the others are useless.

ABLE MAN. After understanding the ABLE MAN qualifications, begin by attempting to determine how nearly you measure up to the maximum level in each case. Your job is with yourself for a few days. Do not accept the advice and opinions of others. Think through each of the qualifications and mark up some kind of score for yourself on each. You be the judge and auditor. Use paper and pencil; you will think better that way. Set down your observations with the idea in mind that you will have to prove to someone else that your inventory has been correct. Have evidence in black and white.

Begin with your assets in each instance. What are they? Are you attractive physically? Good. Are you observant? Do you really believe that you do a thorough job of everything you tackle? You should. Go through all ten of the qualifications and record an honest and thoughtful estimate. This will not be an easy job for you to do. You can find your strong points with little trouble, but when you begin on the liabilities, you will need more careful concentration. Remember Robert Burns' poem with the lines, "Oh, wad some pow'r the giftie gi'e us, to see oursel's as ithers see us."

Through this method of self-analysis you may discover things you never thought about yourself before. It is curious that liabilities and assets often tend in the same direction, and, after thought, you may find that what you have always considered a liability may actually become an asset when made to work *for* instead of *against* you.

Something to say. Having something to say is the best insurance any speaker may secure. Certainly any man who would seek respect as a public speaker will never assume the responsibility of consuming the time of the audience unless he is prepared on his subject to the extent that he may be called somewhat of an authority. Speaking, after all, is a pretty simple matter if the speaker has something to say. If the speaker has a thoroughly crystallized idea that he feels *must* be communicated, he will be able to speak quite effectively without paying much attention to the techniques of delivery. All speaking is a problem of subordinating distractions and emphasizing ideas to be expressed. There is not, however, an abundance of well-informed speakers. This fact is rather well attested by knowing that the average man who seeks instruction in public speaking is worried more about WHAT to say than by HOW to say it.

For our purposes we are concerned with both *specific* and *general* knowledge. Specific knowledge is an accumulation of detailed, accurate, and complete information about a particular subject. Usually it is in the field of business in which you work. It may however be your hobby or any subject that you have studied. The man who can give facts and place himself in the position of an expert will usually receive attention. Specific information, authoritatively presented, leaves little room for arguments against your proposal or questioning of your explanation. Woodrow Wilson once said, "Facts do not threaten, they OPERATE."

General knowledge, on the other hand, includes half-truths and hearsay evidence about numerous subjects, as well as facts. Anyone who reads a newspaper gathers general knowledge in vast quantities, but let it be understood that such reading does not qualify one to speak as an expert. Wide circulation of news through the press has nurtured an astounding number of "arm chair specialists" on politics, national economy, war strategy, and everything else under the sun. It is unfortunate that many people cannot resist a patient listener and become "walking encyclopedias" on all subjects and thus lose respect as authorities in the fields in which they are really well informed. General knowledge should be used only as illustration and as points of reference and analogy in the discussion of subjects well known. However, general knowledge on a great many subjects improves one's intellectual background and makes it easier for one to adapt himself to all situations.

In analyzing your capacity for having something to say as a speaker, make a list of subjects on which you really have enough information to speak as an expert and a list of subjects on which you have a rather high degree of general knowledge. These are assets. Next, make a list of those phases of your major field in which you are not well informed. These are liabilities. There are also many subjects on which you do not possess even general knowledge, subjects that may be related to your chief interest and that might enable you to understand better and to make more efficient the specific job you are now doing. These are liabilities. Your completed analysis should give you a picture of your present speaking capacity, a guide for selecting subjects for speeches, and suggestions for future study.

Ability to say it effectively. Effective expression demands facility with language, skill in analysis and composition, and a vocal and physical delivery free from distractions. Many believe that the ability to express oneself is the sum and substance of success. Our contention does not dispute this belief but merely adds that expression is only the outward manifestation of all the qualities of the ABLE MAN with something to say. With such a foundation expression will cease to be an insurmountable problem.

Many speakers are handicapped because they lack a sufficiently large vocabulary to express specifically and in an interesting manner the abstract ideas that are a result of their thinking. It is common to hear such excuses as, "Well—I know what it is, but . . ." or, "Well—you know what I mean." Insufficient vocabulary is also an obstacle to thought, for even unexpressed ideas must be formulated with words. As your vocabulary increases so does your capacity to think.

In addition to having an adequate vocabulary, the speaker must be able to pronounce and articulate words correctly and clearly. If you "know" a word but cannot pronounce it, it cannot be called a part of your speaking vocabulary nor of your thinking vocabulary. The average person speaks 30,000 words each day. Many words are spoken without evidence of thought, used for gossip, used in anger, used to cover up, or lost for miscellaneous reasons, such as repetitions, incomplete sentences, embarrassment, or apologies for having said the wrong thing. How many do you repeat, mispronounce, grunt, or use improperly?

The ability to speak effectively also demands that a speaker be able to compose his thought and language in such a way as to influence his audience without unnecessary distractions. He must be able to speak grammatically, to analyze his subject in reference to the experiences and interests of his audience, and to achieve an oral style of speech which is clear and appealing.

Finally, his delivery must reveal self-confidence and sincerity. This may be sensed through nuances of the voice and through directness and animation of physical bearing and action.

This third part of the triad, expression or the ability to speak effectively, is usually considered as the complete realm of speech training. It is certainly the means by which deficiencies in the ABLE MAN qualities and lack of knowledge are revealed. For that reason, most of your actual work and study as a student of speech will comprise language, composition, and delivery. But do not forget or minimize the importance of the other two essentials.

Since most of us are not good critics of our own speaking ability, it may be helpful to solicit the aid of a trained speaker or teacher to help you complete the third portion of your analysis. If you are enrolled in a speech class your instructor will see that you get constructive criticism after every speech. Such criticism is invaluable if you make a sincere attempt to take advantage of it. An ABLE MAN would recognize that value and avoid making the same mistakes twice.

Sample balance sheet

The following balance sheet is a suggested outline for self-analysis. It may be used as a guide for your own effort at self-examination and self-evaluation. Analyzing so complex a thing as oneself is not an easy task. It will be necessary to ask yourself specific questions in regard to the various items recommended. For example, the quality of observation may be studied through the use of such questions as, "Do I remember names of the people I meet?" "Do I show an interest in matters outside my major field?" "Am I curious enough about things around me to give them more than casual attention?" Answer such questions as these by noting specific instances that indicate whether you have an asset or a liability in the particular quality. You may rely on

A SAMPLE BALANCE SHEET

(Self-analysis prepared by a young college graduate about to begin work in the sales department of a nationally known meat-packing company.)

Criteria for Speaking	Assets
ABLE MAN Qualities	
Impressiveness	Friendly. Dress in good taste. Good physique.
Observation	
Initiative	Take initiative in things I like to do.
Thoroughness	
Decisiveness	Make decisions quickly and easily.
Adaptation	Adapt easily to new situations. Can do almost anything. Like to meet strangers.
Organizing Ability	
Concentration	
Imagination	
Something to Say	
General Knowledge	Possess general knowledge of politics, business organization and methods, geography of the United States, simple mechanics, history.
Special Knowledge	Specialized knowledge of meat-packing industry, salesmanship, psychology.
Ability to Say It	

Language
  vocabulary
  pronunciation
  articulation
	Pronunciation and articulation satisfactory.

Composition
  grammar
  analysis
  style
	Accurate use of grammar. Good foundation in English composition.
	Speak and write in an easy and interesting style.

Delivery
  voice
  animation
  directness
  self-confidence
  communicative attitude
	Highly animated in conversation.
	Good mental and physical directness.
	Have considerable self-confidence.
	Always have strong sense of communication when speaking.

A SAMPLE BALANCE SHEET

Criteria for Speaking	Liabilities
ABLE MAN Qualities	
Impressiveness	Posture bad at times.
Observation	Not very observant. Poor memory for names. Inclined to hurry too much.
Initiative	Dislike starting difficult jobs.
Thoroughness	Never liked to study. Inclined to be satisfied with getting by.
Decisiveness	
Adaptation	
Organizing Ability	Don't take time to organize. Take things as they come, and therefore waste lots of time.
Concentration	Dislike being alone, so seldom find time for concentration. Would rather talk.
Imagination	
Something to Say	
General Knowledge	Know nothing about literature and the arts. I ought to do more reading in the classics and in contemporary writings.
Special Knowledge	I ought to know more about accounting, marketing, and transportation. Have no system of enlarging my special fields of knowledge.
Ability to Say It	

Language
  vocabulary
  pronunciation
  articulation
	Very small vocabulary. I struggle for words to express my ideas. Should read more.

Composition
  grammar
  analysis
  style
	Have difficulty making an analysis of a subject. I can usually get by on personality, so I do.

Delivery
  voice
  animation
  directness
  self-confidence
  communicative attitude
	Voice is rather high pitched especially when I become excited or nervous. Others have noticed this and remarked about it.

your own critical powers to arrive at a frank and unbiased appraisal, but you will be wise to check results against the judgment of people who may be trusted to make honest answers.

Compensating for Liabilities

Assuming that you have made a complete and accurate evaluation of yourself, you are now in possession of facts that may mean the difference between success and failure in your career. What can be done with this information? There are several things that may prove helpful. First, you may determine to do something constructive about the qualities in which you are weak. You may increase your impressiveness by improving your posture, walk, dress, quality of voice, and manners. You may develop the ability to concentrate by employing self-discipline. Your powers of observation may increase by the simple application of interest in the things about you. And so on through all the qualities of the ABLE MAN. You will find that as you improve in one quality you may consequently improve in another, for the qualities overlap as they weld themselves into the pattern of the ABLE MAN.

If it is impossible to overcome certain liabilities you may compensate for them by developing and capitalizing on your assets. A man without imagination may develop into an effective speaker by increasing his fund of specific knowledge. Conversely, one may develop imagination if he lacks specific knowledge; however such compensation, familiar though deplorable, is the mainstay of too many pseudo-career men with a "gift of gab." If you have a physical handicap you may offset its disadvantages by further developing your abilities in another direction. Do you often wonder at the accomplishments of the average blind person? He has learned to compensate for his handicap by improving the sensitivity of his other senses. Usually his power of concentration is above the average. Alec Templeton's amazing musical ability is the result of a compensation in concentration and application to his inherent musical talent. A careful study of persons who have achieved some success and fame would reveal that most of them have capitalized on some asset, thus compensating for certain liabilities. Politicians may be successful, even though they lack training and background in government, by being unusually friendly and gregarious in their contacts with voters. Actors become famous by playing specific "types" of characters.

Go as far as you can in improving each of the qualities of the ABLE MAN within yourself and then select your strongest assets for special development. Pick at least one quality in which you can excel the average person. Resolve to be an ABLE MAN with something to say and the ability to say it effectively. Having done this, and remembering that the largest room in the world is the room for improvement, you are ready to begin the study of speech, the study that may enable you to sell yourself and your ideas to audiences.

QUESTIONS

1. What is the basis for measuring an ABLE MAN as referred to in this chapter?

2. Why is a person with a high degree of ABLE MAN characteristics a potentially better speaker than a person with a low degree of these characteristics?

3. Discuss the implications of Emerson's statement, "What you are thunders so loud I can't hear what you say."

4. What is meant by the following statement: "Speech is effective, other things being equal, in proportion to the intrinsic worth of the speaker"?

5. Write out an analysis of yourself according to the ABLE MAN qualifications.

6. How much general and how much specific knowledge do you have that would qualify you as a speaker with something to say?

7. Assuming that you have sufficient general and specific knowledge to make a speech, what is your ability to say it effectively?

8. Make out a balance sheet of yourself. Follow the sample balance sheet found on pages 28 and 29. From this balance sheet what may you conclude about your present ability and your potential ability as an effective speaker?

9. What is the "compensating for liabilities" theory discussed in this chapter?

EXERCISES

1. After making a careful self-analysis, prepare a personal balance sheet of your ABLE MAN qualifications, your knowledge of "something to say," and your ability to "say it effectively." List both assets and liabilities.

2. Arrange an orientation conference with your instructor. Use this time to ask questions about the course and to get acquainted with your instructor. He will want to know you and your ambitions. Be prepared to answer questions about your experience, your education, and your plans. This will be your chance to make a good first impression that may be of value to you throughout the course.

3. Arrange a conference with an instructor in your major field or with a man actually engaged in the type of position to which you aspire. Tell him what you want to do and allow him to advise you. After the conference write a criticism of the effectiveness with which you conducted the conference.

SELECTED READINGS

Bingham, Walter van Dyke, *Aptitudes and Aptitude Testing,* Harpers and Bros., New York, 1937.

Hoving, Walter, *Your Career in Business,* Duell, Sloan and Pierce, New York, 1940.

Kitson, Harry Dexter, *How to Find the Right Vocation,* Harpers and Bros., New York, 1929.

Maule, F., *Men Wanted,* Funk and Wagnalls Co., New York, 1937.

Ogllesby, C., *Business Opportunities for Women,* Harpers and Bros., New York, 1932.

Pitkin, Walter B., *New Careers for Youth,* Simon and Schuster, New York, 1934.

Reilly, W. J., *How to Find and Follow Your Career,* New York, Harpers and Bros., 1936.

Rosengarten, William, *Choosing Your Life Work,* McGraw-Hill, New York, 1936.

The Conversational Foundation

I. CONVERSATION AND THE BASIC SPEECH SKILLS
II. SIMILARITIES AND DIFFERENCES IN CONVERSATION, CONFERENCE, AND PUBLIC SPEAKING
   Similarities
   Differences
III. GOOD CONVERSATION AND ACCEPTABILITY
IV. CONVERSATIONAL SITUATIONS
   Conversation by and between friends
   Time-taking-talk-technique
   Conversation designed to improve one's acceptability in society and indirectly to improve one's business and professional status
V. ELEMENTS TO BE STUDIED IN THE ART OF CONVERSATION
   The people
   Material or subject matter
   Vocal and physical aspects of conversational expression
   Rhetorical techniques of conversation
      Ask questions.
      Use common ground.
      Observe the one-minute rule
      Be a good listener.
      Be complimentary.
      Don't argue.
      Don't hit below the belt.

The Conversational Foundation

Conversation and the Basic Speech Skills

THE BASIC speech situation to be mastered is conversation. It involves the elementary skills essential to all types of speaking. It necessitates the use of materials, organization, and vocalization in a manner similar to the use of these skills in conference speaking and public speaking. The major point of distinction in the use of speech skills in these three situations is one of adaptation. In many respects conversation is more important than all other types of speaking. It may be engaged in for the purpose of fellowship; it permits a sharing of ideas; it brings two or more people into harmony. It serves, when well used, as the cohesive force that binds people into social units. It creates, when improperly used, the frictions that cause families, communities, and even nations to fall apart. There is enjoyment and companionship in conversation, as well as information, persuasion, and humor. Conversation is a way of living with others. Its absence would still the minds of men. And yet, since man finds conversation a habit, he seldom recognizes that it involves the skills basic to other types of speech and he rarely makes his conversation an art.

Why does conversation become a habit taken for granted in the same manner as breathing and eating? A new-born baby is confronted with making its needs known to its parents by some vocal method short of conversation. The baby has the lung capacity for forcing air out over the vocal cords, thus creating sound. It soon learns that this sound will secure the attention of the parents, and consequently develops the habit of creating sound merely for the effect on the parents. By the time the child is two years old, one hundred words or more have been acquired. These words result largely from the child's ability to control the vocal organs and to imitate the sounds produced by others. From this point on to the age of four to six years the child continues to acquire new words; he also uses a great number of words without a complete understanding of their meaning. Thus the capacity for speech in the early years is largely a matter of physical effort to produce sound without much regard to meaning. The child develops the habit of speaking as a physiological process with a minimum of mental control over that process.

As in eating and breathing, the act of speaking can be accomplished with a minimum of thought. But also as in eating and breathing, when one is mindful of the physical act, he can control and direct its course. However, since all three are engaged in as a daily routine and can be accomplished with a minimum of thought, they are given but little attention and are seldom developed as an art.

Most people have few inhibitions about the conversational or conference speech situation. A great many people, on the other hand, fear the platform situation. This fear results largely from lack of habit-forming experiences on the public platform. Those who give numerous addresses before public gatherings, such speakers as politicians, teachers, and preachers, often become as unmindful of public speaking as an art as most of us are of conversation as an art. We must first recognize, then, that speech is a physiological process, which can become a habit for any and all of us. We should next recognize that this physiological process when attended to by mindful people can become an art in the conversational, conference, or public speech situation. Finally, since the basic skills of speech are found in conversation the authors present this chapter on conversation as the foundation for good speech.

Similarities and Differences in Conversation, Conference, and Public Speaking

Similarities

Effective conversation, conference, and public speaking result when an ABLE MAN has proper material well organized and the ability to present it effectively. These three types of speech situations are similar in these three respects. There are other speech skills that are common to all speech situations, including the need for concrete, interesting, and vital facts and opinions in the subject matter of the speech. If the subject is advertising, for example, you will want to include specific details about the media of radio, newspapers, magazines, and billboards or details about costs, coverage, and make-up. The extent of the details will vary as greatly between two conversations as they might between a conversation and a conference speech. The material in any speech should also be presented with unity, coherence, and an acceptable style.

In presenting the material, the speaker should be direct. He should speak to and with his audience. He should be alert, both mentally and physically. Nothing retards thought and stimulates lethargy in an audience as quickly as dull and unanimated speech. The speaker's attitude should be one of communicating ideas to others so that those ideas can be understood, enjoyed, and appreciated. The speaker must be sincere. He should portray the impression that the thoughts, ideas, and materials are important to himself as well as to the audience. The voice should be varied in pitch, tone, rate, and volume. By these vocal elements being varied, monotony is avoided and emphasis, clarity, and interests are gained. Since these elements are common to all speaking situations it is essential to note that the student while mastering the art of conversation will be likewise mastering much of the art of conference and public speaking.

Differences

There are four essential differences between the private conversational situation and the public platform speech. For the purpose of clarifying these distinctions the conference speech is considered as more nearly analogous to the conversational situation than to the public speech. These differences are:

CONVERSATION	CONFERENCE	PUBLIC SPEAKING
1. Dialogue	1. Dialogue	1. Monologue
2. Flexible turn of subject matter	2. Pre-determined development of subject matter, but adapted to questions raised by conferee	2. Pre-determined development of subject matter
3. Adapted to one or a few people	3. Adapted to one or a few people	3. Adapted to many people
4. Intimate physical surroundings (home, car, club, and restaurant)	4. Business surroundings (office and work shop)	4. Auditoriums or open air surroundings

In respect to the first two differences the public speech is easier to give than is the conversation or conference, since it is prepared and set in advance. There are no interruptions, no embarrassing questions, no anecdotes to listen to, and no stops to make in the public speech. In the average public speaking situation you prepare the speech in advance, present it in full at the proper time, stop, sit down, and wait for the applause.

It is only in respect to the last two differences listed that the public speech becomes more difficult. Even here the difference is not as great as the average individual thinks. People in an audience merely represent a collective whole; thus the problem of adaptation is that of directing the speech to the average man plus the consideration of group psychology. The fourth difference raises a problem of adapting the vocal mechanism and bodily activity to a larger room and group of people. It involves no difference as far as the basic requisites of good speech are concerned. The conversational manner of speech presentation should prevail in public as well as in private speaking.

Because of these reasons, it is believed that the proper approach to effective public speaking is through the mastery of the principles of good conversation. This approach is doubly effective in perfecting skills in everyday business speech. Here the speech is made in conference with one or a few people, and, except for office surroundings and the specific purpose of the conference, it is identical with conversation in its speech manifestations. It is therefore the plan of this chapter to develop and illustrate those principles and rules basic to good conversation. This is done, first, because there are many opportunities for improving one's acceptability to society by conversation and thus indirectly improving one's status in business and professional fields; second, because these common principles and rules of conversation are basic in everyday business speech; and third, because it is believed that these ends, once gained and perfected, will greatly enhance one's ability to cope effectively with the speech problems of the public platform. With this brief introductory statement on the WHY of conversation as treated in this book, let us turn our attention to the rules and principles of good conversation.

Good Conversation and Acceptability

Step on a bus and sit down in the only vacant seat.   Although you are hoping that your companion will turn out to be an Alexander Woollcott or a John Kieran, you conclude, after a few remarks about the weather, inadequate bus schedules, grafting politicians, utility corporations, or insane automobile drivers, that your companion is something less than a moron rather than the stimulating conversationalist you had hoped for, whereupon you read the advertisements about "Join the Army" or "Wrigley's Chewing Gum" and wish that you could save enough money to own and drive your own car.   Later in the day you attend a formal conference, only to meet your erstwhile bus companion and to learn that he is connected with the bus company and that an accident with his car necessitated his using the bus.   You wonder why he is formal, cool, and uninterested in you or the proposition that you advocate.

Maybe your employer or your instructor invites you to lunch or in an unarranged manner you are afforded a conversational opportunity with one of these.   It may be at golf, or a football game, over a dinner table, on a street car, or in a night club that you meet those with whom you have business and professional contacts.   It matters not where or how the occasion arises.   It matters only that if you are to be forever promoting your business or professional status and interests, you will use these opportunities to create favorable impressions and to refrain from provoking antagonisms that will stymie you in your next business transaction.

Conversation is the most used and abused tool that man possesses.   To many folks a listener serves only as a rhetorical laxative.   They wind up and exhale vocalisms by the thousand. Their ego urges them to be out in front with sarcasm, criticism, intimate and needless details of their doings, anecdotes, exaggerations, interruptions, small talk, and funny stories.   Others, of course, are so overawed by the presence of a listener that it is only after they retire to seclusive haunts that they think, "Why didn't I tell this one?", "I wish I could have said what I wanted to say when I was talking with him," or "I wish I could talk like that man."   It has been stated that the only thing more disastrous to social equilibrium than the man who talks too much is the man who listens too much.

The problem that confronts all of us is how we can participate in a conversation so that it will reflect favorably on us and pay dividends in an improved relationship with mankind. For the purpose of clarifying this discussion, conversation short of the arranged business conference will be divided into three situations.

Conversational Situations

Conversation by and between friends

In conversation by and between intimate friends, liberties may be taken without destroying one's acceptability to society or affecting one's business success. Friends are known more for what they are than for what they say. Detailed revelations of personal matters is a natural subject. Anecdotes, jokes, gossip, and illogical theories on how to predict twin babies do not increase or decrease friendships. Friends understand and enjoy the companionship for the intrinsic worth of the individual concerned. In this situation you are either liked and enjoyed for what you are or in spite of what you are. However, friendships can be gained and improved by following the principles of good conversation.

Time-taking-talk-technique

Much conversation is indulged in for the sake of consuming time. Its principal value lies in consuming time, permitting relaxation, and exercising the physical organs involved in talking. Its principal disadvantage is that it requires the time of a listener who may be bored. This is due to the fact that after a few years' practice talk becomes a habit. Phrases and even sentences are uttered by the speaker without thought. Since this practice seems to follow the laws of nature, it must be tolerated by mankind, but it is appropriate that this type of vocal gymnastics be known as talk for talk's sake or the Time-Taking-Talk-Technique.

This would be a harmless activity if it could be engaged in to one's benefit as much as walking through the woods in the presence of only birds, bees, and trees. But talk has some vulturous qualities; it requires something in the flesh as its victim. Persons who talk for talk's sake are allowed to exist by virtue of the Bill of Rights and the fact that their kind is not in the minority. You can identify a dozen or more of these people in your immediate circle whom you refer to as "Windy," "he can talk a leg off a bald eagle," "he has a line," or "I couldn't get a word in edgeways."

Three rules sho ld be mentioned for this group of conversationalists. First, if they are naive enough to believe that halitosis and B.O. are not offensive to those around them, then they need not worry about their conversation, which may have similar qualities. Second, if they must talk for talk's sake and if they must demonstrate that they are experts at the time-consuming-talk-technique, they should seek out others with the same disease and exchange punishment like men. Third, there are times when the small talk artist can fill in advantageously, preventing silence at parties, dinner tables, car rides, and street corners. In situations such as these, the small talk artist has his merits, but lest he become the conventional bore who, when you ask him how he is, tells you, he should attend carefully to the principles of good conversation.

Conversation designed to improve one's acceptability in society and indirectly to improve one's business and professional status

This third conversational situation involves all conversation where one is attempting to improve his position in life. It includes conversations in group meetings, at parties, on the golf course, on street corners, in the coffee shop, on the train, at conventions, town meetings, and every occasion where one meets his associates or his potential associates. These are the basic conversational situations that warrant the study of conversation as an art.

Elements to Be Studied in the Art of Conversation

The basic conversational situation warrants study in preparation for everyday business speech of both the conference and platform types. This conversational picture consists of four elements, the people, material or subject matter, factors of physical expression, and rhetorical techniques. These four elements hold a conversation together and make for its success. The rules and principles that govern these elements are the rules and principles that, when followed, make for successful conversation.

The people

Conversational ability will improve in direct ratio to one's status as an ABLE MAN. This is true because an ABLE MAN knows that a sure-fire method of impressing the other fellow in a conversation is to make the other man and his doings the subject of discussion. This is known as the "you attitude."

The best conversationalists are not people primarily interested in themselves nor in any particular subject but rather the people who are genuinely and sincerely interested in the other fellow, in what he thinks, and in what he is doing. A few simple statements will illustrate this point. I say to you, "The West is beautiful." The statement indicates that I want to talk about a particular subject and, unless you are unusually interested in the subject, it will not cause any marked response. On the other hand, I might ask, "Have *you* seen Crater Lake in Oregon?" or "Have *you* driven the Columbia River Drive east of Portland and Vancouver?" In this question you and what you have done are the focal points of interest and, unless you are in deep concentration on other matters, you will respond, recalling this and that particular scene. Since the subject concerns you and your doings, you will be more impressed with the conversation in the majority of cases than if it were about some impersonal subject or someone else's experiences. Since your partner in this conversation has recognized you, you will associate pleasant memories with him, and his acceptability to you has thereby increased.

It has been remarked that if a man says, "I think it will rain," he wants to talk, but if he says, "Do you think it will rain?" he wants you to talk. This interest in the other fellow must be sincere, genuine, wholesome, and candid. It rejects any long-nose-poking into another person's business for the sole opportunity of gossip and of undoing his character. An ABLE MAN, of course, is not so tempted.

Try the following questions and statements on people with whom you converse. Keep your own record of responses in determining whether the other fellow is not more ready and more pleased to talk about himself or express his own opinions than any other subject, including your own opinions.

1. "This war is terrible" or "Do you believe that the United States should join an international government?"
2. "I am going to take a vacation" or "Where did you go on your vacation?"
3. "I have stopped smoking since the two-cent tax was placed on cigarettes" or "What do you think of the new luxury tax on tobacco and liquor?"
4. "I have been doing very little these last few days" or "What have you been doing lately?"

This "you attitude" or genuine interest in the other fellow becomes increasingly effective as a conversational aid if enough is known about the other person to permit questions and statements about his most cherished subjects, whether they be himself, his family, his hobbies, his business, or his religion.   Questions about the other man's health, what he has been doing, what he has read in the way of books or seen in the way of plays and movies will nearly always inspire him to talk and to feel more kindly toward you because of your interest in him.   Mark Twain added a provocative thought to this personal factor in conversation when he said, "Good breeding consists in concealing how much we think of ourselves and how little we think of the other person."

Conversation centers itself in the other person's interest, if it is successful.   Two good conversationalists might have great difficulty unless they have common interests—which, of course, they always do.

Material or subject matter

With regard to the subject matter in a conversation there is one rule that has few exceptions: talk about things that you understand and ask questions about those things that you do not understand.   A mutual friend of the authors recently toured to St. George, Utah.   En route through Missouri he discussed with a garage mechanic the possible roads through Kansas.   The mechanic related in great detail the condition of four roads, always pointing out that the roads that the friend wished to take in order to touch certain scenic spots in Colorado were impossible because of recent floods.   The mechanic's stories and details were so inconsistent and confusing that the friend finally withdrew both his car and his business to a more reliable source of in- formation. It was not important that the friend later found that the mechanic knew nothing about the roads more than five miles out of town, but it was important when the mechanic's confused story of unknown facts caused the loss of an automobile repair job.

The following well-known story is worth repeating as an illus- tration of the importance of understanding the material of con- versation. Mrs. Keeler was attending the first annual meeting of the Book Club as a prospective member. The critic of the day, engaging her in conversation, asked her opinion on Scott's *Lady of the Lake.* She responded that Scott was her favorite author and that she thought the book was "simply divine." The critic then asked in turn about *Ivanhoe, Lay of the Last Minstrel,* and others. She showered each with general comments of praise. Finally realizing Mrs. Keeler's ignorance on the entire subject, the critic asked with a smile, "How do you like 'Scott's Emulsion'?" Her response contained more superlatives than before and con- cluded with the evaluation that "this was perhaps the best and most effective of all of Scott's works."

Senator Taber of Colorado, known mostly for his fabulous wealth derived from the mines around Leadville and Central City, was the butt of many anecdotes that further illustrate this point. After contributing freely to the building fund for the opera house constructed in Central City in the 1870's, he was approached by the committee on decorations and asked to contribute one hun- dred dollars for the purchase of a chandelier. Taber replied, "Here, take five hundred dollars and buy the best chandelier pos- sible, and get the best damn chandelier player in the country to play it." The Senator also figured in the following incident: after construction of the opera house was completed and the formal opening was scheduled, Taber was taken to inspect the building. On entering the lobby he observed an oil painting on the wall. He asked "Who is that picture?" When told that it was a picture of William Shakespeare, he replied, "Well, what has Shakespeare ever done for the State of Colorado? Take it down and hang my picture in its place."

The reader will recall from his own experience many attempts on the part of friends to discuss matters about which they had little or no knowledge. In each instance, the result was loss-of-face, a lessening of reputation, and sometimes acute embarrassment. If you do not know, ask questions or keep silent.

A second rule regarding the material of conversation has to do with general and specific knowledge of subject matter. One should have general knowledge about a good many things. Our system of education puts one in touch with all the basic sciences and the fields of literature and the arts. Newsreels, current magazines, speeches, and radio programs present in abundance general information on every subject from spinach to Siberia. Certainly with these sources the ABLE MAN will not be lacking general information. He may not be able to reveal the exact situation regarding Hess' flight to Scotland, but he would know that it was not a figment of Orson Welles' imagination as proclaimed seriously by three undergraduate students ten days after it was first reported. He may not start out reading the sport page of the news each morning, but he certainly wouldn't confuse Joe Louis with John L. Lewis nor Joe Di Maggio with Leopold Stowkowski. General knowledge is easily attainable and a necessary element in successful conversation.

Expert or specific knowledge is not so readily possessed by the average citizen. Almost everyone, however, is an expert on some subject or at least sufficiently informed to ask intelligent questions. Common powers of observation possessed by the average man will give him detailed and specific information about his daily tasks. This is true whether he be a student, drugstore clerk, or gas station operator. Each position requires expert knowledge and this knowledge is the source of material necessary for good conversation. A bank teller of our acquaintance is a most interesting man to talk with. He operates on the principle that banking or those aspects of banking well known to a teller are never thrown into the conversation unless someone specifically requests such information. In addition to having expert knowledge on that subject, this teller has traveled in a good part of the country east of the Mississippi. Having the ABLE MAN powers of observation, he possesses expert information on matters of interest to the tourist. Since he has not traveled west of the Mississippi to any extent, he asks intelligent questions. He possesses detailed information on bridge, bowling, and the mechanics of house and yard upkeep. In these fields he can speak with authority and does so to a limited degree. Otherwise his conversation keeps on the level of general information and utilizes the technique of asking questions. He is a good conversationalist.

Fred Slimp found himself flunking rhetoric his first year in college. His difficulty, as explained by the instructor, was the lack of information about any one subject sufficient to write a theme or essay. Fred had only the most meager general information. He could express all he knew in one hundred words; hence a thousand-word theme assignment was a nightmare for him. The personnel bureau of the college, however, finally informed his instructor that Fred seemed to have two major interests, deep-sea fishing and popular music. These revelations did not put Fred in the ABLE MAN class, but they did open up two fields in which Fred could be classified as an expert. With these two subjects serving as a basis for conferences with Fred, his instructor was able to motivate him to better work in rhetoric.

The expert can give you detailed information on the most menial tasks and you will enjoy it; but, remember this, give the average man an opportunity to relate the detailed operations of his job, his hobby, or his experiences, and he will not only enjoy telling you, but he will enjoy you, and in all probability you will listen to his story with interest and benefit.

The third rule regarding material or subject matter in conversation, and perhaps the most important one, is to have knowledge and understanding of people. One must be able to size up a man and, after a few brief questions and remarks, properly classify his interests, temperament, likes and dislikes. Such knowledge permits adaptation to his interests and attitudes. It avoids insults, offensive comments, and embarrassing situations. One can hardly be a successful conversationalist by scornful remarks on religion to the religious, on athletics to the athlete, or on politics to the politician.

This ability affords one an opportunity to develop a keen appreciation for other people and their problems. The presence of this trait is sensed in some degree by all people; its absence is noted by describing people as "cool," "indifferent," or "uninteresting." Its presence can be further noted by such comments as,

"He is easy to talk with," "He warmed to my remarks," or "He is a real friend." This ability is gained essentially by observations and study of those around you. The ABLE MAN will make these observations and study without the aid of textbook and teacher.

Vocal and physical aspects of conversational expression

Delivery has been defined as all that the speaker does to create an impression or portray an idea to a listener or a group of listeners. This being true, it is necessary to consider not only what we hear from the speaker but also the physical aspects of the speaker that can be seen.

Vocal expression has variety in volume, rate, pitch, and quality. These four factors in combination are the elements of a good speaking voice. Keep the following *do's* and *don't's* before you:

Do's: Speak clearly, distinctly, with sufficient volume and force to be heard and understood. Avoid "lip laziness" in articulation of words. Be direct. Be animated. Let there be life and variety in rate, pitch, and volume. Pause at the end of sentences.

Don'ts: Don't grunt, "uh-uh-uh," "oh-ah-ah," "and-ah," or speak through closed lips or teeth or speak away from listeners.

When we speak we communicate attitudes and ideas through the outward manifestations of our body as effectively as by our oral expression. The difference between direct and indirect eye contact may denote the presence or lack of sincerity, interest, and friendship. A smile or a gloomy face reveals corresponding inner attitudes. The erect body and the slouched sitting position indicate degrees of physical vigor and alertness. These factors and many others so effectively add or detract from our conversation that great attention must be given them if we are to avoid mediocrity.

Rhetorical techniques of conversation

When you engage in the game of conversation with a friend, a business associate, or a stranger there are seven rules that, if followed, will make for success. Five of these are in the nature of rhetorical techniques or devices that should be used. The other two rules deal with *don't's* or rhetorical techniques that should be avoided in the majority of conversations. These rules are:

1. Ask questions.
2. Use common ground.
3. Observe the one-minute rule.
4. Be a good listener.
5. Be complimentary.
6. Don't argue.
7. Don't hit below the belt.

Ask questions. Usually one of two methods is used in starting a conversation. You either toss a subject into the conversation or ask a question or two; the latter is the more certain of receiving a response. Hence the technique of asking questions should be considered as the first and most important technique of successful conversation. The object of conversation, as we have already explained, is to improve one's acceptability to others. This is best done by motivating the other person to talk about himself and his interests and to make him feel that he is the important one in the conversation. Having done this, you will be better received by him.

You can ask three types of questions: first, a question calling for the other man's opinion; second, a question calling for his advice; and third, a question calling for information. Each question compliments him. It is a compliment to be regarded as having an opinion that others seek and it is a compliment to be asked to give advice or information. All such questions indicate that the asker has respect and confidence in the other man's judgment and knowledge. There is no more subtle type of flattery and no surer way of securing a response than by asking questions.

If you are asked to render an opinion on the war, you immediately feel more important and, even if you had no opinion, you would still feel important. You would also probably respond to the question in some fashion rather than permit the impression of ignorance to be created. Ask ten people their opinion on any subject and nine of them will give you an answer. Ask ten people for their advice on some decision which you have to make; all of them will respond, and eight of them will give you some advice.

Ask ten people for information on some subject of which they have knowledge, and all ten will respond with some information. For the sake of good conversation it is not important that the opinion, the advice, or the information be worth having. It is only important that the other fellow feel that you respect him, appreciate his intellect, and have confidence in his judgment. When that state of mind is created you have won a friend to whom you become day by day more acceptable.

Use common ground. You have played either at some game of cards or in some athletic contest. You have observed, without giving particular thought to the idea, that in each contest are players who play the same game with similar equipment and the same rules. Confusion and bedlam would prevail at a card table if twenty cards were from a bridge deck, twenty from a "rook" deck, ten from a flinch deck, and if two cards had no markings at all. What would you play? Or if you prefer, predict the type of athletic contest that would be produced by ten men dressed in track clothes on a football gridiron with ping-pong paddles and a basketball. Yet, without delving too deeply into your experience, you have undoubtedly participated in the game of conversation under similar conditions. Each person present has tossed a separate subject of his own interest into the pot; each person interrupts; each one goes into detail about his or her experience; and each attempts to out-talk the others. Voices become louder until finally the person with the most endurance and least tact prevails. For what purpose? No one knows. Has he made friends or has he only had his say? Did you remember him the next day in a more favorable light or did you remember him only as the man who robbed you of a chance to expound your brilliant exploits in typical Major Hoople fashion?

The use of common ground is the solution to this confusion. If you are to be successful, you will forget that you ran a hundred yards in ten flat or that you read *Gone with the Wind* in one sitting or that your mother is a D.A.R. Not that these are not worthy autobiographical facts, but for the purpose of successful conversation it is the other man and his interests that should become your interest. By so doing you succeed in discussing those things common to both of you, even if only common to you by choice for this particular conversation. If you are to direct the conversation into a successful channel, you will use as the subject matter those topics in which the other man has an interest and of which he has some knowledge or at least a desire to talk.

There will also be common rules to govern this interchange of talk about a common ground subject. The subject when arrived at will be thrown from person to person. There should be no star runner who "carried the ball all the way" by doing all the talking. There will be no unnecessary interrupter who selfishly wants to violate the rules of the game by displaying his special experiences, ideas, or preferences. There will be no thief who steals the show by unwarranted puns, over-dramatic gestures, or loud voice, only to lose it by his own villainy. No, the rules of this game require that you give more time, interest, and attention than you take.

Observe the one-minute rule. Perhaps you will ask how much time one should take with his own remarks in a conversation. Take not more than one minute at a time, but take it as often as necessary to keep the conversation going in the direction of the other person's interest. How many conversations have you heard where one person takes more than five minutes to express an idea that you fully and whole-heartedly listened to? They are few indeed, unless you have listened for the sole purpose of impressing the speaker with your interest in his wisdom. Don't take a chance on long speeches. Stay with the one-minute rule.

Be a good listener. This business of asking questions, talking about a subject primarily of interest to the other man, and the one-minute rule will require your being a good listener. Talk, to some extent at least, is just a vocal explosion of ego. It must have an ear. For those who want to deflate another's ego the best way is to refuse to listen. When a man talks, he thinks what he has to say is important, and you make it seem more important to him by being a good listener. This may seem to be a harsh rule for two good conversationalists, since only silence would prevail. If you are fortunate enough to engage a good conversationalist in verbal play, just waive the rule.

Be complimentary. Man is a vain animal, constantly seeking those who appreciate him. He is possessed with a soul hungry for praise. He is always inspired by kind words and compliments. He is raised from the depths of weary routine by his associations with those who believe in him and say a good word for his efforts. This element in human nature cannot be overlooked in our rules pertaining to conversation. Note the increased heart throb in youth when one of the opposite sex or when one of the same sex drops a complimentary remark about his charm or appearance. Even age does not dissipate the effectiveness of this technique. Pick out a particular feature about your classmate's work, your instructor's teaching, or your employer's management and speak a good word about it. Does it improve your relationship with them? Try it! Should any of these people say a good word to you about your work, you immediately sense a stronger bond. There are few whose heads are not turned by flattery. However, flattery should be used sparingly and always sincerely, never in jest. But it should be used.

Don't argue. The old saying has it "that a man convinced against his will is of the same opinion still." Whether this is true or not, the maxim contains a suggestion for successful conversation. Do not argue or discuss subjects that will give rise to emotional explosions on the part of either yourself or any other person. Such arguments are common and, to some degree, stimulating, but uncontrolled and intolerant discussions accomplish no good end. The best rule is to avoid such subjects.

You may enjoy displaying your superior knowledge on a subject, you may impress others as being a second Aristotle by your logic, and you may be called Demosthenes for your persuasive ability, but you will alienate the people you need for your success whenever they become the object of your argumentative gift. Whenever you attempt to force a man to admit that he is wrong, you have earned the first wage of resentment.

John Brooke, a young lawyer, brilliantly and heatedly pointed out to a friend of his that he, John, had a "three" and not a "four" on the ninth hole at the West Side Country Club; and he was right about the score. Two weeks later when his friend became executor of a $50,000 estate, Brooke was not employed as the attorney.

It is fun to put people in their place and to subject them to ignominy for intellectual dishonesty. But remember that for every person you so indict and prosecute you will have lost a potential friend and that your conversation. day by day, will be giving you the reputation of being a conceited ass and socially undesirable.

Don't hit below the belt. The last rule and the second *don't* is: Don't hit below the belt. This rule, if followed, would prevent a multitude of headaches for all parties concerned. A friend of yours is telling a story. He exaggerates a point here and there and you correct him. So what? Did your correction improve the story? Usually not. Did your correction have any effect on the story? Yes. It probably ruined it! More important than that, it irritated the storyteller and created in his mind an impression of you that was not complimentary. It was his story. Let him tell it! It may be that he follows the rule that truth should not stand in the way of a good story. If so, you have only exposed your ignorance by your correction. Don't correct a speaker unless a highly important matter is at stake.

Refrain from criticism, sarcasm, wisecracks, private huddles in a party of many, and revelations of the intimate details of people's lives that serve only to disparage. The greater part of this hitting below the belt in conversation results from carelessness and a caustic mind. Often after such remarks the person admits that "he just wasn't thinking about what he was saying." An ABLE MAN speaks only after he thinks.

Mrs. Hanks took her ten-year-old son to a neighbor's house for an evening's visit. The host's two-year-old daughter and the son played on the front porch. In the process the doorbell was rung and a potted plant dislodged from the porch railing. The son's mother exclaimed, "It must have been the little girl, because my son wouldn't do a thing like that." The girl's mother held her tongue and only after Mrs. Hanks and little Hanks left the party did she check the doorbell and the location of the potted plant to find them far out of the reach of her two-year-old daughter. Do I need to mention that Mrs. Hanks lost a friend?

Wounds like these do not heal overnight. When you leave nearly all the people you know scarred by your verbal onslaughts, you should easily understand the absence of invitations and real fellowship. Maybe you will not care, if business is good, because with money in your pocket you can take a lot of abuse. However, it is to a great extent these off-the-job, "below the belt" punches that bring the wolf to your door. John Crofts lost a $30,000 order when he wisecracked about "busted-pancake" hats, only to find out the next day that his listener was a buyer from a large department store. History records many who have paid dearly in time, money, energy, goodwill, and reputation by a verbal thrust as deadly as mustard gas.

It must be conceded, of course, that there are exceptions to these seven rhetorical techniques, but the cases are few where any one improves his acceptability to society or promotes his business and professional career by a continual violation of these rules. Therefore, *ask questions, adapt yourself to the interests of the other person, never take more than one minute at a time, be a good listener, be complimentary in a sincere manner, and don't argue or hit below the belt.*

QUESTIONS

1. Do you believe that conversation involves the elementary skills essential to all types of speaking? Explain your answer.

2. What is the major point of difference in the use of speech skills in conversation, conference speaking, and public speaking?

3. What are the essential similarities in the three types of speech situations?

4. What are the essential differences in the three types of speech situations?

5. Why should the rules and principles of good conversation be studied in advance of the study of conference and public speaking?

6. What rules should be recognized in conversation by and between friends?

7. What is the "time-taking-technique"? What rules should be followed in using this technique?

8. Can conversation become an art? How?

9. Would a good conversationalist talk primarily about himself or the other person in conversation? Why? What is the "you attitude"?

10. What are the three rules that should control the choice of material in a successful conversation?

11. What are the "do's" and "don't's" in vocal and physical aspects of conversational expression?

12. What are the seven rhetorical techniques to be followed in making successful conversation?

EXERCISES

1. Note the conversation of your companions at the dinner table. Make a report on why you enjoy the conversation of some and do not enjoy the conversation of others. Hand in a written report on the

principles and techniques used by those who are most successful in their conversations.

2. Report on the techniques and principles used in a conversation with your instructor or your employer. Did the use of these principles and techniques improve the conversation?

3. Apply these rules in conversation with a new acquaintance and report the results.

4. Study the rhetorical techniques of conversation. Use each one on ten different people and report the results.

SELECTED READINGS

Altstetter, Mabel Flick, *We All Talk,* Thomas Nelson & Son, New York, 1936.

Carroll, Loren, *Conversation Please,* Bobbs-Merrill Co., New York, 1939.

Pear, T. H., *The Psychology of Conversation,* Thomas Nelson & Son, New York, 1939.

Wright, Milton, *The Art of Conversation,* McGraw-Hill Book Co., Inc., New York, 1936.

Part II

THE BUSINESS CONFERENCE

CHAPTER IV

Conference Speaking

I. CONFERENCE SPEAKING DEFINED
II. CONFERRER AND CONFEREE DEFINED
III. GENERAL ASPECTS OF CONFERENCE SPEAKING
    The conference an arranged situation
    Time element
    Physical surroundings
    Business levels of those participating
IV. TYPES OF CONFERENCE SPEECHES
    Expository types
      Explanation
      Instruction
      Oral report
      Goodwill
    Persuasive types
      Question of policy
      Inspirational
      Job application
      Sales

CHAPTER IV

Conference Speaking

Conference Speaking Defined

CONFERENCE SPEAKING refers to the speech situation in which a limited number of persons engage in controlled conversation. It involves two or more people; the group, however, rarely being over eight or ten. When more people meet in conference, the speaking is usually in the nature of a public speech, with the listeners not privileged to interject questions. Conference speaking is involved when you apply for a job and may consist only of the question on your part, "Do you have any vacant positions in this plant?" and the answer by a foreman, "No." It may involve several interviews and many minutes of discussion about your qualifications, the employer's policies, and detailed facts about the position. The conference speech may be an oral report on some findings that you have been requested to make. You may be seeking information, as in cases where you see your doctor, dentist, or lawyer. Committee meetings usually utilize conference speaking under some application of parliamentary rules of procedure. Selling over a dry-goods store counter, over a desk in an office, or over a plow to a farmer, all require conference speaking. You may be trying to encourage a fellow student, employee, or friend, or you may be attempting to create goodwill in a prospective customer; the situation is still one of conference speaking. You and a friend may be discussing a joint venture or you and business associates may be discussing some question of policy in your business. These, too, are conference speaking.

Since conference speaking implies conversation in business and professional situations, it will be to our advantage first to recall the similarities between conversation and conference speaking. Effective participation in both involves the following requisites:

57

the ABLE MAN qualities, knowledge of subject matter, and the ability to organize the material and to deliver it effectively. Further evidence of the similarity between conversation and conference speaking is the fact that many businessmen believe that a great deal of their business can be transacted on the golf course or in the downtown club-rooms, where the atmosphere is more conducive to good fellowship and common ground interests. In these latter situations informality dominates the relationship between the participants, and, although business is transacted, the average onlooker would not be able to distinguish between the ordinary conversation and the business conference.

Conferrer and Conferee Defined

In order to discuss the problem of conference speaking clearly, it is first necessary to define the parties involved as the conferrer and conferee. The conferrer is the person seeking the conference. He initiates the speech situation. He may be either desirous of giving or seeking information, of persuading or being persuaded, although in most persuasive conferences he is the one who hopes to do the persuading. It is true that in some conferences the distinction between conferrer and conferee is more a figment of the imagination than of reality. It is also true that the positions of the two or more persons may change during the course of the conference. In situations such as the policy-determining conferences there is no distinction to be drawn between the persons participating. Here the conference is the result of mutual initiative and the objectives are so much of common interest to all that the efforts can be best spoken of as co-operative. Except for these latter exceptions, it will be helpful to keep in mind that it is the conferrer who sets the stage, directs the play, and rings down the final curtain; the conferee participates with a successful conferrer only to the extent that the latter provides, allows, encourages, and directs.

General Aspects of Conference Speaking

There are four essential features found in conference speaking that are not common to ordinary conversation. They occasion special study, if one is to master the skill of successful speaking in the business conference. These features include the fact that the conference is an arranged situation, the time element, the physical surroundings, and the business levels of those participating.

The conference an arranged situation

The conferrer has the duty of making the arrangements. This duty in itself necessitates a conference by telephone, or in person with the conferee or his secretary, or a letter requesting an appointment. The appointment may be made by the conferrer's briefly asking the conferee if he can see him at a given hour or at a time that is convenient for him. The conferee may ask the purpose of the appointment before granting it. He may conclude from the conferrer's conduct or statement of purpose that he is not interested in the proposal or information. This being true, the wise conferrer will prepare his request with care. This request should be designed to arouse the conferee's interest in the conferrer and his proposition and to create an attitude that will be most conducive to the development of the purpose at the time of the conference. It is often advisable to arrange the conference through some intermediary who is a mutual friend of both parties, especially if the conferrer is not known to the conferee.

The conferrer cannot even afford to be careless about arranging an appointment with a business acquaintance or a social friend whom he hopes to engage in some business transaction. It may correctly be assumed that less formality need be employed, but it may be disastrous to avoid the use of skill. Remember this point in arranging a conference: the usual attitude of John Jones, when you request an appointment, is that you want something. This attitude causes him immediately to put up his guard. If he knows you, he may have some basis for that attitude. Furnish him with reasons for believing that he will benefit from your visit or that some other desire will be satisfied. In nearly all conferences, except the sales and job application interviews, you should be able to create a favorable attitude on the part of John Jones for hearing your proposal in conference by making a brief statement of its purpose during the arrangement of it. Even in the sales and job application interviews you will probably create goodwill by stating the purpose of your proposed call on John Jones when you make the appointment. You may lose an appointment or two by telling Jones that you are a sales representative, but you will not lose many sales. The man who will not give you an appointment when properly approached probably will not buy anyway. Furthermore, your refusal or failure to state your purpose will usually cause Jones to develop an unsatisfactory idea regarding you in advance of the interview. He may conceive the idea that you are to be the bearer of some scheme for great riches or he may conclude that your secrecy forebodes a kidnapping plot or a hold-up. In the former case he will want to throw you out when he is told that you are seeking employment or selling tom-toms. In the latter case his imagination creates a thousand doubts and a hundred negative responses to you and your proposal before he sees or hears either.

It has already been stated that the average business conference is an arranged or semiarranged meeting. The latter situation represents those conferences not scheduled by appointments, but rather those that result from the fact that a businessman has an office or a place of business that is designed in part for the purpose of seeing the people necessary to conduct and carry out his business ventures. Thus the average businessman has arranged for conferences, although he does not know exactly when they are to take place. This is true of the lawyer, the doctor, the storekeeper, the corporation president, and the personnel manager. Gas stations, homes, and automobiles may be the scene of business transactions for the salesman and the promoter. Certain hours of the day may be scheduled for appointments whether made in advance or taken advantage of merely when the businessman is not otherwise engaged. All such conferences are thus correctly spoken of as being semiarranged.

In these semiarranged situations, the ABLE MAN will utilize the same skills in gaining the interview and creating goodwill and favorable attitudes on the part of the conferee that he uses in the arranged conference. In this situation, however, he finds that he must adapt himself more rapidly and adjust himself to the surroundings with less plan and preparation, especially when meeting the conferee for the first time. Although the conferee expects to have people call on him and has arranged a place for this purpose, he does not expect any particular person with any particular proposal to make a call. The conferrer can best accept this arranged hospitality and adjust himself to a procedure designed for success, if he has made a careful analysis of the conferee in advance of the conference.

Time element

There may be a few exceptions, but, in general, there are two types of business and professional men. One is a very busy man. The other would have you believe that he is very busy. Both types of men require that the conferrer limit his time in conference. Thus the second unique feature about a business conference is the fact that it is usually limited in time. Only in rare moments should talk be engaged in for talk's sake. Unless the conferee promotes it and the conferrer believes it to be his advantage to indulge in it, talk for talk's sake should not be tolerated. It is well to realize that too many conferrers kill valuable time both at the beginning and the end of a conference by talking off the subject. Since the conferrer has been allowed ten or thirty minutes or such time as will be needed to present his case, he should be prepared to utilize that time efficiently in presenting his case. This does not mean that he must forego conversation about mutual friends and subjects of mutual interest. Conversational techniques should be used by the conferrer to create goodwill and favorable attitudes on the part of the conferee. But they should also be controlled. Since the conferee is good enough to grant some of his time, the conferrer should not abuse it, but rather, use it.

Two illustrations may help in further understanding this point. Joe Thompson is a great golf enthusiast and a good player. He would rather talk golf, practice golf, and play golf than eat. It happens that Joe travels for a tobacco company for a living. Joe relates the following incident: He had an appointment with the buyer for a large chain of drugstores. He had devoted the best part of three days to arranging and preparing for the interview. At last he was in the office. He noticed a golf trophy on the buyer's desk. He used this as a common ground approach. The approach subject was so successful that he had mentioned only in an incidental way the promotional plan for the tobacco goods carried in his briefcase when he found the conference being terminated in what he thought was a successful close. Out

in the corridor he was not certain of just what he had accomplished, but he did recall that the buyer had said, "yes" and
that he would dictate an order immediately. When Joe received
his next communication from the home office, he was bewildered
by the contents, which raised the question, "What are you selling,
golf balls? Report in person to home office immediately."
There he was presented with the order from his conferee. It
read, "Please send two dozen golf balls of the make used by your
pro, Mr. Thompson."

The second story is about John Bridger, the busy executive
for Pan Handle Foods, Inc. When Bridger feels that a conferrer is wasting his time by small talk and unnecessary chatter,
he uses a special buzzer which calls his secretary into the office
with the announcement, "Mr. Bridger, may I remind you of
your appointment with Mr. Plum?" Bridger willingly considers all well-stated proposals, but for conferrers who blunder
and talk around the point, he has developed a very impressive
"I greatly regret that I must interrupt this delightful talk. Mr.
Plum is waiting to see me about a shipment of prunes to Pata-
gonia. Good day." The conference is over. The conferrer is
out with only his social security card to be thankful for.

The first of these two cases is an exception to the "mine-run"
variety. The second case is not atypical of the many businessmen who have developed to a high degree the art of saying, "Is
there anything *else* that you care to see me about?" "Well, that
is very interesting. I'm glad you *came* in," "Your proposition
is interesting. You *may* hear from me," and "I'm very busy
now. Call again when you are in the city." These statements
and others, given with that commanding air of finality as the
conferee stands up from his chair, terminate conferences unsuc-
cessfully for time-consuming conferrers. But if you will state
your case and adapt it to the time element allowed, you may expect better results. This is not an unreasonable requirement
placed on conferrers by businessmen.

Physical surroundings

Except for the conference of the house-to-house salesman, the
average conference is held in the office of the conferee, the office of
the conferrer, or a conference room agreed upon by each. The

office or conference room may be furnished with modernistic indirect lighting and toadstool furniture, or it may be furnished only with the average desk, a few chairs, and a work table. There may or may not be an outer waiting-room where you can remove your hat and coat and find a chair. The office may be occupied by one, two, six, or a dozen people. It may not be an office in the common sense of the word. It may be only a desk and chair in the shop, or the work table of the architect, or the bench of the layout men. It does not matter what the physical surroundings are, except that they belong to the conferee and constitute, in part, the tools with which he does his work. It is this feature of the physical surroundings of the business conference that needs special attention.

Common law rules that a man's home is his castle and as such he can, if necessary, defend it at the price of an intruder's life. Current statutes have placed no such premium on a man's office or his place of business. Fond mothers, Emily Post, and fraternity and sorority social chairmen have a great deal to say about proper conduct, manners, and etiquette in the presence of others. While on many occasions these rules tend to make one stiff and uncomfortable, we all admit the merit of good manners. We further concede that good manners indicate good breeding and that good breeding creates more favorable attitudes and more pleasing relationships than does the lack of it. This trait known as good manners in the home is not, like your Sunday suit, to be left in your closet during the other six days of the week. It is to be worn and exhibited with the same care and grace used by a gentleman in seeing that the lady is seated first or determining that the fork is a better instrument for peas than the knife.

The ABLE MAN then would use the hall tree, a vacant chair, or his lap for his coat and hat rather than deposit them on the conferee's desk. He would remain standing, until invited with either an articulate or an inarticulate expression to be seated. He would refrain from reading letters and other literature on the desk. He would sit in a relaxed but attentive and businesslike manner. It would be improper for him to smoke the conferee's tobacco, or even smoke at all, unless invited to do so by the host. It would certainly be inadvisable for him to be critical of office furniture or business facilities.

The authors appreciate the fact that these precepts are very elementary. But we also realize that they are often violated as is shown in the following incident: An outstanding commerce student, college debater, and law student, entered the practice of law in a medium-sized mid-western city. As is the case with many young lawyers, he found time on his hands and proceeded to use this time to visit older attorneys and the local courts. He had developed the habit of sucking an old pipe, pouring himself into a chair, and either throwing his legs over the arm of the chair or putting his feet on a desk. He became generally disliked by the senior members of his profession for these physical manifestations of indifferences to the privacy of their offices.   But it was not until the judge halted court proceedings in order to give this young attorney a lecture on the ethics of personal conduct in the courtroom that the attorney realized that by his own careless conduct he had greatly deferred his progress in the profession before that court, and even though his record as a young lawyer was good, he felt it advisable to move to another county to continue his practice. The conferrer, then, must conduct himself in a manner that will show respect for the conferee's property and the privacy of his office.

Business levels of those participating

The fourth and most delicate feature about the business conference is the business or professional levels of the persons concerned. There is nearly always a difference in the business capacity of the two people. In many conferences the parties represent different businesses or professions between which there is wide variance in position and influence. This difference in level gives one member of the conference the advantage of being the psychologically dominant figure. Because of this factor, both parties may silently agree that one of the two is greatly superior in intellect, business foresight, and sound judgment. This belief, often unsupported by anything other than supposition, gives the thought-to-be-superior party a great advantage in conference speaking. Since this person is often the conferee, the conferrer is forced to adjust himself mentally or be outdone without knowing why or how.

Hitler is probably the only person today who believes that he has no superior. All human people—obviously a redundant term, but it must be made to allow for exceptions—believe or feel at times and in various degrees that other people are superior or inferior to them. It is interesting to hear the truck driver relate his experience in the last war when he, as a first sergeant, discovered his home town bank cashier as a buck private in his company. It is just as interesting to hear the intellectually inferior student who is an excellent swimmer tell how he saved his Phi Beta Kappa professor from drowning in Lake Yoho and regretted it the next semester. If you have ever applied for a position, you may recall that you were cognizant of the fact that the man with whom you had your interview held a somewhat superior position in the conference. The conferee seemed to be the manifestation of some special capacity. He was a banker, a manager, a buyer, a president, a lawyer, a store owner, a superintendent, or a professor. To you he was a man with special powers or reputation, or the position he held was something big in your mind. He was a "somebody." He was a man who could and did do great things. These thoughts and others, all somewhat vague and very general, developed in your mind the idea of a man that was beyond you. You simply did not feel that you were his equal.

It is this feeling that gives rise to the fact that one person, usually the conferee when the conferrer is immature, is the dominant psychological figure in a conference. It is many times only an illusion, but nevertheless it is as effective in governing the conduct of the parties as if it were a reality. The more mature and experienced person does not conjure up these imaginary supermen as readily as one who is immature and inexperienced. To many experienced businessmen conferee John Jones is not a mythical man, but simply another businessman with special training and aptitudes for the particular business in which he is engaged. For these businessmen John Jones may have a better reputation in the community, his word may carry more weight in arriving at a decision, and he may be drawing a larger salary. These elements are known and evaluated in their true light. They create real differences in the business level between the two men, but they do not give rise to illusions of grandeur or false values.

The ABLE MAN conferrer will evaluate the conferee according to his real and actual business level. He will know his special training and experience, as well as his aptitudes, reputation, and real ability. With this knowledge he can adjust himself to the conference in a normal and natural manner in order to accomplish the maximum understanding and agreement for himself and his proposal. To illustrate the difference in effectiveness on the part of a conferrer who has illusions about the conferee and the one who understands the real qualities, let us examine a few cases.

Jim Blixer, a young lawyer, filed his first case in the Federal District Court presided over by Judge Case. It was Jim's firm conviction that the Judge was a political stooge of H. L. Grein, opposing counsel in the suit. Jim further thought that Judge Case was prejudiced against inexperienced attorneys, very hard to please in the courtroom, dictatorial in his rulings, and wholly uncompromising in requiring adherence to the rules of evidence. As a result of these imaginary concepts, fabricated from hearsay, gossip, and fear, Jim devoted hours to mastering federal procedure and the rules of law. This, of course, was a worth-while study, but in this particular case it consumed a far greater portion of available time than was necessary. As a result Blixer went to trial without having investigated properly his evidence and having failed entirely to brief any law on the questions at issue. Furthermore, he was scared. In his mind the gods were against him. He could not win, but he was determined to put up a good fight. For two days he struggled with imaginary odds against him. He made no objections to Grein's statements and questions, although many were legally objectionable and he knew it. He accepted Grein's objections and the Judge's rulings without argument, in spite of the fact that the law was in his favor on many points. He did nothing that he thought might displease the Judge or indicate criticism of Mr. Grein. After court adjourned the second day, Jim, realizing his inability to cope with the case, secured the aid of T. R. Corson as associate counsel for the remainder of the trial. Corson, an experienced lawyer, knew the Judge to be an expert, experienced in his field, and one having the reputation of being honest and fair on the judicial bench. Corson also knew that Grein was a shrewd lawyer, a master of trial practice, and a persuasive speaker. But he had no illusions about these two men. He knew exactly how to adapt himself to the situation. He objected, questioned, and argued when it was to the client's interest to do so. Thus, for the last two days of the trial the plaintiff was well represented. This resulted not because Corson knew federal procedure or the rules of evidence better than Jim Blixer, for he did not; but Corson correctly evaluated the professional level of the men he had to work with, and, because of this correct evaluation, he was able to adapt himself to the task of trying a lawsuit in the most efficient manner. Although Blixer's client won his case, he did not employ Blixer to represent him in further lawsuits. This failure is just one of the many that result from the inability to gauge properly the business or professional level of men.

Ruth Tarkington remarked that when she prepared her first interview for a position as a food specialist she believed all employers to be cold, hardheaded, inhuman, cross, and difficult to talk with. Because of these illusions she attempted to prepare herself for interviewing just such persons. The effort was futile. "It is like trying to prepare yourself for the electric chair; you just cannot do it and be satisfied." Therefore, Miss Tarkington in conference was inarticulate, afraid, and suffered from a serious feeling of inferiority. However, she stated that in nearly every case she found the conferee human, friendly, and talkative. But each new conferee aroused in her the old fears. She consulted an older friend. With his advice and her experience she was finally able to evaluate a conferee according to his actual business level and personality traits. The subsequent conferences were much easier.

We should note that the ABLE MAN conferrer will recognize the exact business level of the conferee and adapt himself accordingly. He will not create a fanciful, unreal, or chimerical figure, the thought of which will jeopardize his preparation or participation in the conference. He will not handicap himself by taking the psychologically subordinate position any more than you would bet even money against the New York Yankees when they hold a ten-run lead in the eighth inning.

Types of Conference Speeches

The majority of conference speeches may be classified as follows: explanation, instruction, oral report, goodwill, inspirational, question of policy, job application, and sales. The first four types of conference speeches are essentially expository, while the last four types are persuasive in nature. It is true that any business conference, whether it be expository or persuasive, has as its ultimate objective, either directly or indirectly, increased business or improvement of the business and professional status of the members participating.

Expository types

Explanation. This type refers to the conference designed to present subject matter in detail, apart from critical evaluation or argument. An explanation is primarily a "setting forth" for purposes of elucidation, or display. It is given in answer to the question, "What?"

Instruction. This type of conference has as its purpose the imparting of information, knowledge, or skill. It furnishes directions and disciplines to the conferee. It answers the question, "How?"

Oral report. The oral report involves exposition applied to a situation where the conferrer has been requested to make an investigation on a particular subject or where the conferrer in his regular line of duty does investigation work or keeps records. The oral report grows out of the situation wherein this investigator or keeper of records makes a verbal report either to those persons requesting the report or to those persons who, by nature of their position, are particularly concerned with the facts to be revealed.

Goodwill. The goodwill speech is designed to create a favorable attitude toward the speaker or the business that he represents by presenting such information as will produce favorable attitudes on the part of the hearers.

Persuasive types

Question of policy. The term "policy" means a course of action followed or to be followed. Thus the question of policy conference or speech concerns itself with determining or confirming courses of action.

Inspirational. The inspirational conference stimulates the hearers to a higher state of morale and an increased degree of efficiency and productivity.

Job application. The job application conference or interview attempts to secure employment, change of employment, or a promotion in the same employment.

Sales. The sales conference is designed to sell some product, skill, or service other than employment or to promote the sales of these commodities.

QUESTIONS

1. What is conference speaking?
2. What are the similarities between conference speaking and conversation?
3. Define conferrer. Define conferee.
4. What are the four essential features in conference speaking that demand special study?
5. What rules should govern a conferrer in arranging a conference?
6. Why should the conferrer respect the time element involved in a conference?
7. How should a conferrer conduct himself in respect to the physical surroundings in the conferee's place of business?
8. Why is it important that the conferrer gauge properly the conferee's business level before holding the conference?
9. What are the eight types of conference speeches?
10. What types of conference speeches fall into the general class of expository speaking and what types fall into the general class of persuasive speaking?

EXERCISES

1. Hold a conference with your instructor on some problem about which you are seeking his advice. Prepare in advance of this conference a statement in answer to the following questions:
  (a) Who is the conferrer? The conferee?
  (b) How will this conference differ from a conversation with your instructor held while meeting him informally in your home? How will the conference be similar to the conversasation in your home?
  (c) What steps will be taken and what will be said by you in arranging the conference?
  (d) What is your business, professional, or academic level?

What is the business, professional, or academic level of your instructor?

(e) How do you plan on adjusting yourself to the level of the instructor?

2. Hold a conference with some business or professional man in your community. Prepare in advance of this conference a statement in answer to the same questions used above.

3. After having held the two conferences write a report on the following:

(a) Problems involved in arranging the conference.

(b) Problems involved in meeting the time element of the conference.

(c) Problems involved in adapting yourself to the physical surroundings of the conference.

(d) Problems involved in adjusting yourself to the business level of the conferee.

CHAPTER V

Elements of Conference Speaking

I. DETERMINING THE SPECIFIC PURPOSE
II. ANALYSIS
    Conferee—the man
    Conferee's business or profession
    Conferee's attitude toward conferrer
    Conferee's present or potential interest in the subject
      of the conference
III. MATERIALS AND ORGANIZATION
    Materials
    Organization
IV. STRATEGIES AND TECHNIQUES OF PRESENTATION
    "Please-thank-you smile"
    Common ground
    "You attitude"
    "Yes response"
    "Trial close"

Elements of Conference Speaking

BILL MILLER, top salesman for the Reliable Insurance Company, is introduced to Stanley Kuhlman, wealthy farmer with a family of seven. Does Miller look Kuhlman over from top to toe and immediately suggest that Kuhlman buy insurance? No. Only in an exceptional situation would an ABLE MAN salesman try to make a sales presentation without preparation. When you seek employment, do you start to ask every man you see for a job, and "just any" job at that? When you want to explain a matter to Mrs. Nickles, do you not find it easier if you know something about her and what she knows? Noah spent years preparing for a flood that lasted only forty days and forty nights. Joe Louis trains for weeks for a fight that may last less than two minutes. The average college student devotes sixteen years to preparing himself for a job, yet he often fails to get it because he consumes less than five minutes preparing himself for the conference to secure that job.

The study of conference speaking will necessitate focusing our attention on the following four elements: (1) determining the specific purpose of the conference, (2) analysis of the conferee, his business or profession, his attitude toward the conferrer, and his present or potential interest in the subject of the conference, (3) preparation of the material or subject matter, and (4) preparation of strategies or techniques of presenting the material and controlling the conference.

Determining the Specific Purpose

Speaking, like any other serious activity, should be engaged in with a specific purpose. The most successful men in all walks of life are men who have selected a goal and worked energetically toward that goal. A majority of the failures in this world are not men who have too little ability but men who have too little direction and purpose in what they are doing with their abilities. Employment bureaus as well as college personnel bureaus are beginning to emphasize this fact by asking job seekers and students to state their purpose in life and to state the specific goals that they wish to attain.

When you start traveling for your vacation, do you just start out and go? You probably select a destination. You determine the route that you will take in order to reach that destination. Petroleum companies throughout the country recognize this need for a specific purpose and a specific route in traveling and furnish excellent "tour-aids" with particular emphasis on the points of destination and how to arrive at those points.

The attorney-at-law files a charge against some defendant. If the charge is vague and so general that the defendant is not apprised of the exact nature of the charge, then the court will, on proper motion, require the attorney to make his charge more specific and definite. This is just another way of saying that a legal charge must be specific and must be stated with a high degree of accuracy.

Do not be satisfied with the determination of only a general purpose for your speech. If your only purpose in life is the general purpose of living, then remember that rodents, porcupines, fish, and toadstools have that same purpose. If your only purpose in speaking is to talk, then remember that morons, parrots, and artificial talking-machines are in the same category.

The first element to be mastered in preparing for a conference speech is to select the specific purpose. Determine exactly the objective to be worked toward in the conference. Formulate this objective with certainty. It is often helpful to write a complete sentence that expresses your purpose, to memorize it, and then throughout the conference to keep a constant check on your speaking to see that everything you say contributes to the accomplishment of that specific purpose.

There are two primary advantages in selecting the specific purpose at the start: it determines what you intend to accomplish in the conference and it permits you to prepare the most efficient plan.   Although you must consider your ability, the factual material in your possession, the conferee's likes, dislikes, abilities, experiences, and other factors, they have little or no bearing on the conclusion of the conference until you have selected the specific purpose.   Once this purpose has been selected you are ready to measure, evaluate, study, and prepare all other factors so that you can drive a true course toward that purpose and thus insure a successful conclusion.

Analysis

The engineer works with steel and concrete.   The doctor works with medicine, broken legs, and cancer.   The laborer works with tools, machinery, and his muscles.   The conferrer works with people.   His results are determined not by the bridges that he builds, not by the lives that he saves, not by the houses that he constructs, but by the people whom he influences, instructs, informs, inspires, persuades, or in whom he creates goodwill.   Thus the second element to be mastered in preparing for a conference is that of analyzing the man with whom you are to confer.   This problem of analysis should be divided into four parts: (1) analysis of the man, (2) analysis of his business or profession, (3) analysis of his attitude toward you, and (4) analysis of his present and his potential interest in the subject of the conference.

Conferee—the man

An individual starts out in life as a squirming mass of protoplasm.   By the time he is old enough to vote he has become the product of our democracy which allows him an opportunity for education, freedom of worship, a chance to earn a livelihood, and the right to gain some social status.   His environment has conditioned him with likes and dislikes, beliefs and disbeliefs.   He is either energetic or lethargic, intelligent or ignorant, optimistic or pessimistic, talkative or taciturn.   These intrinsic characteristics must be analyzed and studied by the successful conferrer.

Many factors influence a man's response.   His age is an important element.   Youth is optimistic, enthusiastic, careless in exercising judgment, and willing to take a chance. Maturity creates conservative tendencies, a degree of pessimism, disappointments, and sounder business judgment. Education, formal or otherwise, tends to increase the scope of information possessed and the ability to reason and understand a proposition. It tempers fear, emotion, and prejudice in a man's mind. Experience in traveling, reading, having contacts with people, and living among others broadens one's point of view, makes one more tolerant and easier to talk with. Family status, club and fraternity associations, hobbies and special skills in sports will develop special interests. Particular experiences, such as automobile accidents, fires, deaths, divorces, relatives who have succeeded or failed, wars, bank crashes, unemployment, stock market success or failure, and happy home life will all leave their imprint on the conferee or on the conferrer. Such experiences, when known to the other person in a conference, can be used to promote interest in a proposal or avoided to prevent failure.

One often hears the remark, "If I knew the man, I wouldn't have any trouble talking with him." Maybe you have a friend who comes to you or to whom you go with this request, "I don't know the man. Won't you talk to him for me?" These statements represent an element of fear on the part of the speaker, a fear based on lack of understanding and knowledge. It can be most easily dissipated, when actual acquaintance is impossible, by completely analyzing the man. The next best thing to knowing Roosevelt, Willkie, Wallace, Knudsen, Ford, or Churchill in person is to study, read, and talk about them from and with sources that do know them. Think of your analysis in terms of scouting the enemy. Study of the opponent is always a prelude to competition in baseball, football, prize fighting, or horse racing. Baseball catchers are as important as pitchers, since it is the man behind the plate who studies the merits and weaknesses of the batter and tells the pitcher where to throw the ball. Military units of the government spend millions annually studying opposing military forces. We can take a lesson from all this, and, if we profit from this lesson, we will analyze our man before we engage him in a business conversational duel. The following outline may be used as a starting point in this problem of analysis:

SUGGESTED OUTLINE FOR CONFEREE PRE-ANALYSIS

Factual Information

Age
Position
Salary
Family background
Memberships
  Nonprofessional
  Professional
  Recreational
  Traveling experience
  Education
    Degrees
    Publications
    Academic Activity
  Hobbies
Outside Interests

Appraisals

Intelligence level
  General knowledge
  Special knowledge
Sense of humor
Patience
Talkativeness
  Opinion of self
  Mental attitudes, complexes, likes,
    dislikes, etc.
  Personality traits
  Anything else you can discover

Conferee's business or profession

From the point of succeeding in a conference it is important to know the conferee, but it is of no less importance to know the particular business or profession with which he is connected. In most business and professional conferences, the conferrer knows at least the type of business in which the conferee is engaged; that is, he knows whether the business is manufacturing, teaching, or the practice of medicine. But the analysis of the business should not stop with this surface information. Suppose you are applying for a position with the Mansfield Products Corporation. You should know the policies regarding salaries, retirement, sickness benefit payments, labor unions, unemployment compensation, and opportunities for advancement. These policies will tell you much about whether you want the position, provided it is offered to you, and will acquaint you with the terms and conditions under which you will be asked to work. You should have knowledge of the specific products and services made and rendered by the Mansfield Products Corporation. You should know about their main office, their branch offices, their main plant, their branch plant or plants, their advertising program, their educational program, their markets present and potential, and you should have ideas that will help promote the corporate business and goodwill. With this information you can make yourself appear to be an asset to the corporation, if employed.

Conferee's attitude toward conferrer

The conferee's attitude toward the conferrer may be expressed either in terms of confidence, trust, appreciation, respect, faith, and mutual understanding or in terms of lack of confidence, distrust, disrespect, disbelief, and lack of understanding. The conferee may have no opinion of, or attitude toward, the conferrer before meeting him in conference. However, he will have opinions and attitudes in the process of formation the minute he sees and shakes hands with him. In part, the success of the conference will depend on these opinions and attitudes. If they are favorable, you may, of course, expect more success than if they are unfavorable. In any given case you should try to gauge your partner's attitude toward you and conduct yourself accordingly.

Conferee's present or potential interest in the subject of the conference

In many conferences you will find that the conferee has a high degree of present or potential interest in the subject of the conference. In the oral report conference this interest is evidenced by the fact that the conferee has usually requested the information that you are presenting. In the exposition, instruction, goodwill, question of policy, and inspirational conferences the conferee's interest in the subject will be as high as that of the conferrer, if the subject is properly presented. In all such conferences, the conferee has as much to gain from the conference as has the conferrer. In many of these conferences the conferee has more to gain from the conference than has the conferrer. Your oral report may be the basis for building a new plant or opening a new store that will increase the stockholders' yearly income to a greater degree than it will increase your salary. Your instructions may serve to increase the bookkeeper's efficiency to the point of increasing his salary without necessarily increasing yours. The question of policy speech has the welfare of the company foremost in consideration and this will contribute to the benefit of all participants. The goodwill speech should produce profitable relationships for the business that you represent with the public as the beneficiary of your increased service.

You can easily understand the present or potential interest that the conferee has in such conferences, though you may not realize that the same factor holds true to only a lesser degree in the sales and job application interviews. Broadly stated, all business is interested in buying and selling either a physical commodity or a service. This involves essentially the process of first buying materials and labor; second, producing some goods or services; and third, marketing these goods or services to consumers. The consumers are interested in their purchases, since by them they are able to satisfy their wants and desires. It should, then, be recognized that Sam Bowers is as interested in buying the services of a carpenter to build his house, a bookkeeper to keep his books, or an engineer to plan and direct his construction work, as John Peel is in selling his ability as a carpenter, bookkeeper, or engineer. Bowers has as great an interest in buying lumber for his house, equipment for his office, or steel for his construction work as John Peel has in trying to sell the same commodities.

The problem that confronts John Peel in both the job application and sales interview is to impress Sam Bowers with the fact that it is his, John Peel's, services or commodities that will best satisfy Bowers' needs. Therefore, a proper analysis of needs, wants, and desires should be undertaken. When this is done, in preparing for his job application interview or sales conference, Peel can present himself or his commodities in such a manner as to make the strongest appeal. A careful analysis guarantees a mutuality of interest in the subject matter and tends to remove conflicting interests or objections on the part of the conferee that might disrupt conference harmony and prevent success.

Materials and Organization

Materials

If you are baking a cake or building a bridge, you would do two things before starting the baking or the construction: you would gather the necessary ingredients for the cake or the materials for the bridge and you would determine in advance the order and method of putting them together to bake a good cake or build a useful bridge. In constructing a speech these steps are not to be overlooked. To do so will cause your explanation to be lacking in clarity, your argument to be groundless, and your job application to be devoid of any real reason why you should be employed. Both gathering and organizing the material are essential to successful conference speaking.

One cardinal rule should govern the material that you will use in a conference speech, whether it be expository or persuasive in type. Your material should abound in concrete and specific illustrations and examples. Should you be asked on applying for a position what you can do, be prepared to answer that you can take shorthand, type, sell shoes, operate a drill, drive a truck, or take care of babies. Don't answer that you "can do anything." You may be taken at your word and asked to run a chemical analysis or perform an appendectomy. Be specific. To do this you must be prepared with specific materials in advance of the interview. In the question of policy conference you may be asked to justify your support of the thesis that the advertising budget should be increased. If your answer is merely that you know what is good for the company, or that it will make more money, or that some other companies are doing it, or that you like some sponsored radio program and you thought your company ought to try a similar program your answer will probably be met with the further question, "How do you know that it will make more money?" or "What specific facts support your contention that the company ought to increase the budget?" Not only will you be unable to answer these questions, but also you will have no influence on the conferee. You cannot drive tacks with a fly-swatter or a golf ball with a broom. You may touch on the subject superficially and you may attract some attention to it, but you cannot be successful with it when using generalities. In a conference you can make a hit that counts only when you have specific facts, illustrations, and examples at hand.

Many people confronted with the problem of speaking, in either the conference or the public platform situation, realize the importance of this rule but feel that they are unable to find material suitable for such occasions. This is particularly true of those lacking maturity and experience. However, adequate material is not difficult to secure, provided you have the necessary energy and ingenuity and use a systematic approach. Sources of material may be classified as follows: firsthand knowledge, observation, experience, and recorded information that may be studied. The ABLE MAN will have the ability to observe and will observe many things that can be used in speaking situations. He will read the newspapers, periodicals, trade journals connected with his field, and other publications that come to his attention and read them with the ability to detect and remember the important and pertinent information. He will hear speeches presented on the radio, from the public platform, and in conference from which he will remember significant facts and opinions. He will recall that his formal education presented much in the way of information about history, political science, literature, geography, world trade, domestic economics, and the exact sciences. For him, past conversations in the home and on the street will have contained worth-while facts about local, state, and national affairs. All of this information will be at his disposal when he needs it.

The ABLE MAN will know that if he does not have the necessary information at hand, he can probably secure it from some person who has expert knowledge on the subject. These experts will be approached in an effort to secure the material needed. The local banker, lawyer, dry goods store manager, Community Chest director, Farm Bureau director, and school teacher are all experts in their field. Business, government, and educational institutions abound in directors, experts, and information bureaus whose sole purpose is that of supplying information to those who request it.

Nor will the ABLE MAN shun the task of doing individual

research to provide himself with adequate material. This consists primarily of doing one or both of two things: original investigation or experimentation and reading what others have discovered or think about the subject. As a result of William Knudsen's experimentation with welding while director of OPM welding has replaced riveting in ship building and in other construction. Knudsen secured his information by original experimentation with welding in an effort to discover a method of speeding up the construction of ships for the defense program. Should the reader not have the opportunity for original research, then he can turn to the thousands of reports contained in books and magazines and read the best opinions and results of other people's research and thought. In order to locate the information and material desired, it will be helpful to consult your local library catalogues, guides, and indexes. The general references and guides to be found there are the card catalogue, the Reader's Guide, the Industrial Arts Index, and the Public Affairs Information Service. These in turn will direct you to books, general publications and periodicals, scientific and technical publications and periodicals, and special reports and publications issued by various governmental and business units. The Public Affairs Information Service, for example, contains reports of business firms and associations that should be particularly helpful to one seeking information for a business conference. In addition to these general sources, the trade and business journals and professional magazines are helpful in securing special information about particular fields.

Organization

Material once secured and recorded on cards, note paper, or in record books will, as a general rule, not be sufficiently organized or arranged to justify presentation in that form. It should be organized to gain the maximum clarity, understanding, and conviction in its presentation. The main organization will consist of an introduction, discussion or body, and a conclusion. The introduction serves two functions: it should introduce the subject matter and gain favorable attention and interest. The discussion or body of the material should be organized around the specific purpose. This can best be done by selecting the two, three, or four main reasons or central points that support the specific purpose.   These should be set out distinctly and apart from other materials in order that the conferrer can concentrate on their development.   These main points selected to support the specific purpose will in turn be supported and developed by using the numerous concrete and specific illustrations and examples that the conferrer has gathered.   The above organization of the discussion will be made subject to necessary adjustments during the presentation.   However, this point should be kept in mind in conference speaking: if the conferrer fails to develop his material along some planned course directed at accomplishing the specific purpose of the conference, he may reasonably expect to fall short of that specific purpose.   Thus, even though the discussion allows for adjustments and adaptations during the conference, it must pursue a definite course.   The conclusion should usually serve two functions: first, it should summarize the subject matter as developed in the discussion, and second, it should appeal for a favorable close.   In the exposition conferences, this favorable close is usually gained by a summary of the main reasons or central points developed in the discussion.   However, in the persuasive conferences, the favorable close involves a distinct appeal for belief or action in keeping with the conferrer's specific purpose; and if that is not obtainable, then the appeal should be of the sort that will create goodwill and leave the door open for future favorable associations with the conferee.

Strategies and Techniques of Presentation

There are a few easily mastered rules that can be followed advantageously in presenting a conference speech: (1) The "Please-Thank-You-Smile," (2) common ground, (3) "you attitude," (4) the "yes response," and (5) the "trial close."

"Please-Thank-You-Smile"

You may recall the old fairy story which set forth the characters "Please," "Thank You," and "Smile." These characters symbolized success, manly traits, pleasing and forthright relationships with others, and, above all, courteous, polite, and well-bred people.   We thus believe that the first and foremost technique to be used in a conference is what we shall call the "Please-Thank-

You-Smile" technique. This does not mean that you are constantly smiling. It simply means that your whole attitude and bearing during the conference is one denoting genuine appreciation for the conferee's time and attention. It further denotes that you are in a healthy mental and physical state. When this "Please-Thank-You-Smile" technique is employed you may anticipate a more congenial reception on the part of the person with whom you are conferring.

Common ground

In the chapter on conversation we stated that the subject should be one of interest to the other persons participating, if their attention is to be maintained. This principle was referred to as the use of common ground. The use of common ground in conference speaking has three important aspects: It serves to hold the interest of the conferee. It presents subject matter, facts, and opinions on which the parties to the conference have the same point of view; thus some element of agreement and mutual understanding is insured. It further offers the conferrer the opportunity of turning the discussion away from subjects on which there is conflict of emotions and opinions, since most persons prefer to discuss matters on which they can agree and to avoid disputes that would partially or wholly destroy success in the conference.

Common ground is used to prevent disagreements, negative responses, and unfavorable attitudes and, at the same time, to increase agreement, mutual understanding, and co-operation. It can be illustrated in the discussion of policy conference. All parties in the conference are interested in making profits for their company. They may not agree on some particular question of policy. If you are attempting to secure agreement on a certain policy, you can use profit, the common ground subject, as the appeal that will harmonize the group and bring agreement. If you are applying for a position, you can discuss company policies of particular interest to your conferee. On these points you may rest assured that the conferee will agree, and you may hope that out of this state of agreement may come a willingness to agree on the question of your employment. If you are explaining a new mechanical process, you may expect better results if you develop said explanation in terms understood and examples already known to the conferee. A blueprint can be most easily explained to the layman by making reference to a building that corresponds to that shown in the blueprint and with which the layman is already acquainted.

"You attitude"

Mark Twain increased his reputation as a humorist by writing in his early years a satire directed at a state supreme court justice and entitled, "Professor Personal Pronoun." The essential theme in this satire is the justice's constant use of the pronoun "I." There are two conditions of mind that will permit a person constantly to use the pronoun "I." These are conceit and indifference. Neither is designed to promote voluntary agreement or respect in either a conversation or business conference. Dizzy Dean and Tony Galento were colorful newspaper copy while they lasted, but the sporting world will remember the deeds of men like Joe Louis, Joe Di Maggio, and Carl Hubbell far longer.

Whereas the use of "I" will only irritate the conferee, especially when used too often, the use of "you" will serve as a stimulant in the majority of cases. The "you attitude" means not only using the pronoun "you" but also developing any given proposal in terms that will indicate to the conferee that it is being presented for his interest and benefit rather than for the interest and benefit of the conferrer. A large number of job seekers make the mistake of simply stating that they need a job rather than showing the employer that they can be an asset in his employment. Too many people are prone to advance arguments in a discussion of policy conference with "I think," "I believe," or "I know." Since the success of the conference depends on what the conferee thinks, believes, and knows, it is much more advisable to present the subject in terms of his thoughts, beliefs, and knowledge.

The "you attitude" also allows the subtle and effective use of compliment. The conferee is pleased when the conferrer states that knowledge displayed in the conference is that of the conferee's. Every conferee is human enough to enjoy having himself and his doings and ideas the subject of the conversation. The ABLE MAN conferrer will state to the conferee, "Your score was below par yesterday" rather than, "*I* shot a 68 yesterday"; or,

"Our company made a good profit by following your advice in the purchase of the XYZ plant"; or, "Mr. Jones, you want a good investment to protect yourself in later years," rather than, "I tell you, I think you ought to buy this insurance."   Many a successful housewife attributes her success to the fact that she manages her husband by making him think that he manages her.   It matters not that you had the good ideas or the better golf score, that you really believed the conferee should buy the insurance or that you really needed the job.   It matters only that you secure agreement from the conferee.   If this can be done by making him feel that he is the important man in the conference and that he will benefit from the action that you recommend, then the desired response is assured.

"Yes response"

The "yes-response" technique is as old as the institution of marriage.   When Adam approached Eve in the garden, his conversation must have progressed in somewhat the following manner.   "Eve, you have beautiful eyes."   Eve silently reflects a "yes."   "Eve, you are a gorgeous creature."   Eve thinks, "Yes." Then Adam asks Eve, "Do you like me, honey," and Eve answers, "Yes."   By this time Eve is so much in the mood of agreeing with Adam that when he asks her to marry him, the answer is naturally "yes."   Thus the theory of the "yes-response" technique was tried with success and has been used more or less successfully every May from that day to this.   Stated theoretically the technique involves asking questions, and only those questions, that will receive an affirmative answer from the conferee.   You thus create in the conferee the spirit of agreement and the habit of saying "yes."   The spirit so disarms the conferee that when you ask for agreement on the main proposal he will find it difficult to say "no."

Two advantages grow out of the use of this technique: First, if you are phrasing your questions and stating your proposition in a manner to secure agreement, you are probably developing the proposal in terms of conferee interest.   Second, after the conferee has agreed to the many separate parts of your proposal, as he must do if you are using the technique, it will be much easier for him to agree and respond with a "yes" to the whole of the proposal.

If he says "yes" to *A* and "yes" to *B* and "yes" to *C*, then it will be easier for him to say "yes" to *D*, which represents the whole of *ABC*.

"Trial close"

The last strategy to be presented is the "trial close." This is not to be confused with the conclusion of the conference, although it may result in that. It may be compared to a trial balloon sent up to determine the direction of the wind. The purpose is to determine the state of progress toward a close for the conferrer. It consists in asking questions to which the conferee's answer will indicate whether or not he is ready to accept the conferrer's proposal. If you are selling automobiles and you have presented most of your sales points, you may ask the following questions as a "trial close": "What color car do you desire?" "Do you wish a two-door?" "Do you want the standard or deluxe style?" "Do you plan on paying cash or will it be more convenient to purchase on the installment plan?" The buyer may answer "yes" or "no" to all, or none, or part of, the questions without committing himself for or against the purchase. The important thing to note in these questions is that the conferee is making a choice by his answers and he is further telling you whether or not his mind is made up. Should he indicate that he has decided on a green two-door of the standard style and that he will pay cash, you can assume that he is ready to buy and you close the deal. If he states that he does not know just what he wants, you can continue with your sales presentation. The point is this, he has told you that he is not ready to buy without committing himself to that position; thus the door is still open for a possible sale. This same principle holds true in all persuasive conferences.

QUESTIONS

1. What is meant by "determining the specific purpose of a conference"?

2. Why should the specific purpose be selected and specifically worded at the beginning of the preparation for a conference speech?

3. What is meant by "analyze the man with whom you are going to confer"?

4. What four factors should be considered in analyzing the man with whom you are going to confer?

5. Why is it necessary to select and organize your material before you enter into the conference speech?

6. What one cardinal rule should govern the material to be used in a conference speech?

7. From what sources can speech materials be collected?

8. What are the three main divisions in a well-organized speech? What are the main functions of each of these three divisions?

9. What are the five strategies and techniques of presentation in conference speaking?

EXERCISES

1. Select six different types of conference situations and write out the specific purpose of each conference.

2. Select six men in different business or professional activities and write an analysis of each.

3. Name ten sources or guides that would be helpful in finding material for conference speeches.

4. Go to the ten sources or guides listed in answer to #3 and select specific illustrations and examples that will tend to develop one specific purpose listed in answer to #1.

5. Select a specific purpose for any given conference speech. Collect material to develop this specific purpose. Prepare this material in outline form.

6. Assume that you are to take part in three different conferences with three different types of conferees.

    (a) Select a specific purpose for each conference.

    (b) Write an analysis of each conferee.

    (c) Name the sources from which you will secure your material for said conferences.

    (d) Write an outline of your material for each conference.

    (e) Write a short discussion on how you plan to utilize each of the five strategies and techniques of conference speaking in each of these three conferences.

CHAPTER VI

Exposition in Conference Speaking

I. PRECISE EXPOSITION
  Words
  Examples and illustrations
  Visual aids
II. PICTURESQUE EXPOSITION
III. EXPOSITION IN TERMS OF AUDIENCE EXPERIENCE
  Reference to experience
  Presentation of new in terms of the old
  Pre-analysis necessary
IV. INSTRUCTIONAL AND EXPLANATORY TYPES
V. THE GOODWILL SPEECH
VI. ORAL REPORT
  Types of oral reports
    The informative report
    The examination report
  Steps in making an oral report
    Determining specific purpose
    Gathering material
    Organization of material
    Outlining the report
    Presentation of report

Exposition in Conference Speaking

EXPOSITION is the art of explaining or interpreting a subject. It involves revealing, displaying, and exposing. It is the answer to the questions "what?", "when?", "how?", and "where?" Exposition is not to be confused with exhibition or demonstration, although these two acts may be used as a supplement in explaining or interpreting a subject. If you present an object such as a stem-winding watch for examination without comment as to the winding, then you are exhibiting and not explaining. If you wind the watch for your observers, you have given a demonstration.

Expository speaking may be done with two purposes in mind. The first purpose is to present precise information about a subject. The second purpose is to present a pictorial understanding or interpretation of a subject. The instructional, explanatory, and oral report speeches fall in the first category, while the good-will speech falls in the second. We shall refer to these types of exposition as *precise* exposition and *picturesque* exposition.

The words and materials used in precise exposition must be specific, clear, concrete, and concise. Such exposition is based on facts. It is not the colored fabrication of a salesman nor the panacea of a politician. It must be something definite, something upon which all agree as the facts, cut-and-dried statistics, measurements, in other words, concrete evidence. You do not give instructions in terms of rosy descriptions; you do not try to sell something in an oral report; you do not attempt to influence the conclusion an auditor may draw from your report. You should be concerned only with giving clear and objective exposition.

The words and material used in picturesque exposition must

be concrete and concise, but they must also present information that will be of such use and interest to the auditor that he will be impressed by both the speaker and the organization that he represents. Goodwill speaking is based entirely on picturesque exposition. Here the exposition requires accurate but also colorful facts, specific but also vivid details, and clear but also pictorial language. This type of exposition is well demonstrated by the speeches, moving pictures, and booklets presented by gasoline and oil companies for tourists. The information contained in these services must be accurate and clear in regard to the roads, routes, and accommodations for the trip, but they must also be colorful, vivid, and picturesque. They contain fascinating details about towns, parks, points of historic interest, and geographical aspects of the territory. The first purpose in furnishing such information is to inform the tourist; a second purpose is to create a favorable impression, which will motivate the tourist to buy the products and services of the company.

Precise Exposition

Words

If you are confronted with the problem of explaining a subject, you may decide to use only words. In this instance, your effectiveness will vary in direct proportion to the number of specific and concrete words used that carry a correspondingly specific and concrete meaning to your listener. You may say, "He went down the street." So what? Who? When? What street? Effective exposition would require the following statement: "John J. Jones ran on the sidewalk from Race Street down the north side of Green Street to Cedar Street in the City of Urbana, Illinois, at 8:15 a.m., Saturday, June 1, 1941." You might use other words describing the manner in which John moved, such as staggered, waddled, slunk, or crawled. Each word in turn presents to the listener a different understanding regarding John's movement.

You may wish to describe a building for a real estate listing. You might say, "There is a building on the corner." This statement at most presents the vaguest kind of idea. It is somewhat, but not much, improved by saying, "There is a house on the northwest corner." The following statements present with increased specificity the subject of the building on the corner: "There is a home on the northwest corner." "There is a private home on the northwest corner of Race and John Streets." "There is a private home of brick material on the northwest corner of Race and John Streets in the City of Banff." "There is a two-story, private home of red brick material on the northwest corner of Race and John Streets and facing on Race Street in the City of Banff in the Province of Alberta." "There is a seven-room, two-story, private home with a large front porch and a well-landscaped front yard at 501 W. Race Street, Banff, Alberta, Canada. This home, located on the northwest corner of Race and John Streets, is constructed of red brick material and is covered with a gray slate roof. There are seventeen windows showing, fifteen of the regular size and two of the half size, each having fastened thereto green shutters. The lot on which the home stands runs 150 feet on John Street and 97 feet on Race Street. The home itself has a foundation running 57 feet on the Race Street side and 63 feet on the John Street side." We could go on with this series of word descriptions of the house, but the point should be clear. Each statement gives the reader a clearer understanding and a more accurate picture of the house than did the preceding statement. This results entirely from the increased use of specific and concrete words.

Examples and illustrations

Better than words alone is the use of concrete and specific examples and illustrations in expository speeches. Let us apply this method to the subject of the house. For this purpose we select a house with which the auditor is acquainted and compare it with the house in Banff. We use Peter Smith's home, which the hearer has seen many times and which is located on a beautifully landscaped lot, 125 by 135 feet, on the southwest corner of Prairie and Vine Streets in the city of Joliet, Illinois. Smith's home is a six-room, red brick house, 47 by 59 feet, having a front porch, green shutters, and a slate roof. We say, "The John J. Jones' home in Banff, which we have described, is similar to Peter Smith's home, which you know, except that the Jones' home is a seven-room house on a slightly larger lot." Since the auditor has a rather clear mental picture of the Smith home, he gains a fair concept of the Jones home. But since the two homes do differ, there is a large element of uncertainty about the Jones home. He still wonders about the kind of shrubs and flowers, the kind of homes across the alley, the kind of wood in the floors, the type of furnace in the basement, and whether it has a bath on each floor.

Visual aids

A picture of the house would further increase the understanding. If it were a colored picture, it would present an even better basis for studying the effect gained from green shutters on red brick under a gray slate roof. More would be known of the trees and the landscaping. Windows, doors, and porch would take on more meaning. This picture could be augmented by a blueprint setting forth in detail the dimensions, floor plan, and the location of utility closets, light sockets, and staircases. A map of the city showing streets, alleys, railways, bridges, business district, industrial areas, rivers, and highways would assist the auditor in understanding the location of the home and its position relative to other buildings. A model of the house might still add to the explanation and interpretation of the subject. These aids would give the auditor a far better understanding than words alone or even words augmented by illustrations and examples.

However, to gain a full and comprehensive knowledge of the house an exact reproduction of the house and the surrounding locality should be presented and explained, or the house itself might be shown and explained. As a matter of fact, it would be necessary for one to live in the house for some time, devoting study to matters of construction, sticking windows, flooded basements, and termites, before a complete understanding could be attained. Unfortunately time and space do not usually permit the conference speaker and especially the public platform speaker the opportunity of presenting the actual subject when engaged in speech. But there are very few speech situations wherein the speaker cannot avail himself of some of the aids described.

Such aids are largely visual. Other sensory aids are equally effective, although not as available for use. The chemist knows that he can explain test tube results in terms of the olfactory image; the baker knows that the gustatory image will assist him in introducing his goods; the scientist has for years been calling into play the tactile, motor, and thermic senses; nature lovers study birds as much through the auditory sense as through the visual. You may remember the sense of touch and motor response gained from your experience in riding a bicycle or driving a car. This response is sometimes referred to as "the feel of the car." These motor images might be used, for example, in instructional speeches on flying an airplane or operating a hoisting crane. Your furnace dealer and air-conditioning salesman know how to explain their products in terms of thermic imagery. The insurance salesman will explain the benefits of insurance through the media of graphs, charts, and pictures; the engineer will report on a technical advance in terms of heat, light, motion, and hardness or softness of substance; and the culinary artist will give instruction about new foods in terms of taste and odor. The successful speaker will use any or all of these aids, as well as literal, exact, concrete, and specific words, and illustrations and examples in presenting precise expository speeches.

Picturesque Exposition

The small box camera records in shades of black and white the figure of the man, his dog, and the trees and hill in the background. The fast speed camera, using fast film and a better lens, gives you more detail and depth. It may catch some action and life. Add color film to this camera and you have further increased the details, the beauty of the landscape and the warmth of the sun. Put a colored film into a good movie camera and you have an effective and impressive reproduction, not only of the man, his dog, the trees and the hill, but life itself. Thus technicolor has become the best seller in the movie industry today. Add sound to the movie and you have life in a still more picturesque, colorful, and vivid state.

The business and professional speaker can take a lesson from this illustration. Picturesque exposition may not persuade or sell, but it does stimulate the vision and grip the emotions so that one is impressed or in the mood for suggestions and appeals to action. It serves the same function as flowers on the dinner table, goatees on professors, and brass buttons on monkeys—not the real meat, of course, but very impressive. It stimulates the imagi-

nation, and, as T. V. Smith so ably states, "Man's imagination is
the real source of comfort and enjoyment in life."

Let us look at a few samples of picturesque exposition and contrast these with the precision type.   John Muir gives the following description of the Grand Canyon of the Tuolumne River and
Waterwheel Falls in Yosemite National Park:

It is the cascades or sloping falls on the main river that are the crowning
glory of the canyon, and these, in volume, extent, and variety, surpass those
of any other canyon in the Sierra.   The most showy and interesting of them
are mostly in the upper part of the canyon above the point of entrance of
Cathedral Creek and Hoffmann Creek.   For miles the river is one wild,
exulting, onrushing mass of snowy purple bloom, spreading over glacial
waves of granite without any definite channel, gliding in magnificent silver
plumes, dashing and foaming through huge boulder dams, leaping high in the
air in wheellike whirls, displaying glorious enthusiasm, tossing from side to
side, doubling, glinting, singing in exuberance of mountain energy.[1]

One with more interest in precision, might express it like this:

The Waterwheel Falls may be reached by a good trail 5.5 miles from the
Tioga Road down the Tuolumne River Gorge to the Glen Aulin High Sierra
Camp, where meals and overnight accommodations are available, then 2.8
miles down the river to the falls.   Saddle animals may be rented at Tuolumne Meadows for the trip.   Below the Waterwheels the Tuolumne Canyon
descends abruptly, the river running through the mile-deep gorge.   Trails
built a few years ago down the canyon from the Waterwheel Falls to Pate
Valley penetrate the heart of the gorge.   The Muir Gorge, a vertical-walled
cleft in the canyon a half mile deep, is, as a result, but 2 hours below
Waterwheel Falls and the same above Pate Valley by the new trails.   The
entire canyon may be traversed with ease either on horseback or on foot.[2]

The Grand Canyon of the Colorado River in Arizona has likewise been variously described.   John Muir writes:

It seems a gigantic statement for even Nature to make, all in one mighty
stone word.   Wildness so Godful, cosmic primeval, bestows a new sense of
earth's beauty and size.   But the colors, the living, rejoicing colors, chant-
ing, morning and evening, in chorus to heaven.   Whose brush or pencil,
however lovingly inspired, can give us these? [3]

A minister would say, "Today I saw the works of God."   A ten-
year-old child would probably tell you, "Today I stood on the rim

---

[1] *Yosemite National Park* (bulletin), United States Department of The Interior,
United States Government Printing Office, 1938, p. 8.

[2] *Ibid.*, p. 9.

[3] *Grand Canyon National Park* (bulletin), United States Department of The
Interior, United States Government Printing Office, 1938, p. 1.

of the Grand Canyon and spit a mile." Contrast the above with the following precise statements:

The Grand Canyon of the Colorado River, located in Arizona, is 217 miles long, 4 to 18 miles wide, and approximately one mile average depth. The Colorado River is the second longest river in the United States and cuts nineteen major canyons along its course. Where measured at the gauging station in Grand Canyon, it is 300 feet wide and flows from 2½ to 10 miles per hour in speed. Measurements indicate that it varies from 12 to 42 feet in depth and carries past the gauging station an average of nearly 1,000,000 tons of sand and silt every twenty-four hours. This river has two main sources, one in southwestern Wyoming, the other in northern Colorado. Many large tributaries add to its volume as it flows some 2000 miles to its delta at the upper end of the Gulf of California.[4]

Someone recently presented this picturesque definition of intoxication:

I had 12 bottles of whiskey in my cellar and my wife told me to pour the contents of each down the sink or else! So I proceeded with the task. I withdrew the cork from the first bottle and emptied the contents down the sink with the exception of one glass, which I drank. I extracted the cork from the second bottle and did likewise with the exception of one glass, which I drank. I then withdrew the cork from the third bottle, emptying the old booze down the sink, save for one drink which I drank. I pulled the bottle from the cork of the next one, drank one sink out of it, and poured the rest down the glass. I pulled the sink from the next glass and poured the cork down the bottle. I pulled the next cork out of my throat, poured the sink down the glass, bottled the drink and drank the pour. When I had emptied everything I steadied the house with one hand and counted the bottles and corks and glasses with the other, which were twenty-nine. To make sure, I counted again when they came by, and I had seventy-four, and as the house came by I counted again and finally I had all the houses and the bottles and corks and glasses counted except one bottle, which I drank.

On the other hand, the precise statement would be:

Intoxication, the state produced in the system by the excessive use of a stimulant, such as opium, chloral, belladonna, and alcoholic liquids. The intoxication is acute when a considerable quantity of poisonous substances are taken at once, especially by a person not accustomed to its use. In the first stage of slight intoxication the blood circulates quite rapidly and the nervous and mental processes are stimulated. This state of excitement is soon followed by the second stage, in which the baser traits are manifested and the sense of propriety is lost. In the third stage an intoxicated person suffers from dizziness, stupor, double vision, and greatly weakened consciousness, and in some cases fits of delirium. Delirium tremens often result from habitual intoxication and sometimes it causes alcoholic insanity. The exces-

---

4 *Ibid.*, pp. 2–3.

sive use of liquor frequently induces vomiting, especially in those not accus-tomed to it.   A cathartic, an emetic, or a Turkish bath may relieve a person when becoming drowsy from intoxication, and in extreme cases a stomach pump may be employed.

Let us remember, then, that to be clear one must use specific and concrete words, specific and concrete illustrations and exam-ples, and that word descriptions may be augmented by maps, charts, diagrams, models, and actual demonstrations.   If your pur-pose is to impress, then you will use colorful, picturesque, and vivid words, illustrations, and examples.   These likewise may be supplemented with picturesque and colorful pictures, maps, charts, diagrams, and demonstrations.

Exposition in Terms of Audience Experience

Reference to experience

We must keep in mind that our speech is effective only in terms of the results gained from our audience.   Therefore, we state again, and this is particularly important in exposition, that words, examples, illustrations, charts, maps, pictures, diagrams, and dem-onstrations must be familiar to the audience or easily understood by them.   The audience's understanding depends on its previous experience, present knowledge, and capacity for interpretation. This point is well presented in the story of "The Six Blind Men of Indostan" who went to see an elephant.   They each in turn examined different parts of the elephant's anatomy.   The man examining the tail understood the elephant to be like a rope.   On feeling the legs, the second man exclaimed that the animal was like a tree.   The third, after feeling the ears, compared him to a fan.   The fourth, noting the tusks, argued that an elephant was like a spear; while the fifth, coming in contact with the trunk, insisted that it was a snake; and the sixth, after touching the skin, thought that an elephant was a wall.

Presentation of new in terms of the old

It has often been said that we understand the new only in terms of the old.   This being true we wish to state one rule which should always be kept in mind.   New ideas will be best under-stood only in relation to the previous knowledge of the audience. We understand new methods of road construction when they are

compared with our previous knowledge regarding road construction.   We know how to create new production techniques or use
old techniques on new products by a study of known techniques.
We explain air-cooled and liquid-cooled airplane motors to our
audience in terms of knowledge already possessed by them regarding automobile and motorcycle motors.   Thus insurance will be
discussed as an investment to a banker who understands investments; it is presented in terms of retirement income to the civil
service employee who knows about pensions; it is described in
terms of low cost for administration of estates to the lawyer who
understands ordinary administration costs; it is couched in terms
of trust investments to the trust investment manager; and it is
presented in terms of guaranteed income to the farmer and laborer who have experienced both certain and uncertain income.

Pre-analysis necessary

The extent of the audience's previous knowledge is determined
by making an adequate pre-analysis of that audience.   You search
for the information, knowledge, and experience that can be used
as a basis for comparison with ideas to be presented in your
speech.   The chart for audience analysis found in the preceding
chapter offers a systematic basis for a general audience analysis.
However, it is the specific and concrete facts related to the subject
of your speech that will be of greatest value in expository speaking.   The following incident will lend clarity to the point just
made:

A traveling salesman found himself far out from town and unable to determine which road to take in order to arrive at his
destination.   He stopped a farmer and asked for directions.   The
farmer answered, "You go east one mile, then you turn south for
about 200 rods; at that point you jog west for about a quarter,
then go south until you cross Slippery Creek.   Just beyond the
creek you turn east for three miles, taking the second crossroad
south until you come to Bill Bainer's place.   After passing this
farm you take the first fork to the east and go straight south-by-
east into town."   Do you understand?   Well, neither did the
salesman.   Why?   He didn't know the distance represented by
200 rods; he wasn't sure of the term "jog"; he couldn't tell Slippery Creek from the Mississippi River; he didn't know Bainer's

place from Jones' or any other place; and finally, what did the old gentleman mean by "first fork to the east and go straight south-by-east?" Fortunately for the salesman, the farmer's son came out and gave the following instructions: "Do you see that telephone wire running alongside the road? Well, you start east from here and you can follow that telephone line all the way into town." Clear? Effective? Yes. It was simple and in terms that could be understood.

Instructional and Explanatory Types

Of the four types of expository business speeches, two, the instructional and explanatory types, follow, in general, the rules and suggestions already presented. They require clear organization. The material should be developed under three or four main points, between each of which there should be a logical relation. The transitions between the main points as well as the minor points should be smooth and clear. It may help in these two types to list each point as, "one, two, three, and four" or, "first, second, third, and fourth." The material can usually be arranged in a time order, a space order, or in divisions and classifications already known to the audience. For example, if you are giving instructions about the care of an automobile, you can follow the known divisions of "tires, engine, radiator, carburetor, wheels, transmission, and body." If you are explaining price fluctuations, you can use time divisions such as, "years, months, or seasons," or time periods, such as, "before the depression and after the depression" and, "before the war, during the war, and after the war." If your discussion turns to freight rates you will find space divisions very helpful. Your explanation would be divided into, "first zone, second zone, and third zone" or, "Illinois, Indiana, and Iowa" or, "eastern states, middle western states, Rocky Mountain states, and Pacific states." In conclusion, remember that the instructional speech is given in answer to "How?", while the explanatory speech is in answer to "What?"

The Goodwill Speech

A new neighbor moves in next door. You go over, introduce yourself, and offer to help. The next morning you give your new

neighbor a ride to the office. He reciprocates on the following
day by asking you to ride with him. By your acts you have added
to your list of friends. You have given free service and helpful
information. The friend is moved to return the favor. Goodwill has been created. What is true of neighbors regarding goodwill and its results is equally true of business and professional
men and their associates, clients, and customers.

A salesman may willingly explain a new product and its use
although he knows an immediate sale is impossible. A company
representative may explain the services of his company. Every
attorney knows that a helpful suggestion to a potential client may
turn him into an actual client. Alert businessmen are constantly
giving helpful hints to others, thus creating goodwill for their
organizations. This type of conference speaking not only attempts to make a matter clear but also to leave a favorable impression on the auditor. Although goodwill speaking finds
greater use on the public platform, it cannot be disregarded by
the conference speaker.

Oral Report

In every business and profession there are innumerable times
when specific and detailed information must be discovered, analyzed, organized, and presented for use as a basis for deliberation
or action. Such reports of information may concern the financial
condition of the company, marketing and distribution, investigation of personnel, matters of engineering, or any other situation
pertinent to the efficient operation of business. In each instance
the purpose is simply to present the results of investigation and
study. No attempt is made to persuade or influence action or
belief, except in the recommendations at the end of the report.
However, the report itself is nearly always the basis for action or
change of belief.

While the written report is peculiarly the instrument of the
engineer and the scientist, the oral report is the instrument of
the business and professional man. It should be recognized that
most written reports are also presented orally, although usually in
much briefer form, and that a number of oral reports find their
way into writing on a much expanded scale. This means that

there is no essential difference between the two except in the medium of presentation and length.

Types of oral reports

There are essentially two major divisions under which all reports may be classified: (1) informative reports that concern past facts, and (2) examination reports that present and interpret new facts resulting from a special investigation. In many instances the two types overlap. However the distinction is helpful because it is closely allied with the two major purposes of all reporting: (1) knowledge of past happenings, and (2) knowledge that serves as a basis for future action. These two types of reports have also been designated as the historical and the research reports.

The informative report. This report, somewhat easier to prepare than the examination report, requires the gathering of historical data. It is made primarily in answer to the question, "What has happened in a given period of time or in a given place?" It may involve a monthly report on finances, a daily report on sales, or a report on the growth of advertising during the past 150 years. It may be one of a series of reports on the same subject over different periods of time, or it may be one of a series of reports all on different aspects of the same subject at the same period of time. In a business field it is usually rather simple and brief. The daily quotations of the market reports or charts showing weekly sales for the past ten years are illustrative of such brief and simple informative reports.

The examination report. The examination report involves exploration into the unknown for the purpose of revealing and interpreting facts that may serve as the basis for future action. This is the type of report made by engineers previous to the construction of Boulder Dam, previous to the conversion of an automobile plant into an airplane factory, or previous to the use of plastics and plywoods in airplane construction. It is the type of report that is utilized by the scientist in giving the world the advantages of his research. This type of report will precede the location of a new rubber plant in Arizona or a new dry goods store in Kewanee. While the informative report tells a businessman where he has been, the examination report gives him information for determining where he is going.

Steps in making an oral report

Much greater emphasis must be placed on the preparation for an oral report than on the presentation. This preparation involves four separate considerations: (1) the statement of the specific purpose of the report, (2) the gathering of the material, (3) the organization of the material, and (4) outlining the report.

Determining the specific purpose. The oral report is usually presented in response to a specific demand by a group that has some special interest in the findings revealed. Informative reports are often routine matters, such as annual financial reports, yearly or monthly reports on sales, and yearly or monthly reports on personnel. The salesman's daily or weekly report falls in the same category. Other informative reports are of a special nature. These result when the management of a company details one of the executives to collect specific data regarding past events. A special request for information regarding a particular plant's operation or a report on a particular sales branch record would fall in this category. In any event the oral report will be made in direct response either to a routine request or to a specific request.

Examination reports are made to meet two situations. The first situation involves a request for specific material that would be used as a basis for determining future action of the business or profession concerned. Such reports provide the data for policy-determining committees. They may, for example, constitute the basis for action in converting plants to the production of new products, in determining the type and style of bridge to span a river, in deciding on real estate developments, or in determining whether or not a new store should be opened in a given community. The second situation involves reports on research of a purely experimental nature. These latter reports come out of the research laboratories of industrial concerns, universities and colleges, medical and dental schools, and technical schools of all types. The report may or may not be made in response to a request. It may or may not be offered as the basis for future action. It may result solely from the fact that a particular experiment has been completed and it is appropriate that the results of the experiment be reported to the parties sponsoring or interested in the experiment.

In all reports it is necessary first to determine the specific purpose of the report. What information is desired? What facts must be determined to portray accurately past events? What facts must be known to determine accurately future action? What facts are necessary in completely revealing the nature of a purely experimental project? The first step, then, requires a statement of the specific purpose of the report; this purpose will guide the reporter in his collection of the facts. With this specific purpose in mind the reporter will be aware that he is to collect only data that will reveal accurately, clearly, and completely the subject under consideration; he is not concerned with gathering data primarily to interest his audience.

Gathering material. The data that make up a report will be collected primarily from one of three sources: (1) data already available and to be had by personal interviews, correspondence, and reading; (2) data available from field investigation; and (3) data available from laboratory research. These sources of data should be utilized in the order listed. If the reporter can secure the data required from someone already in possession of it, he not only can secure the necessary facts, but he can also secure an interpretation of the facts from an experienced person in the field.

Field investigation combines firsthand observations as well as those observations made by others. Thus the engineer, asked to report on a proposed dam site, will collect data already prepared by government and private agencies on such factors as weather conditions, rainfall, geographical and geological considerations, other dams, construction materials, transportation facilities, labor supply, and cost. These data will be used to supplement the specific data that will be gathered at the site of the dam. All data will go into the notes of the reporter's preparation.

Laboratory research combines field investigation plus experimental observation. Thus the industrial chemist, seeking a solution to the problem of need for synthetic rubber, will collect all data available from other experiments on synthetic rubber. He will then gather such data as his experiments produce. His report may consist of a summary of the data collected by others, the data collected from his own experiments, or the data collected from the combined sources. In any instance the collection of material should be complete before it is organized into a report.

Organization of material. Two major considerations should govern the organization of material in the body of the oral report. First, select only significant data or summaries of significant data for presentation. Second, present and interpret the data or summaries of data in the order of their significance. These requirements are particularly true of the oral report. The reporter should bear in mind that the auditor is often interested only in the final summary of the report. Should the auditor be interested in the more elaborate details, a written report containing these details should be presented to him for study. It is impossible to present a great volume of detailed information in a speech and have it remembered. Therefore, keep the final organized report brief and to the point.

Satisfactory organization can be best secured if the reporter will first select the main ideas to be presented in his report. If possible these main ideas should not exceed three or four. To use ten or more main ideas is to use none at all, for so many will not be remembered. The three or four main ideas may be selected along chronological or logical lines, depending on which classification lends itself best to the development of the report. Once these main ideas have been selected, the data to be presented should fall naturally under one or the other of the ideas. Use only such data or summaries of data as are necessary to develop clearly, concretely, and completely each main idea. If these main ideas are well selected and the data judiciously used, the report should result in clear understanding by your auditors.

After the main body of material has been organized, the reporter should prepare the introduction. Since the report is going to be presented to an auditor or auditors who either have requested it or who by their position are specifically interested in it, the speaker need not concern himself too much with securing attention. However, in order that the data be accepted as accurate and in order that the audience may best understand the report and its significance, it will be necessary for the reporter to present the following information in the introduction: (1) the reason for the report, (2) the purpose of the report, (3) the source of the data contained in the report, and (4) the method of securing the data. The introduction should contain a state-ment of the main ideas to be presented; such a statement will provide an easy transition to the body of the report.

The conclusion should contain a summary of the data and a summary of the significance of the data and/or a recommendation for action based on the facts presented. The information report will contain in the conclusion only a summary of the data and a summary of the significance of the data. The examination report will contain the same type of summary, but it may also present a recommendation for action where it is justified. Such summaries of data should follow the same lines as the main ideas included in the body of the report.

Outlining the report. After the reporter has organized the material it will be of value to him to outline the report. This outline should contain the material as organized in the sample form:

Introduction

   I.   Reason for report
  II.   Purpose of report
 III.   Source of data
 IV.   Method of securing data
  V.   Statement of main ideas

Body

  I. First main idea
    A. Sub idea
      1. Data
    B. Sub idea
      1. Data
 II. Second main idea
    A. Sub idea
      1. Data
    B. Sub idea
      1. Data

Conclusion

  I.   Summary of data
 II.   Summary of significance of data
III.   Recommendations

Presentation of report. Three important considerations must be made in reference to the presentation of an oral report. First-the speaker should use the elements of effective delivery desirable in any public speech.

Second, the speaker must recognize that the report is being presented to an audience that has more than average interest in it. Thus the speaker need not sacrifice clarity for the element of interest. The speaker need not indulge in dramatic mannerisms to secure audience attention. He need not employ vivid or figurative language to hold attention. He needs only to present clear, concise, concrete and complete data in an understandable way.

Third, the speaker should adapt his vocabulary and style to the technical-layman capacity of his audience. If the report is being presented to a technical group, the speaker can assume complete audience interest; he can use technical terms and jargon; he can maintain a scientific point of view; and he can assume that the audience will be able to give significant interpretation to a substantial part of the data presented. If the report is being given before a group of laymen, the reporter may assume audience interest to a lesser degree than that that would prevail in the technical group; he should therefore use fewer technical terms and more common, everyday terms; he must also use more illustrations, examples, charts, diagrams, and demonstrations to make his meaning clear. He may even be justified, in some instances, in using special devices for holding attention and interest.

QUESTIONS

1. What is exposition?
2. What is the distinction between precise exposition and picturesque exposition?
3. What type of exposition is involved in the instructional speech? the explanatory speech? the oral report speech? the goodwill speech?
4. What kind of words, examples, illustrations and visual aids can be used in effective precise exposition?
5. What is the basis for effective picturesque exposition?
6. What is meant by the statement that "exposition to be effective must consist of terms familiar to the audience"?
7. What is meant by the statement "we understand the new only in terms of the old"?

8. How does the pre-analysis of your auditor help in expository speaking?

9. What rules should govern the instructional and explanatory types of speech conferences?

10. What is the purpose of the goodwill conference? How may this purpose be accomplished?

11. What is an oral report speech? What are the two major types of oral reports? What is the general purpose of each type?

12. What four steps are involved in preparing an oral report?

13. How should a report be outlined for oral presentation?

14. What considerations should guide the reporter in presenting his report?

EXERCISES

1. Select a single subject. Write one paragraph developing this subject and illustrating precise exposition. Write one paragraph developing this subject and illustrating picturesque exposition.

2. Write in outline form a set of instructions in answer to one of the following questions: "How does a freshman register in your college or university? How do you grease a car? How do you operate a lathing machine? How do you file an income tax return? How do you air condition a private home? Other questions requiring instructions may be used.

3. Write in outline form a speech in answer to one of the following questions: What is coal? What is a certified public accountant? What is institutional advertising? What is the Reconstruction Finance Corporation? What is the Constitution of the United States? What is time and motion study? Other questions requiring explanation may be used.

4. Assume that you represent one of the following institutions: an automobile manufacturer, a tire manufacturer, an airplane transport company, a construction engineering company, a chain drugstore, a small clothing store, or some other institution. Assume further that you have been asked to contact the officers of the State Educational Association, the State Bar Association, the State Medical Association, the State Labor Association, and the State Agricultural Association. Outline a goodwill speech that would be suitable for each conference with the officers of each group.

5. Prepare an information report on one of the topics listed on page 269. Include tables, charts, and diagrams in the final outline of the report. Enlarge these tables, charts, and diagrams so that they may be used effectively before one or more auditors.

6. Prepare an examination report on one of the topics listed on page 269. Use field investigation as your source of information for the report.

SELECTED READINGS

Baker, Ray Palmer, and Howell, Almonte Charles, *The Preparation of Reports,* Revised edition, The Ronald Press Co., New York, 1938.

Gaum, Carl G., Graves, Harold F., and Hoffman, Lyne S. S., *Report Writing,* Revised edition, Prentice-Hall, Inc., 1942.

Nelson, J. Raleigh, *Writing the Technical Report,* McGraw-Hill Book Co., Inc., New York, 1940.

Stevenson, Brenton W., Spicer, John R., and Ames, Edward C., *English in Business and Engineering,* Prentice-Hall Inc., New York, 1936. (Chapter IV, "The Written Report").

Sypherd, W. O., and Brown, Sharon, *The Engineer's Manual of English,* Scott, Foresman and Company, New York, 1933.

Persuasion in Conference Speaking

Persuasion in Conference Speaking

Introduction

GORDON BURNS will be graduated from college in June. He will no longer be able to look to his father's purse for support. He secures a lead on a position and makes an appointment with the personnel manager. At the appointed hour Burns goes to the scene of the interview. What he says in the ten or fifteen minutes after his entrance will determine his work for the following few months, perhaps for his entire life.

Advertising Manager Truet goes to the annual board meeting for the purpose of presenting next year's budget. He finds that the board believes that his budget should be cut 25 per cent. What he says in the next hour not only determines the size of the budget, but also affects the welfare of the business, the dividends of the stockholders, and his own future salary.

John Mason builds a home on "C" Street. Two days after he moves in the September rains fill his basement with sewer water. He arranges to appear before the city aldermen to request drainage repairs. What he says in the thirty minutes allowed him to present his problem may determine the livability of his new home.

Sales Manager Hedden is having a poor year with the men in his territory. He calls a district meeting. What he says during that meeting will affect future sales, future incomes, future earnings for stockholders, and perhaps his job.

You have shown interest in an insurance program and, although you have already talked with three other salesmen, you agree to an appointment with a fourth. What he says in his conference with you determines whether you buy from him or from one of his competitors.

Each of the above mentioned persons is confronted with a problem in persuasion. Everyone meets similar problems during his life, and success and happiness depend to a large extent upon mastery and skill in the use of the principles and techniques of persuasion.

Definition and Types of Persuasion

Persuasion is the art of influencing others to believe or act as desired by the speaker. You may be influenced to believe or act because of the speaker's personality, his enthusiasm, or because his obvious conviction in his beliefs gives you confidence in him. Your favorite milliner or clothing clerk may sell you that new hat or sport sweater more because you like her or him than because you need the article or had planned to buy it. This is persuasion through personality.

After having had a series of pains in your abdominal section for a few weeks, you are rushed to the hospital for diagnosis and treatment. The doctor explains that you have an infected appendix. He further states the consequence of the infection and the possible remedies. You immediately agree that he had better perform an appendectomy. The doctor did not use persuasion on you in causing you to arrive at that conclusion—or did he? He merely explained the case. You drew your own conclusions. The need for the operation was implied from the facts presented. Thus we have persuasion by explanation.

Bruce Boyer was graduated from State Law College and passed the bar examination. He thought that he wanted to open an office and establish a practice in Logansburg. He presented his plans to an older friend, the president of the county bar association, who pointed out the following facts: Logansburg was rapidly declining as a business center because its principal source of income, mining, was no longer profitable. Three other attorneys had opened offices there in the past five years and each one had moved elsewhere within eight months because of lack of clients. These facts, and a few others, served as the basis for the fatherly advice that Bruce open his office in Trenton rather than Logansburg. The truth of the conclusion was inferred from the facts presented. Logic, in this case, was the unit of persuasion.

When your neighbor buys a new car, you begin to want one.

When someone shows you the new suit, topcoat, and hat he has just purchased for spring wear, you begin to think about your own needs for new clothing. It is the old vicious circle which keeps us in debt and makes possible the continued operation of large finance and loan companies. Your friend tells you that Bill Moran is a lowly, despicable, undersized runt. You do not like lowly, despicable, undersized runts, and so you do not like Bill Moran. A local politician shouts, "Down with taxes on the poor, oust the crooks, elect honest representatives, and preserve democracy." Well, you like these ideas, so you vote for him. In these latter cases, you are moved to action because of appeals to your fundamental needs, wants, and desires.

There are, then, five methods of persuasion: *persuasion* (1) *through the personality of the speaker,* (2) *through explanation,* (3) *through logic,* (4) *through suggestion,* and (5) *through appeals to fundamental needs, wants, and desires.*

Persuasion Through Personality

Personality is the sum total of an individual's traits and characteristics. A superior personality is represented by the same traits and characteristics attributed to the ABLE MAN. As you will recall, the ABLE MAN is a man of sound judgment, one whose opinion is respected, one who is energetic and sincere, one who is a leader, one who has a reputation; and because of all these traits he is liked and followed. When the ABLE MAN is confronted with a problem of persuasion, there will be many who will believe and act as he desires them to believe and act, simply because he IS an ABLE MAN.

This has been clearly illustrated by two service station operators in a mid-western community. May we refer to them as Wally and Jim, working respectively for ILLSO and TEXSO Oil Companies? There are approximately ninety oil and gas stations pouring gas and servicing cars and trucks in this community, thirteen of which are ILLSO and nine of which are TEXSO. However, Wally and Jim serve about ten per cent of all the cars served. Why? Personality! People like them! Customers enjoy being called by their first names, by their professional titles, or by Mr. and Mrs. So-and-So. Customers appreciate the special attention given their machine by the head man in these stations. Both these operators are welcomed into homes of customers, because they are good conversationalists and because they mix well with other people. Their gas and oil are certainly no better than those of other operators selling the same product. They fill tanks, radiators, tires, crankcases, and transmissions in exactly the same manner as these containers are filled elsewhere, but because they include a little personality in each sale and each contact, their incomes permit them to join country clubs and go to California or Florida on vacations. When Wally or Jim tells you that your car ought to be greased or that you need a new air filter, you do not say, "Why?"; you just say, "When can I have it done?"

Many times during the Lincoln-Douglas debates people were heard to remark, "Douglas is a great speaker, much more colorful than Lincoln, but somehow Old Abe seems to be right." Lincoln's personality demonstrated sincerity and honesty. His exposition and logic were good. His humor was devastating to an opponent. He could make an appeal to emotions, as he did in his arguments to juries. But more important than all these factors was the faith held in him by those who heard him. They accepted his conclusions because of the MAN. Franklin D. Roosevelt and Wendell L. Willkie are men of commanding personalities. As has been demonstrated, Roosevelt cannot pass on to others his ability to win votes, even though he strongly urges the other man's election. It is Roosevelt that people accept and not those that he recommends.

If it is your purpose to utilize your personality in speech, then it will be necessary for you to speak with conviction, sincerity, and some degree of dynamic presentation. Without these outward manifestations of intrinsic worth as a man, your listeners will not be greatly concerned about your conclusions. They must first be impressed by you as an individual.

Persuasion Through Explanation

A large life insurance company has recently adopted the policy of requesting that their agents first attempt to sell insurance through the medium of explanation. If this fails, then, and only then, are the agents urged to use the more motivating means of persuasion. It is the theory of this insurance company that most people want reliable investments and, further, that most people do not want to be *sold*. Therefore, the agent's approach to the customer is one of explaining investments, retirement incomes, disability incomes, beneficiary benefits and incomes, costs, interest rates, and guaranteed and secured programs. These factors are explained in terms of the customer's needs and ability to pay for insurance so that the conclusion which the agent wishes the customer to accept is implied. That insurance will best satisfy all the requirements is obvious. This technique is designed not only to sell insurance by letting the customer sell himself but is also designed to create goodwill so that the customer will sell the company's service to others.

Many employees have been stimulated to greater efforts after the boss has explained their future in terms of advancements. The professions of law, medicine, and dentistry have codes of ethics that prohibit direct selling of services. Therefore, the members of these professions rely to a great extent on explanation for persuasion with clients. The lawyer's problem is one of explaining to the client whether or not he has a case, whether the facts and the law give rise to a cause of action against the defendant, and whether the case should be settled out of court or should go to trial. Doctors and dentists explain their diagnoses. The patient concludes from the explanation that he should or should not have treatment. There are, of course, many "ambulance chasers" in these professions and many who have but little regard for a professional code of ethics, but, for the most part, explanation is the means of persuasion used.

Persuasion Through Logic

To most students of speech logic is something that Aristotle wrote about 2,000 years ago and that is taught today in courses by impractical-minded college professors. It is rather difficult for some to realize that the most scientific, the most exacting, and the most durable means of persuasion is logic or reason. We agree with others who have referred to this form of persuasion as argumentation and defined it as the art of influencing others through the medium of reasoned discourse. Here by using evidence you prove the truth or falsity of the conclusions that you are presenting.

Evidence

Evidence should be defined as any fact, opinion, or statement used to support the conclusion. Acceptable evidence is that evidence that comes from reliable sources. The source is reliable when the man back of it is in a position to know the facts, when he has mastered the facts, when he has no reason for misinterpreting them, and when he is able to understand the presentation of facts at the source.

Direct evidence. Direct evidence is identical with the conclusion that the speaker wishes the audience to accept or that, in other words, immediately substantiates the conclusion without the necessity of making any inference. In direct evidence you need only to test the accuracy of the source. For example, if Browner states that "Davis shot and killed Jones," and your belief is that Davis shot and killed Jones, then you have needed to make no inference from the evidence to arrive at your conclusion. You should, however, test the reliability of Browner. Was he in a position to know? Did he actually see the shooting? Has he any reason for misinterpreting the shooting? If the answers are "yes," "yes," and "no" to these three questions, then you should accept the conclusion. This same evidence is only circumstantial in respect to other conclusions. It proves only by inference that Browner is guilty of murder. Since other facts must enter the picture for you to conclude that this is legal murder, you arrive at that conclusion only after all the evidence points by inference to that conclusion.

Indirect evidence. Indirect or circumstantial evidence supports a conclusion only by inference. When Johnny comes out of the kitchen with bread crumbs and jelly on his lips you know that he has been eating bread and jelly. You know this because it is the only reasonable conclusion that can be drawn from the evidence.

When the cash register in Jack Robinson's store shows a day's receipts of $250 and the money in the cash drawer amounts to only $195, you may conclude that someone failed to put the additional $55 into the register, that it was put in and then removed, or that the cashier has made a mistake in operating the machine. A check against the day's sales slips and inventory would supply evidence from which you could test the accuracy of the conclusion that the cashier had made a mistake. A check on the amount of money possessed by the cashier would provide some additional evidence to support the conclusion. Other examinations would reveal further evidence. But unless you could produce direct evidence that the cashier took the $55, you could establish your conclusion only by circumstances that point to that conclusion. When the evidence can be explained only by the conclusion, then the process of explanation, or reasoning from the evidence to the conclusion, is known as inferential reasoning. Such reasoning may be arranged in four patterns of proof.

Patterns of proof

Proof may be defined as indirect evidence plus inference. The four patterns of proof are inductive, deductive, analogy, and causal relations.

Inductive pattern. The inductive pattern is reasoning from specific facts to general conclusions. The Belton Mining Company found Smith of B College a very satisfactory employee. Jones of B College and Brown of B College were also satisfactory employees. Therefore, one may conclude that all B College men can be employed with satisfactory results. A salesman might present his product in the following inductive manner: "Mr. Carter purchased one of our cars and was satisfied. Mrs. Mays was greatly pleased with the car that we delivered to her last spring. J. B. Collins told us that he was so enthusiastic about our cars that he would never think of buying another make. Therefore, it appears that everyone buying from us believes our cars to be real buys."

All of the above specific facts lead to or infer general conclusions. We assume or infer that what is true about a few examples in a class is true of the entire class. Our logic is good *if* we have examined enough typical cases in the class. The general conclusion that we have drawn from the specific facts becomes a rule that we now apply to all new cases found in the class. Thus we begin to experience the use of deductive reasoning.

Deductive pattern. The deductive pattern is reasoning from general conclusions or rules that cover a class of subject matter to the specific cases within the class. To illustrate this pattern of proof we may take the conclusions arrived at in the inductive cases already mentioned. If all B College men make good employees, as shown by the experience of the Belton Mining Company, then it may be assumed that Jack Sierra, a B graduate, will make a good employee. Since "it appears that everyone buying from us believes our cars to be real buys, you may be assured of satisfaction if you buy your new car from us."

Analogy pattern. The inductive and deductive patterns are often used together. After setting forth several cases which point to the general rule, you may assume the rule and state that what is true of the cases examined is true of the case at hand. Having found that Close-Shave Cream is good for Tom, Dick, and Harry, you may logically state that it will be good for your customer, George. This combined use of the inductive and deductive patterns of proof, where the general rule is assumed rather than stated, is generally known as analogy.

The pattern of proof known as argument by analogy is one of the most often used means of persuasion. It is based on the inference that what is true of one or more cases is true of all similar cases. If the individual cases are identical in every respect, then, of course, the inference is correct beyond doubt. Since it is impossible to have identical cases, the inference is never correct beyond doubt, but will vary according to the degree of identity between the cases. If aspirin tablets will cure Mary's headache, it may be inferred that they will cure Betty's headache. Your last B-8 car was a good car; therefore, you should buy another B-8 car, because it, too, will be a good car. Zink & Co. used radio advertising with success; therefore, we ought to be able to use it with success. Coulee & Co. stimulated their men to greater production by paying a bonus at Christmas; therefore, our company ought to pay a bonus at Christmas. Joe has a new suit; therefore, I ought to have a new suit. Neighbor Turk went to California on his vacation; therefore, we ought to go to California.

All of these cases are based on argument by analogy. Its probative value lies in the similarity of the two things compared. It has persuasive value in addition to its logical values, in that the same pattern contains much suggestion and emotional appeal, regardless of the similarity between the two cases being compared. Your income may not equal that of the Turks who went to

California, but since the Turks went, you and your wife—well, you just cannot let the Turk family get ahead and do things that you cannot do—so you go. Then there is that suit that Joe bought and the sport clothes that Jean purchased. Well, if they buy them, so will you. Your purchase here is not logical, but is made as a response to wants and desires created by seeing your friends with their new outfits.

Causal relations pattern. It is a law of nature that every effect is produced by some cause and that every cause produces some effect. This being true, we can infer from known causes the effects that will be produced, and from known effects we can infer the causes that produced them. When Fine-Cut Tobacco Co. spends $100,000 on a radio program in 1937 and their sales increased that year 12 per cent over the 1936 sales, they conclude that radio advertising increases sales. When the experience is repeated in 1938 and 1939, they are certain that radio advertising increases sales. In 1940 the radio advertising budget was eliminated and sales fell off 10 per cent. At the 1941 Board of Directors' meeting the advertising manager presents the above facts. His pattern of proof is causal relations. He knows that if the company will give him an adequate budget for radio advertising in 1942, sales will increase. He knows that if the Board will produce the "cause factor" (budget), the "effect factor" (increased sales) will be made.

You are ten days out on your vacation. Twenty-five miles out of town on the eleventh morning the car seems to pull to the right. This pulling to the right is the "effect factor" in your pattern of proof to determine the "cause factor." Having had previous experience with the car pulling to the right or being able to reason out what might cause it to pull to the right, you conclude by inference that your right front tire is in need of air. This conclusion leads you immediately into another pattern of causal relations. You know that flat tires will cause accidents. You know also that if you drive on a flat tire you will cause the tire to be cut and completely ruined. Knowing these causal relations and not wishing to suffer either effect, you stop your car and change the tire. In these two situations you have arrived at conclusions through the process of reasoning, first, from *effect to cause,* and second, from *cause to effect.* These same patterns of proof may be used by your gas station operator in an attempt to persuade you to change tires, to have tires repaired, or to sell you a new set of tires.

Persuasion Through Suggestion

When you see a colorful advertisement showing a beautiful and well-known movie star smoking a common brand of cigarettes and languishing in the luxury that only Hollywood can supply, you begin to associate that brand of cigarette with all the appealing aspects of the pictures. Your attention is centered on the beautiful movie star and the luxurious surroundings, but indirectly you also sense the relation of the cigarette. When next you buy cigarettes you may ask for that particular brand, not because you know it is a good brand, but because a strong positive suggestion has been planted. Such suggestion is widely used in advertising and it shows no trend toward losing its effectiveness.

Suggestion defined

Suggestion is the process of establishing an idea indirectly in the mind of another person. It is based on the fact that people build up a pattern of responses to certain stimuli. It is like yawning, smoking, or eating. You see another doing one of these three things and you immediately want to yawn, to light a cigarette, or to eat. In addition to these physiological responses built up in individuals, there are several mental responses to word stimuli. These habitual responses to word stimuli serve as the basis for the use of suggestion in persuasive speaking. If the suggestion is such as to receive a positive answer, then it is called positive suggestion. However, if the response is negative, even though you intended a positive response, then you have used negative suggestion. You would never insert the following advertisement in the local newspaper.

> Ratty's Clothiers needs your business. The sheriff served us with bankruptcy papers last night. Your purchases will keep us open a few more days. Our stuff is no worse than anyone else's. Come on in; give us a break.

This statement is loaded with negative suggestions. It has unpleasant connotations. The name "Ratty" suggests nothing desirable about a clothing store. The reader of this advertisement would question the quality of goods after the store has been served by the sheriff. The word "stuff" lacks dignity and color. "Come on in" sounds like a carnival barker, while "give us a break" suggests that the buyer pays more than the goods are worth in order to save the seller. This notice would interest only the tightest of bargain hunters. The customers from whose purchases the store could profit would shop elsewhere.

Modern advertising makes constant use of suggestion. It relies, in most instances, upon the association of the most desired things with the product that is being sold. Movie stars are associated with everything from cigarettes to fishing tackle. When you see Charley McCarthy you think of Chase & Sanborn Coffee, while "One Man's Family" brings to mind Tender Leaf Tea. These pleasurable associations suggest that you use the product sponsoring the program. That this is effective persuasion is clearly demonstrated by the fact that both these programs have been running for several years.

The first element of a speaker that suggests responses to the auditor is the speaker himself. He may have a positive and aggressive manner or his bearing may appear anemic and negative. The auditor responds positively to the first and negatively to the second. The speaker's dress may elicit either a positive or negative response. The truth of this is fully recognized by the producers of dramatic productions both in the movie industry and on the stage. Make-up men and costume directors spend hours preparing the characters in order to produce the desired responses. Huey P. Long, William Jennings Bryan, Billy Sunday, and Robert G. Ingersoll gained effective, positive responses in their audience because of a positive, dynamic, and aggressive manner on the platform. When the speaker is sincere, he suggests that he can be trusted. When the speaker is well informed and bases his arguments on sound reason, he suggests that his decisions and judgments can be accepted. When the speaker presents his ideas in terms of taking the initiative, he suggests that the audience follow his leadership.

Rules for use of positive suggestion

The business or professional man may use the following rules in conference, on the platform, or wherever he seeks to secure action from other persons.

Let manner suggest confidence.   Let your manner suggest that you are confident and that you have a strong belief in your own convictions.   Regardless of what you say, your appearance and manner must reveal an inner sureness or you will be unable to gain the desired response.   The voice must be pleasant and strong.   The bodily action must be meaningful and sincere. The audience must feel safe in accepting what you say.

Use direct and positive language.   In general, avoid using the negative "don't."   When you say to a child, "Don't touch the radio buttons," you are really suggesting the idea to the child that radio controls be touched.   Perhaps it had not even occurred to the child to touch the radio in the first place, and each time thereafter that you say "don't" to him you merely resuggest the action.

The weak and vacillating chairman who says, "Friends . . . friends . . . please, friends, may I have your attention?   I would like to ask your kind indulgence in maintaining order," will not secure the desired response, particularly if the words are spoken in such a way as to suggest that the chairman doubts the effectiveness of his own request.   The direct and confident command, "Friends, this meeting will come to order!" suggests no other alternative.   When you reply "Yes" to a question and your voice reveals a questioning attitude through a rising inflection, you are making a negative suggestion.

Use suggestion easily and unobtrusively.   The use of suggestion is an acquired art.   For that reason, the overimpatient may try too hard to make the suggestion work.   The speaker who says with great pompousness, "Now, I know I have proved to you that it is necessary to accept my terms," makes his pleas too obvious. The auditor becomes aware of this effort and naturally looks for reasons why he should not accept the terms.   The job seeker makes good use of suggestion when he asks, "When will the position be available?"   The salesman shows his ability when he asks the prospective purchaser, "Would you like to have this suit delivered to your home or will you call for it?"   The foreman who wishes to stimulate the men working under him knows that the following will gain the desired response, "I heard one of the boys in the front office say that a few of the most productive men would receive a raise in salary the first of the year."

Avoid mention of the contrary idea. "One cannot sow faults and reap virtues." A man running for election to public office should not spend time throwing mud at his opponent. To do so will suggest to many listeners that he himself is that type of candidate. The salesman cannot sell his wares by simply declaiming the demerits of his competitor's products. When you concentrate on faults and demerits, you suggest that your audience think only of faults and demerits. But when you concentrate on virtues, your audience will see only virtues.

Persuasion Through Appeal to Needs, Wants, and Desires

Aristotle said in the year 322 B.C., ". . . men will satisfy their longings." If by any stretch of the imagination the audience can believe that your proposal will satisfy its needs, wants, and desires, it will register positive responses. How else can we explain the profitable operation of matrimonial bureaus, dude ranches, and bootleggers? This rule in reference to the use of suggestion is closely associated with what many speech teachers have called the basic element in all persuasion, that is, direct appeal to the needs, wants, and desires of the audience. Therefore, let us turn our attention in the remaining part of this chapter to these basic appeals.

These appeals to the basic motives for action do not depend on the accuracy of the facts presented nor on how well the facts support the proposal being considered. They do depend on the fact that the individual is motivated to action in an attempt to satisfy his needs, wants, and desires. Authors on the subject have presented many and varied lists, all of them correct, but none of them complete enough to account for the entire scope of individual differences. Therefore, it is necessary to concentrate on those needs, wants, and desires that are most nearly universal.

What are the things that most of us talk about? What do we work for? What do we take pride in? We are all interested in maintaining our health. We want to make money and own property, a desire that most businessmen recognize as the most fundamental of all in the business world. To many people the desire to play safe and to take no chance leads the list. And yet the same people cannot resist taking a chance or assuming some risk, when it is presented in an interesting light. We love our children. We work for a reputation. We want to be somebody. We want to occupy our time. We are curious about new inventions. We read the newspapers to get the "low down" on other people. Some people are interested most in helping others and doing the right thing in a business deal. All of these things, and many more, we do because we are compelled by our needs, wants, and desires.

These desires are basic to the motives that control our every action. They determine our pattern of life. They must, therefore, be considered by the speaker in addressing his audience and in attempting to influence their actions. The following list, with discussion following, makes no pretense to completeness; the authors believe, however, that it covers the ordinary range with which the business and professional speaker will have occasion to concern himself in both the conference and platform situation:

1. Self-preservation
2. Self-esteem
3. Acquisition of property
4. Constructiveness
5. Safety

6. Pugnacity
7. Curiosity
8. Attractiveness
9. Imitation
10. Love of family

Most of these fundamental desires are double-edged; that is, what you consider to be important today may be unimportant tomorrow, or what you consider important in one sense may be immaterial in another sense. It may be that the individual has desires which point in two directions. The desires may motivate one to follow two courses of action that are in direct conflict. Consequently, in the following discussion of fundamental desires, we shall also consider the accompanying opposite.

Self-preservation

Self-preservation has properly been called the first law of nature. In an attempt to find a fountain that would impart perpetual youth to all who would partake of its waters, Ponce De Leon discovered Florida in the year of 1512. It is said that the first life insurance agent in China suffered great consternation when, upon the death of the first person he had insured, he learned that all the local inhabitants expected him to bring the man back to life.   Show anyone how he can prolong his life and he will accept your proposal.   Many people when asked to do something, respond with the question, "What do I get out of this?"   When a national advertiser says that his product supplies a certain vitamin "necessary to strong bodies," he is appealing to the reader's desire for self-preservation.

Self-preservation has a very broad application.   The satisfaction of many other fundamental desires depends upon the satisfaction of this one.   A college president speaks to a group of high school seniors.   His purpose is to persuade them to attend college.   He says that a college education will not only increase one's personal happiness, but it will also greatly increase his chances of making a living.   His basic appeal is to self-preservation.

Though we devote a majority of our time attempting to preserve ourselves, we also wish to be helpful to others.   We contribute to public and private charities.   We contribute to churches.   In times of distress we are free and willing in our efforts to bring comfort and relief to those who are less fortunate. We contribute money and goods to aid the Chinese or the Finns. This is the desire to be helpful.   We wish to help the oppressed and the needy.   This desire is less instinctive than the desire to promote our own well-being as is clearly illustrated by the slogan, "Defend America by Aiding the Allies."

Self-esteem

Just as a matter of personal pride, folks desire to "amount to something," to excel in a particular thing, to encourage the respect of other people, or, in other words, to occupy the "limelight" of public and personal favor.   Self-esteem is the motive power that in many cases moves a wealthy person to donate money for the erection of some public building or shrine that will bear his name or to do any number of things in order to establish and preserve his identity.   College students by the hundreds turn out each year for dramatic productions.   Children want to be cowboys, policemen, baseball players, engineers, and prize-fighters. This desire, closely related to the desire for increased personal prestige, can be used as the driving point for hard work on a particular project or in an organization.   Thus, a speaker who wishes to promote a message of inspiration to the members of his organization may say that the men who devote themselves to their work and to the welfare of the group are the ones whose names will appear on the letter-heads ten or fifteen years hence. Perhaps, if you have read this book as far as this page, you have done so because you saw opportunities for improving your ability to speak, for becoming articulate, and thus establishing yourself in business groups and in your community.

You may drive a large and expensive car, not because it "gets you there" any faster or with any more comfort, but because you feel a certain sense of pride in owning such a beautiful car. You like to have your friends remark on the luxuriousness of the back seat and the "classiness" of the car's appearance. Such attention flatters your ego, gives you a feeling of prestige, and promotes your self-esteem. It is a universal tendency and, as such, can be used in many cases by the ABLE MAN speaker.

The opposite of self-esteem is self-abasement. It is a strong and important emotional drive. Unlike the desire to be helpful, self-abasement is less instinctive than it is acquired. We all have our low periods, times when we can be made to believe that we have failed, that all our work has been wasted. When in this state of mind, we invariably magnify our troubles beyond all reason. We depreciate our true worth. We want to get away from everything, change friends, start over in some different place. At these times we are moved by appeals to these desires to get away and start anew. These desires are not those that will last, but they are, nevertheless, those that the speaker may use. If the audience is experiencing a particularly black moment, the speaker may use an appeal to self-abasement in order to secure attention and set the stage for more lofty appeals.

Acquisition of property.

Why do people collect stamps, old coins, bottles, odd dishes, and numerous other less valuable things? Why do we pinch pennies and work furiously to build up an estate? Of course, we build estates and save money to keep alive in our old age and to take care of emergencies as they arise, but, beyond that, we acquire property for the simple reason that we want to own and possess.

The desire for property goes further than acquiring real estate, furniture, stocks, bonds, and gadgets. It extends to the point of wanting to save what you already have, that is, to avoid waste. A refrigerator agent can move the housewife to buy a new refrigerator by showing her how much it will protect and save food. When you advertise that you are having a sale on furniture, many people will buy because they see only the chance to buy an article cheaply. Many an attic and storeroom are filled with such bargains that have never been used. The customer's desire for property and savings overrules his better judgment based on need. Have you not often heard the housewife say to her hardboiled husband, "But, dear, it was on sale and it really is a wonderful bargain at that price." They are "penny wise and pound foolish." But that does not decrease the value of the sale to the seller or the value of the appeal to the speaker. It works!

Conscientious as we may be in our thrift, we also have moments of pure extravagance. When our desire to spend becomes stronger than our desire to save, we throw good judgment to the four winds and go on a spree. Isn't it thoroughly enjoyable to spend money foolishly once in a while? It serves as an emotional release. There are times when money seems to burn our pockets. We can't be satisfied until it is gone. We all have moments when we want to break loose from our routine moorings and spend lavishly. "A fool and his money are soon parted." When the auditor is feeling foolish, the speaker can take advantage of this appeal.

Constructiveness

This tendency refers to the instinctive desire to be creative. Every person at some time during his life has had the desire to write a book, build a bridge, plant a garden, or organize a group to promote better parks in the city. This motive helps account for such community organizations as the Chamber of Commerce, Kiwanis, Rotary, and Exchange, groups that work for community betterment, support community centers, public improvements, and charities, and attempt to create a better reputation for the community. The desire to do, to create, and to promote should not be overlooked by the speaker.

Opposed to constructiveness is the desire for destruction, to tear down and to destroy. Hallowe'en, the evening before All Saints' Day, for many years has been the occasion for American youth to give way to this motive. It sometimes appears after football games when the victorious take goal posts, uniforms, and everything else that they can put their hands on. The defeated sometimes give way to this motive and destroy a good deal of property belonging to the victorious school. Destruction is the sole objective of the saboteur. It is the basic philosophy of nihilism, which underlies the doctrines of the Nazi State. It is a throwback to man in a primitive state. However, every individual is motivated by this desire at some time or other. Witness the pure enjoyment we receive in belittling and breaking down old social and business traditions and standards. Note the satisfaction that comes to some people from gossip and slander. Some secure great satisfaction from destroying what is possessed by others, simply because they do not have as much. Insofar as the speaker finds occasion to use this appeal, it should be used with discretion and sound judgment.

Safety

"Safety First," "Stop, Look, Listen," and many other trenchant slogans are manifestations of our desire to play safe. A speaker can make good use of this instinctive desire, perhaps while opposing a change in the organization of a company. He will caution the other board members to take no chances and to oppose all change when they cast their votes. This appeal is used by the stockbroker when he urges you to buy only from the old reliable companies. It is used by the political campaigner when he states, "Never change horses in the middle of the stream." On the other hand, if you are promoting change, you can appeal to the desire for something new, the desire to take a chance, the feeling that any change will be better than what we now have. The statement, "You will never know, until you try," has often been used with effective results.

Pugnacity

This is the "will to fight." Some people are much more pugnacious than others, but most of us enjoy a good fight once in a while. The speaker's approach will be most effective if it is an emotional one. He will taunt his audience with provocative questions, "Are you going to stand by and allow your wages to be cut?", "Do you want these people to reduce your position to one of slavery?", "Are you a quitter, or will you fight for your rights?" These questions provoke negative replies and pave the way for the final plea, "Then lend me your support in this struggle!"

The appeal to peace and quiet is of equal effectiveness. Who does not enjoy the comfort of an evening at home in an easy chair with no troubles to worry him, no fights to wage, and no arguments? A well-known insurance company advertises with a picture of an elderly couple enjoying the declining years of their life in perfect security and peace. The caption reads, "You also may enjoy peace and security after sixty." The advertisement is effective.

Curiosity

The average person has a great interest in new things. He likes to discover, experience, learn, and explore. Put a "wet paint" sign on any piece of wood and nine out of ten people will determine to their own satisfaction that the sign speaks the truth. The radio announcer says, "Listen in tomorrow at this time and you will hear a most unusual announcement." The speaker builds up suspense, plays on your curiosity, and holds your interest.

On the other hand, contentedness is a joy and a comfort to many. "Precedent is the lawyer's first law." Some people have lived within thirty miles of the Grand Canyon of the Colorado without going to see this wonder of nature. Many a young man has said, "Well, it was good enough for my father, why should I change?" Elderly people, in particular, are as a class, conservative. They have a love for the old and the familiar.

Attractiveness

Attractive things appeal strongly to individuals. This accounts for lipstick, rouge, platinum blondes, red automobiles, technicolor films, elaborate flower gardens, neon signs, and brightly colored artificial fish bait. The opposite factor, repulsiveness, produces negative responses. If the speaker will attribute attractive qualities to the proposals that he desires his audience to support and repulsive qualities to those proposals that he wants them to reject, he will find that his effectiveness has increased.

Imitation

This desire is more strongly developed in young people than in old; yet if we should analyze the number of things that are done each day in imitation of others, we would discover that older people are not immune to this desire.   Fads usually spread like wildfire.   Homes are built in new subdivisions because neighbors build there.   You visit the south and come back talking like a Southern Colonel.   Mrs. Jones purchased a bargain at Q & W Store.   You run down and make a purchase.   Yes, imitation goes deeper than most of us would care to admit.   Therefore, it is a desire that the speaker should not overlook in making his persuasive appeal.   Sheep herders know that if they keep a bell on the "head man," they can find the entire flock, because the others will follow.   Play producers used to hire "claques" or professional applauders to start the applause, knowing that once it was started, others would follow and all would feel that they had seen a successful show.   Your story about the traveling salesman may not produce a single laugh when told to several friends individually.   But tell it to them in a group.   When one starts to laugh, they all laugh.   Sheep?   Yes, that is, a good part of the time.

Love of family

If you can show an audience that a certain action will safeguard the health of their families, you have made an appeal to their love of family that will in most instances secure for you the response that you desire.   Insurance is sold on this appeal.   Protect the wife.   Educate the child.   Do not leave the family without a guaranteed income.   Advertisers use this appeal repeatedly to sell "certified" foods, safe medicines, automobiles with steel bodies and safety glass.   Parents devote themselves to their children and their love and affection is returned.   Albert W. Whitney makes an appeal to this love of family in his war against reckless driving:

The story, however, cannot be told in bare numbers.   It must be told also in human terms, in the lifeless forms of little children, in crushed and bleeding bodies, in ruined hopes, in broken hearts.

The love of family is one of the most precious desires held by mankind. It should be used by the speaker, but, we hope, not abused.

In summary, these final observations should be made regarding the speaker's appeal to desires as a means of persuasion: These desires vary with each individual and with each audience on different occasions; it is necessary for the speaker to analyze them before giving each speech. He then prepares the speech so that its appeal will be effective. Work out in advance of the speech the particular word images, examples, and illustrations that you plan to use. They can then be presented with a degree of confidence and spontaneity not otherwise obtainable. *Your use* of these fundamental desires *must be sincere.* If the audience detects insincerity, if they believe that you are being facetious, if they sense dishonesty, you will have lost them and you *should* lose them. But if you speak as an ABLE MAN, you will win them and they will act as you desire them to act.

QUESTIONS

1. What is persuasion?

2. How may your mastery of the principles and techniques of persuasion influence your success in business?

3. What is persuasion through the personality of the speaker?

4. What is persuasion through explanation?

5. What is persuasion through logic?

6. What is persuasion through suggestion?

7. What is persuasion through appeals to fundamental needs, wants, and desires?

8. What is evidence? Direct and indirect?

9. What tests should be applied to determine the validity of evidence?

10. What are the four patterns of proof available for arranging indirect evidence in support of a given conclusion?

11. What are the rules for use of positive suggestion?

12. What are the fundamental needs, wants, and desires possessed by all men that can be appealed to in persuasive speaking?

EXERCISES

1. Cite examples of occasions when you were persuaded to a belief or action because you respected the integrity and personality of the speaker.

2. Explain a recent motion picture you have seen in such a way as to persuade another person to see it also. Use no other method of persuasion.

3. Make a list of ten situations in which persuasion may be achieved through explanation.

4. Conduct a discussion of policy on a question of timely interest. Demonstrate your knowledge and skill in the use of logic as a method of persuasion.

5. Find five advertisements in magazines that illustrate the use of suggestion (positive or negative).

6. In conference with a classmate make use of suggestion to persuade him to some belief or action.

7. Confer with a friend on the selection of a name for some new product or organization.

8. In five good advertisements find to what fundamental wants, needs, and desires the major appeal is being made.

9. Imagine yourself in one of the following situations. Prepare for a conference along the lines indicated by one of the situations. Make use of effective conference techniques and the methods of persuasion. Hand in a brief sketch or outline of your conference before you speak.

(a) You are a minister attempting to persuade a recalcitrant member of your congregation to conduct a Sunday School class.

(b) You are a sales manager endeavoring to secure better sales from a salesman.

(c) You are an accountant in a small business firm attempting to secure a raise in salary from your employer.

(d) You are a fraternity member trying to persuade a freshman to believe your fraternity is the best on the campus.

(e) You are a football coach speaking to the captain between halves of a game. The score is 20 to 0 in favor of the opponents.

(f) You are a radio announcer seeking permission to interview a visiting celebrity on the air.

(g) You are an Army Recruiting Officer talking to a boy who would like to join the Marines.

(h) You are in debt to the local clothing store. Your bill is three months overdue. You have come to see the manager about a further extension.

(i) You are a student speaking to an instructor who gave you a *C* grade instead of a *B*, which you think you deserved.

(j) You are a labor union organizer talking to a workman who has just been employed in a nonunion shop.

(k) You are the play director of the local dramatic club trying to encourage a member to try out for the new play.

(l) Select any other conference situation in which you must use persuasion to secure belief or action.

SELECTED READINGS

Higgins, Howard Hubert, *Influencing Behavior Through Speech,* Expression Company, Boston, 1930.

Overstreet, H. A., *Influencing Human Behavior,* W. W. Norton and Company, New York, 1925.

Sarett, Lew, and Foster, William Trufant, *Basic Principles of Speech,* Houghton Mifflin Company, New York, 1936.

The Question of Policy Conference

I.   INTRODUCTION AND DEFINITION
     Question of policy and facts
II. POLICY-DETERMINING CONFERENCES
     Defining the problem
     Discovering the causes
     Finding a solution
     Procedure illustrated
III. POLICY-CONFIRMING CONFERENCE
     The statement of policy
     Preliminary forms of support
        Definition of terms
        History of the question
        Immediate cause for discussion
     Development of supporting issues
        Is there need for a change?
        Is the change practical?
        Will the change be beneficial?
     Concluding appeals for confirmation

The Question of Policy Conference

Introduction and Definition

YOU ARE a member of a summer soft ball team. Last year your team played in the Commercial League. Since you were the league winner, your team has been asked to join a league that plays a better class of soft ball. The team manager calls all the players together for the purpose of determining whether or not you will accept the invitation. Each player is asked to state his views on the question under consideration. The discussion in which you participate concerns a question of policy.

Your local city council has had several requests from property owners in the new Valley Subdivision for relief from surface water during the periods of heavy rain. The mayor of the city calls the council together on a Thursday to consider the problem. The discussion that follows concerns a question of policy.

J. C. Nickle Co. operates some 300 retail dry goods stores throughout the nation. It has been the policy of this company to pay the local store managers a straight salary for their services. At the thirty-seventh annual meeting of all the managers, someone proposed that the managers be placed on a combination salary and commission basis. This plan is presented to the board of directors. Its pros and cons are discussed. This discussion is a question of policy.

You have been employed in the personnel division of the Blue Steel Co. Having been put in charge of labor relations, you have completed a study of working conditions, wages, insurance and retirement benefits, and hours of employment. You are now an expert on these particular questions as they pertain to the Blue Steel Co. In conference with the first vice-president you present an oral report on your findings. Two days later he calls you into conference on the question of unemployment insurance.   In this discussion of policy conference with the first vice-president you decide that the company should adopt a program including unemployment insurance benefits.   The first vice-president requests that you attend the next board of directors' meeting, present the program, and urge its adoption.   Your speech before the board is an attempt to seek confirmation of a policy already determined.

From these illustrations it should be apparent that *the question of policy concerns itself with a line or course of action in relation to some particular issue or subject.*   The situation, whether it involves one speaker or a half dozen, is a question of policy situation if it attempts either to determine a course of action to be followed or to win approval for a course of action already determined.   The first situation is classified as a *policy-determining* speech; the attempt to win approval of it, on the other hand, is *policy-confirming.*

Question of policy and facts

Basic to the determination or confirmation of any question of policy are the underlying facts.   What do the facts reveal?   Can you win more glory, have more fun, and increase your self-esteem by playing ball in the Class "A" league?   Is it practical for the city to provide temporary surface outlets or should the city contract for a complete drainage system?   Will a combination salary and commission payment for store managers increase the profits of the company or the quality of its service?   Will unemployment insurance increase the workers' morale at the Blue Steel Co.?   What are the facts?   Considerable research must precede any successful question of policy conference or speech.   Many conferences are adjourned because no one has the facts and many speeches are a total waste of time because the speaker fails to present facts.

You state, for example, that new machines should be installed in the shop.   The conferee asks you if the old machines can be repaired.   How much do new machines cost?   How long will it take to install them?   Can the company afford to wait until the low production season to install them?   Your conferee will want the facts; he will need the facts in order to make a decision.   Suppose the conferee says, "I think that about ten of those machines should be replaced." You say, "I think that thirty-three need replacing." Does it help solve the problem to *guess* the number of needed replacements? Does it help solve the problem to state that you are right and he is wrong? This does not mean that you cannot arrive at a decision. The problem in determining a policy is a co-operative method of finding the best solution, and only through consideration of the *facts* can a satisfactory decision be reached.

Policy-Determining Conferences

The policy-determining conference is the type of speech situation most commonly confronted by boards of directors, committees, groups of elected officials, and executives in conference. These groups are constantly trying to improve the status of the organizations that they represent. To do this they must chart courses of action, determine budgets, advertising problems, marketing questions, taxes, production methods, and other important problems. Three steps in the determining of policy are recommended: (1) the problem must be resolved and accurately defined, (2) the causes of the problem must be discovered, and (3) possible solutions must be considered.

Defining the problem

The first step involves the isolation and definition of the exact problem. "Wherein lies the difficulty? What is wrong?" Walker & Son's profits for 1941 are equal to those of 1940. Competitors have increased their profits. What is wrong? What is the problem? You might say that the problem in this instance is the failure to increase profits. Yes, but there are other problems back of this one. They may be poor marketing, greater competition, increased cost of raw materials, or ineffective advertising. In order to determine the course of action that should be followed, it is first necessary to locate the precise problem that needs to be solved. The doctor attempts to locate the trouble before he recommends treatment to a patient. This same scientific approach should be made by the businessman when determining a question of policy.

Discovering the causes

The second step in determining a solution is to discover the causes. Walker & Son's profits have failed to increase. Suppose the difficulty lies in poor marketing. What causes this poor marketing? If the problem is increased cost of raw materials, what caused this increased cost? If the advertising was ineffective, then the question is "why?" Further consideration of the problem may reveal to the group that the advertising was ineffective because the advertising manager is not qualified. It may be that the advertising budget was too small. The wrong medium may have been used. The results may have been a combination of more than one of these factors. But in all cases the group must find these causes to be able to solve the problem.

The advertising manager may be asked to present his explanation of the causes. The marketing experts will be asked to make their reports. Field men may be consulted for information not found in the home office. Buyers may be asked for their opinions. From these sources and from the information possessed by the board members the true state of affairs will come to light. The real cause will be known. If, however, the facts at hand are not sufficient to disclose the real cause, the group should adjourn until the facts are made available. If the real cause is a small budget, then it will not solve the problem to fire the manager. If the manager lacks ability, the company may make less profits the following year if the board decides to keep the manager and change the medium. The problem will be solved only by removing the cause or counteracting its effect upon the system.

Finding a solution

There are at least two theoretical solutions to every problem. The factor that gives rise to the problem may be removed or its effect may be counteracted. If it be assumed in the above hypothetical case that the advertising is ineffective owing to poor management, then the board can solve its problem either by replacing the manager with an efficient manager or it can increase the advertising budget to a point where it will overcome the manager's inefficiency. The first of these two methods, if employed, would remove the cause, while the second would counteract the cause.

In this case, as in most cases, the most practicable solution is to eliminate the cause. This matter of finding the most practicable solution to the problem is, then, the third step to be taken in the policy-determining speech situation. The Walker & Son's case presented above represents a fairly simple application of the three steps.

Procedure illustrated

Let us reiterate these steps and examine, by way of illustration, their application in a more difficult and complex policy-determining situation. They are: first, locate the problem; second, determine the cause or causes of the problem; and third, determine the most practicable solution for removing the cause or causes, or for counteracting them.

Producer's, Inc., have had a good year. The men in charge of the firm are in their annual meeting. Jones makes a motion that dividends be paid on all stock. At that point Smith takes the floor and states, "I am going to vote against that motion." Smith explains that he is not sure just what the trouble is, but he feels that there will be a very poor year ahead and therefore the company should retain a large reserve. After Smith is seated, two other members agree with what he has stated and conclude that they will vote against the motion. At this point Jones makes a real contribution to the meeting. Jones says, "You boys feel that something is wrong. Rather than asking for a vote on my motion before we investigate the difficulty, I'll withdraw the motion until this problem is determined and solved." The group now enters into step number one of the policy-determining speech situation.

All members now devote their attention and remarks to the matter of determining the felt difficulty or the problem mentioned by Smith. Smith thinks that business will suffer because of the war. Brown thinks that business will be better than ever if the company will only take on some war contracts. Day suggests that the real problem that confronts them is the loss of available young men through the draft; therefore, a problem in both labor cost and labor efficiency exists. Jones believes that with orders increasing every day, business will be better than ever. Doss believes that Jones is right in what he says, but that that is the problem. It will mean plant expansion, if the orders are to be filled; this step would be disastrous with the loss of business when the war is over. These men, having all the necessary facts at hand, devote the next three hours in locating the exact problem felt by Smith. They finally conclude that the company cannot conduct its "business as usual" for the duration of the war.

They then turn their attention to the exact causes of this problem. The major cause is, of course, the war. There are many minor factors or causes that also enter into the picture. Cost factors, increased taxes, labor shortage for special types of work, factors of distribution, and factors of demand all present themselves as contributing causes. Further, it is impossible to predict with any degree of accuracy the duration of any of these causes. Since the difficulty arises out of many causes and a combination of causes and since the duration of these causes is unpredictable, the board finds no easy solution. However, they still have the responsibility of running the business at a profit. Thus, their next step in this policy-determining situation is to present and adopt a practicable and workable solution.

They first ask themselves the question, "Can any of the causes of our problems be eliminated?" They can hardly eliminate war as a factor. There is but little that can be done about increased taxes and labor shortage. It might be that a good attorney could figure out some method of keeping taxes down, but they would still increase with the rates being adopted in Washington. They might set up a training program for labor which would supply their requirements for skilled employees. This will take both time and money. Costs might be cut in some departments, but with increased prices it will be difficult to cut total costs. Distribution might be handled more effectively and demand might be stimulated by increased advertising.

The conclusions show clearly that the major cause, war, and some of the minor causes, increased taxes and costs, cannot be eliminated. Some of the other minor causes, such as shortage of skilled labor, might be removed, but this will require time and money. In view of these conclusions, the board decides that the course of action to be followed will have to counteract the causes rather than remove them. This will be difficult. It may even be impossible. But the board members finally agree that the most practicable solution will be a combination of the many courses of action previously presented. Consequently, they vote to pay a small dividend, retool a small part of the plant for government orders, train skilled laborers, and send the first vice-president down to Washington in an effort to cut taxes.

This case is typical of the thousands of problems with which business throughout the country is confronted. It further represents the typical group question of policy situation. All members of the group make a contribution to the discussion and to the final solution. All members will find it helpful if they will follow the three steps in their policy-determining situations. The reader will note that in the preceding case, the board members were confronted with the problem of finding a solution to a felt difficulty. Except for Smith's proposal that dividends be paid, all members of the group started this policy-determining situation by trying to locate the problem and its causes before voting on a course of action to be followed.

In concluding our remarks on the policy-determining speech situation, it should be stated that an individual in presenting a speech on policy-determining matters should follow the same three steps. He should work through these steps in advance of the speech. He should then prepare his speech with these three steps serving as the main ideas. When this is done, the presentation of the speech will reveal to the audience the facts and evidence showing the problem, its causes, and the most practicable solution. When the speaker presents his case in this manner and asks the audience to accept the solutions, his method of persuasion has been persuasion through explanation and through logic.

Policy-Confirming Conference

Whereas the purpose of the policy-determining speech situation was to *find* a course of action, the purpose of the policy-confirming speech is to secure audience acceptance of a course of action which you, the speaker, want them to adopt. It may be that you have conducted an investigation along the policy-determining lines and have thus arrived at the most practicable course of action. It may be that you simply desire a certain course of action to be followed. It may be that you want your proposition accepted for reasons not concerned with the company. It matters not what your reasons are: it matters only that you are able to motivate the audience to accept your proposal. This involves the utilization of the same principles and techniques discussed in the chapter on persuasion.

Every businessman shares a public trust as well as a private trust. He is stimulated to action by both the profit motive and the public service motive. From day to day he must make decisions and advocate their acceptance. When a lawyer is engaged by a client, the first decision to be made is whether or not the client has a cause of action. Once that decision has been made in the affirmative, the lawyer's entire efforts are devoted to ways and means of having his decision accepted by the opposing litigant, judge, or jury. His course of action is clear. He must influence others to accept his decision. He will use any or all of the forms of persuasion presented in the last chapter.

The same situation holds true of the members of a deliberative assembly. Once a proposal or bill is introduced, the duty of the supporters is to influence others to accept their judgment as regards the course of action to be followed. Many business conferences are devoted entirely to hearing and/or discussing a course of action advocated by the advertising manager, sales manager, or other executive. In all of these instances it is customary for the other members of the group to advocate opposing courses of action. The following discussion contains helpful suggestions on organizing the material for presentation in the policy-confirming situations.

The statement of policy

When a course of action has been determined, its advocate should state the course of action desired in a clear declarative sentence. The language should be simple. The statement should avoid ambiguous terms and should be worded in the affirmative. The following statements will illustrate these requirements:

Jones and Company should increase its advertising budget by 20 per cent for the year of 1942.

Allied Products, Inc., should pay a 4 per cent dividend at the end of the present operating year.

Grover College should require entrance examinations of all new students.

When the advocate's statement of policy conforms to those requisites his position can be clearly understood. This understanding is essential to adoption. It limits and determines the material needed in support of the policy.

Preliminary forms of support

Definition of terms. As stated in the last chapter, explanation is one of the important forms of persuasion. Definition of terms embodied in a statement of policy is a form of explanation. It leads to an understanding between the advocate and his conferees or audience. It places all parties on common ground regarding the policy and makes for harmonious action. In many instances the only factor preventing joint action is lack of understanding. By clearly defining the terms of a statement of policy, the speaker charts his course for his audience in a manner comparable to the course charted by a navigator. Travelers go more willingly when they know *where* they are going. Audiences will be persuaded more easily when they know where the speaker is taking them.

History of the question. Without exception we all can exhibit better foresight after having indulged in hindsight regarding a particular proposal. We predict, judge, and gauge the future in light of the past; we interpret future affairs in terms of our understanding of them in the past. Therefore, it is advisable for any advocate to review the history of the particular problem before him and to use such historical facts as are available to point to the wisdom of adopting the policy. The history of mass production, advertising, marketing programs, sales techniques, and foreign trade all point to policies that must be followed in the future. The history of labor problems points clearly to the general policy that labor will exercise greater control over the production agencies of our country and, therefore, business must provide a labor relations department that will utilize labor contributions for the maximum improvement of the entire industry. This historical approach to a question of policy is essential persuasion through explanation. State the history of a given case and the future course of action may often be implied.

Immediate cause for discussion. This preliminary form of support serves as a point of departure for the presentation of the basic reasons and appeals for accepting the advocated policy. Its chief value lies in the fact that it justifies the discussion at the time and place that it is presented. In times of war we find it inadvisable to discuss many peacetime questions. Priorities, for example, make discussions of production schedules meaningless for many small industries. It is then advisable for every advocate to state the immediate cause for discussion of the problem if he would gain a sympathetic conferee or audience. The audience must feel that the question of policy presented is proper as regards time and place.

Development of supporting issues

Is there need for a change?   When seeking approval in a policy-confirming speech situation it is advisable first to consider the reasons for changing from the *status quo*. Man, by nature, is slow to adopt a new course of action until the old course of action fails. We are victims of habit, conservatism, and lethargy. In some instances we prefer to go about our work in the old routine manner because it takes less effort, but in most instances the old routine is followed merely because we lack imagination and initiative. Therefore the policy-confirming conferrer or speaker should first show his audience the need for a change. This is illustrated in business by the many shifts in policy owing to the national efforts in time of war. Small organizations must reorganize their production energies or go out of business. Automobile dealers are forced to discharge their salesmen and increase their repair and service departments.

The "need for a change" issue is easily understood in the above illustrations. It may not be so obvious in the case of labor's demands for increased income or the demands of business for governmental contracts on a cost-plus basis. In these last two cases it will be necessary for the advocate to first show that the old course of action fails to satisfy present needs and problems. When this need issue is firmly established, one is ready to consider the practicability of the new course of action.

Is the change practical?   This issue is developed mainly by explanation of the proposed policy in terms of how it will work to solve the needs presented in the first issue. It involves a detailed outlining of the plan to be followed under the new policy. This issue deals with finances, plant facilities, labor supply, materials needed, and so on. The successful advocate will establish the particular features of his plan to prove that it will be a practical solution to the problems presented.   Charts, diagrams, statistics, and other aids to understanding will be helpful in presenting this phase of the policy-confirming speech.

Will the change be beneficial?   This issue allows the advocate of a policy to appeal for action on the basis of benefits to be derived from its adoption.   These benefits may be stated in terms of profits, successful operation against competition, greater service and goodwill, improved conditions for employees, increased market, or increased efficiency.   This portion of the policy-confirming speech will also deal with questions of increased expenses, cost of operation, plant expansion, and other burdens that the company may assume by adopting the policy.   The advocate of the new policy will want to answer all objections by showing that they are outweighed by the benefits gained.   The issue of benefits deals with the future; therefore the conferrer or speaker has a good opportunity for appeals to needs, wants, and desires of his auditors and thus to motivate action.

Concluding appeals for confirmation

The conclusion to a policy-confirming speech, whether public or in conference, has two functions.   It should contain a summary of the main ideas and a final appeal for adoption.   The summary of main ideas will correspond, in general, to the three supporting issues.   The conferrer or speaker can, with proper preparation in advance, analyze the audience and the material supporting his proposal and thus base his final appeal on those ideas that will have the greatest motivating influence.

QUESTIONS

1. What is a question of policy speech?
2. What is a policy-determining speech as distinguished from a policy-confirming speech?
3. Explain the statement "The question of policy business conference depends on facts."
4. What are the three major steps to be followed in a policy-determining conference?
5. In what order should the material be developed in a policy-confirming speech?

EXERCISES

Policy-Determining Speeches

1. Select two questions of policy. Write in outline form a speech which will determine the policy to be followed in each case. These outlines should follow the three steps presented under this section of the chapter.

2. Conduct a policy-determining speech discussion in some group to which you belong. Follow the steps recommended. Make a report of the discussion and the success of the policy-determining aspects.

Policy-Confirming Speeches

1. Select two questions of policy. Write in outline form a speech that will confirm the policy that you think should be accepted in each case.

2. Be prepared to present a policy-confirming speech in class.

CHAPTER IX

Sales

I. FOUR FACTORS IN SELLING
    Ability of the customer to buy
    Competition
    Price
    Salesman
        Salesman and a pleasing personality
        Salesman and his product
II. BASIC IDEAS IN EVERY SALES SITUATION
III. THE SALES PRESENTATION
    Securing the interview
    The approach
        Indirect
        Direct
    Presentation of needs, wants, and desires
        Needs, wants, and desires possessed and recognized by
        the prospect
        Needs, wants, and desires possessed but not recognized
        by the prospect
        Nonexisting needs, wants, and desires that salesman
        may create
    Explanation and demonstration of product
    Confirmation of product
        By authority
        By reference to specific cases
        By sample and demonstration
    Closing the sale
    Devices preparatory to closing
        Assumed approval
        Summarized close
        Dramatized close
        Command approval
IV. THE PROMOTIONAL SITUATION

CHAPTER IX

Sales

IN 1918 a nationally known insurance agent was serving as First Lieutenant with the 33rd Division in Texas. The government wished to introduce its plan of war insurance to the soldiers. The men were to sign an insurance contract and authorize the payment of the premiums out of their monthly pay checks. The Commanding Officer, knowing that his Division had among its members this "crack" insurance agent, delegated to him the responsibility of explaining the program to the soldiers. On the following morning several hours were devoted to an explanation of the program. The agent had little success. The men understood insurance, but they also understood that the premium was to be taken from their earnings. Only four had signed the authorization papers when Private Jones stepped up and said, "Pardon me, Lieutenant, y'all know a lot about insurance, but," he hesitated, "y'all don't seem to know much about these here soldiers. I believe these men ought to sign up. How about letting me talk to them?" Hoping that something might happen to make his efforts successful, the Lieutenant consented. Private Jones faced the company and made these remarks, "Boys, over in France there's going to be two types of soldiers. One type is up on the front lines getting killed off by the enemy. The other type is going to be 'way back of the front lines taking care of the mules. Y'all know Uncle Sam ain't putting any man carrying ten thousand dollars' worth of insurance up on those front lines." The entire company had signed up by mess call.

The agent, in reporting this story later, stated that this single experience taught him more about the art of selling than any other thing that he had ever heard or read. It is hoped that the same result will be produced on the reader. The art of selling can be stated in two sentences: present a need, want, or desire possessed by the buyer; show the buyer that the product for sale will satisfy that need, want, or desire.

Four Factors in Selling

Four factors enter into every sales situation. These are the ability of the consumer to buy, competition, the price of the goods being sold, and the salesman. If you can cope with these factors, you are a salesman. If you cannot, you are at best an occasional delivery boy.

Ability of the customer to buy

In regard to their ability to buy, customers may be grouped in two categories, those who have actual ability and those who have potential ability. The salesman can do but little with the customer without the actual ability to buy; in fact, he should not be considered as a customer or a prospect. The salesman's problem here is to complete a good prospect list of those individuals who have the cash or credit necessary for the purchase of his goods. This requires time and effort; it also requires a careful study of incomes, expenditures, budgets, and credit capacities of the persons being prospected. Without this information much time is lost in actual sales presentation. Obviously it is foolish to present a product if the conferee does not have the ability to buy.

Persons with potential ability to buy present a different picture to the salesman. With this group his problem is largely one of influencing them to accept his product as the one on which they should spend their money. This group includes the people, businesses, and companies who spend their income and use their credit in the normal course of their regular activities. If you are going to sell to this group you must either hold them as customers or take them away from other sellers. The salesman can do nothing about this group's ability to buy; he can only compete with others in an attempt to sell.

Competition

There is only one thing the salesman can do with competition if he wishes to eat three square meals a day—he can work harder than the competitor. This means better prospecting; it means a better analysis of a customer's needs, wants, and desires; it means a better knowledge of the products being offered for sale; and it means better sales presentations.

Price

Since the price factor in the sales situation is determined by the home office or the local manager, the salesman can do nothing about it except to get the customer to agree to pay the price set. The salesman can work out terms for cash and credit. If the customer's resources warrant consideration he may be permitted to open an account. Warranty or guaranty contracts may be acceptable. Such terms sometimes make it easier to sell the customer and in many instances make the price less objectionable. But the fact still remains that the customer must agree to the price before a sale can be consummated.

Salesman

The last factor, and in many cases the most important in the sales situation is the salesman himself. The challenge to the salesman is, can he create favorable attitudes? Can he make the customer cognizant of needs, wants, and desires? Can he show the customer that his product will satisfy these needs, wants, and desires to a higher degree than the product of his competitor? For the ABLE MAN the answer is "Yes." But there are many salesmen who will answer, "The customer didn't have the money," or "Competition is too great," or "The price is too high to sell anyone." To these people the sales manager will say, "You are not a salesman. Your services are no longer needed."

Salesman and a pleasing personality. In the chapter on persuasion, you will recall, the first method discussed was persuasion through personality. Personality in selling is invaluable. The customer's attitude toward the salesman must be a favorable one. Attitude is as much a result of the subconscious mind as the conscious mind, and personality makes its mark on the subconscious mind. Prospects, being victims of their subconscious minds, either like or dislike the seller the moment they see him. Since the prospect buys more often when favorably impressed, the seller cannot afford a personality that produces negative responses. Therefore, the salesman must be alive, be happy at his work, put enthusiasm into his effort, and present outward manifestations of the ABLE MAN qualities.

Salesman and his product. A consistent record of sales cannot be made unless the salesman knows his product. If you have worked as a clerk in a store, you will recall that your first duty was not to sell but to familiarize yourself with the stock. You may have talked with an employer who told you that the training course for all his salesmen began with work in the plant so that each salesman would know the product—from the wool on the sheep's back to the double-breasted suit. You may recall your recent experience with the clerk in the local dry goods store. You asked for percale sheets; she brought out cotton sheets. You asked for infant sweaters; she had to ask the floor man where to find them. You asked the price on a dozen handkerchiefs; she had to call the main office. You went to another store. She— well, she is looking for another job.

Basic Ideas in Every Sales Situation

In general, the sales speech should be developed around two main ideas. These ideas, as already stated, are first, the presentation of needs, wants, and desires, and second, the demonstration of the salesman's product as a solution to these needs, wants, and desires. We buy food not because we want to collect food but to satisfy our hunger. We buy clothing not for the purpose of having clothes but for the purpose of keeping warm or remaining in style. We buy land not in order to hold land but in order to make money or to possess security. Thus, as salesmen, we should not try to sell food, clothing, or land, but we should sell hunger, low temperature, lack of style, poverty, or insecurity. Once the customer feels the pressure of these uncomfortable factors, he will be possessed by wants and desires. These wants and desires can then be satisfied by the purchase of food, clothes, or land.

It has been reported that a certain mouth wash increased 63 per cent in sales when the producers stopped emphasizing mouth wash and started advertising "Your best friend won't tell you." The people were sold halitosis; they were sold the idea that halitosis made them social outcasts. Bad breath! No friends! Failures! Immediately, people everywhere developed a driving want and desire. They wanted to destroy this monster that prevented success, this thing that was so distasteful that even your best friend would not tell you about it. The advertisement suggested the answer to these problems and sales jumped. It is also reported that the sales of a certain soap rose precipitously when the producers stopped advertising the soap and started to advertise "B. O." Pick up the daily newspaper or turn on your radio. Are the advertisers asking you to buy? Yes, but only after they attempt to make you conscious of some need. You enjoy the radio program and you buy because you want "the skin you love to touch," "the smile of beauty," or "the cigarette that satisfies."

The Sales Presentation

Securing the interview

There are many devices used for getting into a home or office for a sales interview. Some organizations send out questionnaires by mail to be called for at a specific hour by their representative; such questionnaires raise the question of needs and wants of the customer in reference to the product being sold. The salesman sends his prospect a telegram indicating important business at a specified hour; he is then readily received by the prospect. Another salesman may call and leave a sample to be examined by the prospect; he expects this device to gain a favorable conference at a later date. Still other salesmen gain their entrance on some pretext of donating to charitable organizations or representing service companies or repair men. The less ingenious may gain an entrance by sheer perseverance. The story is told of the busy executive who refused to see sixteen insurance agents on a given day but who finally permitted an interview with the seventeenth. The executive started the conference by stating. "Young man, you are extremely fortunate in gaining this interview. I have refused to see sixteen insurance agents today." The agent replied, "Yes, I know, and I appreciate this conference. You see, I was all sixteen of those agents."

In many instances it is necessary for the salesman to utilize some devices for gaining an interview. However, selling has been elevated to a dignified profession in the past two decades. Buyers recognize that salesmen render a valuable service in the field of distribution. Consequently as a general rule, it is not advisable to use devices or schemes in gaining the interview for the simple reason that the prospect is put on his guard. This creates a wall of resistance which must be overcome later in the sales presentation. It is therefore recommended that the salesman use straightforward methods in gaining his interviews. These consist of appointments made by telephone, by letter, or by a previous conference in which the purpose of the proposed interview is stated. Such an appointment may be made with the help of a third person. This latter method is a particularly advantageous one when dealing with a new prospect. Salesmen will be given interviews in the majority of instances if this straightforward attitude is maintained. It can be maintained as long as salesmen are honest and ethical in dealing with customers.

The approach

The term "approach" is used to indicate the first part of the sales conference wherein the salesman introduces himself and the purpose of his interview. In any sales approach the salesman has two objectives to accomplish: first, he must create a favorable impression upon the prospect and secure positive interest and attention, and second, he must shift the positive interest and attention of the prospect to the article of sale. In many interviews the salesman has a third objective to accomplish; he must secure information about the prospect or amplify or reject information previously secured. When these objectives are secured the salesman is ready to proceed to a discussion and demonstration of the needs of his product.

Two types of approach may be used in accomplishing these objectives. The *indirect* approach involves the use of questions and statements pertaining to matters and needs of general interest to the prospect. This type of approach is being used when the salesman starts talking about the weather, politics, the customer's health, football, baseball, or the war. From the customer's replies the salesmen can gain new information or confirm or reject information previously gained about the customer and thus, holding his interest, he can lead him toward a discussion of his needs and wants as they pertain to the goods being sold. The principal advantage of this approach is that it is easy to use.

There are always timely topics of interest to a customer. The principal disadvantages of this approach are that it may take too much time if not carefully used and that it requires a transition from matters of general interest to those of specific interest as related to the product being sold.

The *direct* approach involves the use of questions and statements pertaining to matters and needs of specific interest to the prospect and definitely related to the salesman and his product. In using this approach, the salesman, after a proper introduction, will start talking or asking questions about specific illnesses, investments, clothes, or wants and needs for specific goods. To do this successfully, a careful analysis of the customer must be made in advance of the presentation. The principal advantages of this approach are that it allows both individuals to "get to the meat" of the conference in a minimum of time and that it avoids abrupt and difficult transitions from the approach to the main discussion of the conference. Its principal disadvantages are that it requires more time in preparation, more skill in execution, and more confidence on the part of the salesman.

Both the direct and indirect opening should utilize concrete examples and illustrations. The salesman should use the type of opening that will best accomplish the objectives to be attained. Therefore, his use of either the direct or the indirect approach or a combination of both will depend to a marked extent on the prospect and the circumstances surrounding the interview. When time is of the essence or the prospect is a man of few words, the direct approach is preferable. When the reverse circumstances prevail, use the indirect approach.

Presentation of needs, wants, and desires

Types of needs, wants, and desires can be roughly grouped into three categories: (1) those of whose existence the prospect is well aware, (2) those that the prospect has but does not recognize, and (3) those that do not exist but that the salesman can create.

Needs, wants, and desires possessed and recognized by the prospect. This category of motives for purchasing goods includes the need for food, clothing, and shelter. These needs are ever present and always felt. They vary in degrees in accordance with differing circumstances. The "have-nots" are more concerned than the "haves." But everyone has these needs and everyone is concerned with goods that may be used to satisfy them.

In selling goods that satisfy needs, the salesman's problem is not so much that of explaining the needs themselves as of demonstrating that his particular product can best satisfy those needs. Thus the baker adds vitamins to bread, the clothier adds style to suits, and the contractor adds automatic heat, air conditioning, and more utility closets to the house. The successful salesman will break down the general need into specific needs and associated needs. He will not discuss hunger but rather hunger for particular foods. He will present at the same time problems of diet deficiencies, iced coffee in preference to hot coffee, recipes for tasty foods, and economy factors in both purchasing and cooking. He gains recognition from the customer of the latter's specific and associated needs in relation to the product being sold. If he can gain this recognition for his product to a greater degree than that gained by his competitors, he will naturally make more sales.

Needs, wants, and desires possessed but not recognized by the prospect. This category of motives for purchasing goods includes need for deluxe foods, clothing, shelter, luxuries, specialties in all lines of goods, and nearly all items that can be broadly called investments. These needs are always present and often recognized to some degree, but do not constitute a buying motive without some form of promotion being exercised by the salesman. This category may be explained in another manner. It consists of general needs, wants, and desires not translated into specific needs, wants, and desires and for which no specific goods or services come to the mind of the customer as a possible solution. Thus a tired and overworked prospect might or might not realize the need for a rest. He might recognize that he should take a rest but might not know how to translate that need into specific action. The travel service agent or health resort representative will present this need to the prospect in terms of avoiding sleepless nights, indigestion, lack of domestic tranquillity, nervous collapse, and loss of business. This need would then be translated in terms of a specific solution in the nature of a particular trip or vacation at a particular resort. A housewife burdened with washing and ironing will have her general needs translated into specific needs for fewer weary hours over the scrubbing and ironing boards and for more hours with her family and friends, for wider social horizons, and for cleaner and neater clothes and prettier hands. Utility salesmen will translate these needs into specific solutions in the form of new washing machines, mangles, and other electric equipment.

To a considerable extent the work of the salesman dealing with this type of appeal is educational in nature. Labor-saving and safety machines are installed in industrial concerns, insurance is sold, real estate is purchased, books are read, and cows are harnessed with mechanical milking machines, all because the ABLE MAN salesman educates the public by making them aware of specific needs, wants, and desires that the salesman's goods or services can satisfy.

Nonexisting needs, wants, and desires that the salesman may create. Many people are completely satisfied. They reach this state of mental complacency as a result of custom, tradition, ignorance, lack of experience, or lethargy. Such people follow a routine of buying today what they bought yesterday. They live on the thesis, "What was good enough for father is good enough for me." Such people are therefore hard to sell. They lack imagination, vision, foresight, and progressive outlook. To sell a member of this group the salesman must actually create a need, want, or desire in the member's mind. The situation may be illustrated by the following example. Mr. Jones has used a hand-fired furnace for years; he is able to heat the house; his coal bill is not above the amount that he expects to pay; he expects to tend the furnace twice a day. He is satisfied in all respects. His thinking regarding furnaces has stopped at this point. It is up to the stoker or oil-burner salesman to create needs, wants, and desires in the mind of Mr. Jones, if he is to succeed in making a sale. Thus he presents to Mr. Jones the need for more time to do other work around the house, the need for saving the expense of hiring someone else to fire the furnace in the owner's absence, the need for clean heat, and the need for clean basements.

This category of prospects can be touched by increasing their capacity for consuming goods. If a man doesn't like music, you cannot sell him a piano. Educate him to enjoy playing and he will buy your piano. The sale of airplanes will increase following the war for the reason, among others, that more people will know how to fly an airplane. Many needs, wants, and desires are created by giving samples to prospects. Many grocery stores keep salesmen who give shoppers sample cuts of cheese, meats, cakes, and candy, thus creating a desire that produces a sale. As in the second general classification of prospects, the salesman's job in this category is largely one of education in meeting competition. The better the education, the less competition.

Explanation and demonstration of product

The purpose of explaining and demonstrating products is twofold: first, to show how it satisfies the need, want, or desire of the customer, and second, to show that it is a more satisfactory solution than a competitive one. It is true, of course, that an explanation or demonstration of the product often helps in producing the need, want, or desire for the product and such explanations or demonstrations may also help to close the sale. Once the customer is convinced that a problem exists, he immediately wants to know how to solve it. Explanation and demonstration answer the question "How?" In selling shoes, for example, you explain or demonstrate the construction, the style, the arch support features, and particular combination widths. If you are selling farm real estate, you explain the type and quality of soil, the nature of crops that can be produced, the arrangement and capacity of barn and tool shed, features of the house, and profits from owning the farm. Knowledge of your product is imperative if your explanation and demonstration are to be complete.

It is always desirable, if possible, to let the prospect use the product by way of demonstration in a sales situation. In doing this the salesman should make sure that the prospect is informed on how to use the product. If injury or accident should result from the prospect's use while the demonstration is being made, a sale might be lost and a lawsuit gained.

Confirmation of product

This step in the sales presentation is essentially one of proving that the goods or services being sold will satisfy the customer and do the things that the salesman states that they will do. This confirmation may be established in one or more of three ways. *First,* recommendations by recognized authorities may be presented to support the claims made by the salesman. Testimony of famous people is used to confirm many products. Advertisers use the same device when they secure endorsements from movies stars or baseball players.

The *second* method of confirmation is to present actual cases where the product has performed as represented. Here the salesman will use the case of a friend of the prospect if at all possible. The confirmation may run like this: "Your neighbor, Mr. Jones, averaged twenty-two miles per gallon on his trip last summer," or "Mr. Smith, who lives around the corner from you, saved twenty-seven dollars on his stoker last winter."

The *third* and best method of confirming the salesman's statements is to let the customer have a sample or demonstration of the service or goods. He can thus tell from his own experience whether the salesman is right or wrong. The proof of the utility of this method of confirmation is the fact that few products are sold today without some sample or demonstration being used to promote the sale.

Closing the sale

You may be perfect in your approach, you may be silver-tongued in your presentation, you may be a magician in your demonstration, but if you cannot close the sale you are not a salesman. If you use the "trial-close" technique presented in the chapter on conference speaking, you will have some idea of the proper time for closing the sale. If you study the prospect carefully during the sales presentation, you may detect some question, statement, or physical expression that will indicate his readiness to buy. If you have planned and presented your sales story effectively, you may expect to close immediately following the demonstration or confirmation. The time for closing may be difficult to determine, but the real difficulty results from failure to attempt a close rather than from failure to close at the right time.

Devices preparatory to closing

Every salesman should use the "yes-response" technique, common ground, and the "trial close" as devices preparatory to a final close.[1] The "yes-response" technique will not only condition the prospect into saying "yes," but will have him in agreement on a number of the reasons why he should buy before the final appeal for a sale is made. The use of common ground will create a degree of mutuality of interest between seller and prospect that will help in securing an affirmative response. The "trial close" will not only indicate a favorable time to close, but will narrow the prospect's choice and lead to an implied consent to purchase.

Assumed approval. If your sales speech has been well presented, you may assume approval on the part of the customer. This may be done by saying, "You'll want these canned goods delivered tomorrow, won't you?" or "Just sign this contract on the line marked with the X." If the customer gives you a negative response, you should attempt to show him that saying "no" to your proposal is saying "yes" to some other proposal that is less satisfactory than yours. If, for example, the customer says "no" to your food products, he is saying "yes" to hunger, poor health, and an anemic condition. If he says "no" to your clothing goods, he is saying "yes" to cold weather, poor appearance, and lack of friends. This technique of making "no" mean "yes" to an unsatisfactory solution gives the salesman an opportunity to restate his case for a sale. It may often result in an immediate sale.

Summarized close. Select the one, two, or three main reasons why the prospect should buy. Restate these points briefly, but in positive terms, with your final statement containing a request, invitation, or appeal to buy.

Dramatized close. Here the salesman points out in vivid, picturesque, and colorful terms the benefits and comforts of owning the product, following immediately with a request to

---

[1] See Chapter IV.

buy.   He may use overstatement or vital examples of others who have purchased.   He should step up his enthusiasm and animation in showing great concern for the customer's welfare.   He may use a motivating story or picture to secure a close through impulse or emotion.   These and other "high pressure" means are often used with success.   They should not be used, however, if you expect follow-up sales with the same customers.

Command approval.   The last method of closing to be presented may be called the "command approval" close.   Here you ask the customer to buy.   Here you state definitely, "Mr. Jones, you should buy this article."   This close should be used when you believe that the customer is favorably inclined to your proposal but that he just cannot make up his mind to say "yes."   Remember that if the sale is not made, you are not a salesman.

The Promotional Situation

In many situations it will be impossible for the salesman to complete a sale in one interview or one speech.   Nearly all platform sales speeches are given under circumstances that prevent or do not warrant taking orders or making the actual transaction of goods for money or credit.   These occasions should be considered as promotional sales situations to distinguish them from situations where sales may be consummated.   The promotional speech will follow the same steps as the sales speech, except that the conclusion will not contain specific attempts to close a sale but will contain specific appeals to the audience in terms of future purchases.   This speech should inform the prospective customers on the questions of where and how they can buy the goods being sold.   It should close with an appeal for action definite enough to cause the customers to make future purchases or accept appointments and interviews from salesmen selling the goods being promoted.

QUESTIONS

1. Can you express in two sentences the basic art of selling?
2. What four factors enter into every sales situation?
3. What can the salesman do about the following three factors: (1) ability of the customer to buy, (2) competition, and (3) price?

4. Why is the salesman the most important factor in a sales situation?

5. Must you know your product to be a good salesman?

6. What are the two basic ideas in every sales situation?

7. What is the best way of securing a sales interview?

8. What two types of approaches may be used in starting a sales interview? Under what circumstances should each be used?

9. Types of needs, wants, and desires can be roughly grouped in three catagories. What are these catagories?

10. How does explanation or demonstration of the product help the salesman complete the various steps in his sale?

11. What methods of confirmation of product are available to the salesman?

12. What devices may be used preparatory to closing a sale?

13. Why is "trying to close" a sale the most important factor in closing a sale?

14. What is a promotional speech as distinguished from a sales speech?

EXERCISES

1. Select some product that you believe you can sell:
   (a) Write a paragraph on the customer's needs, wants, and desires that can be used as a guide for preparing your sales presentation.
   (b) Write a paragraph that explains how the product satisfies these needs, wants, and desires.

2. Select some article that you can bring to class and sell to your fellow students. Prepare a sales speech outline.
   (a) Be prepared to sell this article to a fellow student in a conference.
   (b) Be prepared to give a promotional speech on the article.

SELECTED READINGS

Borden, Richard C., *How to Deliver a Sales Presentation*, Harper & Bros., New York, 1938.

Borden, Richard C., *How to Make a Sales Point Hit!*, Prentice-Hall, Inc., New York, 1938.

Brisco, Norris A., *Telephone Selling*, Prentice-Hall, Inc., New York, 1940.

Brisco, Norris A., Griffith, Grace, and Robinson, O. Preston, *Store Salesmanship*, revised edition, Prentice-Hall, Inc., New York, 1941.

Fernald, Charles H., *Salesmanship*, Prentice-Hall, Inc., New York, 3rd Edition, 1942.

Ivey, Paul W., *Successful Salesmanship*, Prentice-Hall, Inc., New York, 1937.

McCord, Jack, *Selling Is a Game,* Prentice-Hall, Inc., New York, 1939.

Robinson, O. Preston, and Robinson, Christine H., *Successful Retail Salesmanship,* Prentice-Hall, Inc., New York, 1942.

Roth, Charles B., *Secrets of Closing Sales,* Prentice-Hall, Inc., New York, 1941.

Russell, Frederic A., and Beach, Frank H., *Textbook of Salesmanship,* 3rd Edition, McGraw-Hill Book Co., New York, 1941.

Sandford, W. P., and Yeager, W. H., *Practical Business Speaking,* McGraw-Hill Book Co., New York, 1937.

Tosdol, Harry R., *Principles of Personal Selling,* A. W. Shaw Co., Chicago, 1925.

Vining, Vernon E., *Selling Slants,* Prentice-Hall, Inc., New York, 1938.

Wheeler, Elmer, *Sizzlemanship,* Prentice-Hall, Inc., New York, 1940.

Wheeler, Elmer, *Tested Direct Selling,* Prentice-Hall, Inc., New York, 1942.

Wheeler, Elmer, *Tested Retail Selling,* Prentice-Hall, Inc., New York, 1941.

The Application Interview

CHAPTER X

The Application Interview

PROGRESSIVE LEADERS in education are becoming more and more convinced of the necessity of incorporating into the school curriculum an efficient course of study in the principles of occupational orientation and job finding. They have discovered that a large proportion of their alumni are baffled when faced with the problem of securing a position in the field for which they have supposedly been trained. These alumni, although well qualified to work in their chosen professions, often fail to secure employment because they do not understand or they fail to recognize the basis upon which job applicants are selected.

Surveys among leading personnel directors indicate that the personal interview carries the greatest weight in determining whether or not an applicant will be hired. They recognize the value of the information included in the application letter and data sheet, but rely upon the personal contact as the chief means of selection. It follows, then, that job finding is largely a speech problem, for only through utilization of the principles and techniques of conference speaking can a person hope to create a winning impression.

Preparation for the Application Interview

George J. Lyons and Harmon C. Martin, both of whom are recognized authorities in personnel management, write:

The problem of the job seeker is to sell his personal wares—his abilities, his services, and his ambitions. His primary job is to satisfy a prospective employer that these wares are adaptable to a particular business or profession. The merchandising problems of the job applicant can be compared to those of the business man. Prospective employers, like customers, must be located. Each job seeker must find a market for his product. He must develop methods by which he can familiarize the buyer with the benefits of the product.   Advertising partly fulfills this function.   The contact point, however, is where most goods are sold.[1]

The authors' purpose in this chapter is to outline a method of preparation for the "contact point" or interview that will take the reader's applications out of the realm of mere chance.   The method advocated requires careful and systematic work, but the person who wants a satisfactory position and is not content to spend his time in hit-or-miss pavement-pounding will find it the wise procedure to follow.

Application essentially a sales problem

If job seekers are familiar with the company to which they apply, acquaint themselves with the specific requirements of the job they want, and also know something about the man they will interview, they will be able to plan an effective "sales approach."   They will know how best to appeal to the needs, wants, and desires of the purchasing powers.   A selling technique is the applicant's best insurance for success.

In making application for a job you are literally selling yourself.   If you were selling automobiles, you would want to know everything possible about the particular machine.   Has its past performance been successful?   Is it trouble-free?   Does it have speed, power, and endurance?   Does it really give value for money received?   These are the general questions that you might be expected to consider.   You would also have to back up your statements with an actual demonstration and explanation of engineering, materials, and workmanship that go to make the machine what it is.

So, if your product is yourself instead of an automobile, is it not logical to assume the same approach?   You will want to use what you learned through self-analysis to aid you in planning your campaign.   Perhaps your self-analysis revealed that you were an ABLE MAN with some deficiencies in imagination.   Should you seek an advertising job?   If you are low in thoroughness, the chances are you will not be very valuable in an accountant's office.   If you lack initiative, do not seek a job that

---

[1] Lyons, George E., and Martin, Harmon C., *The Strategy of Job Finding*, Prentice-Hall, Inc., 1940, pp. 5–6.

puts you on your own responsibility. Salesmen need the powers of adaptability and expression. Engineers must have imagination and thoroughness. Executive positions require decisiveness. Every job, in fact, requires particular proficiency in at least one of the ABLE MAN qualifications. Be sure you have what it takes.

Try to have a chat with some person who is now employed in the kind of a job in which you are interested. Select a person who has been rather successful and who has received regular promotions and raises. Ask him about the peculiar abilities required. Find out what quality he considers most important. But do not stop there. Consult two or three reliable guides to occupations. They will give you authoritative facts about duties, history, chances for development, promotion possibilities, and salary. The Department of Labor has published a *Dictionary of Occupational Titles,* which describes 17,452 different jobs. You may find copies of this *Dictionary* in nearly all public and university libraries.

Just as the automobile may be sold for a specific use by the owner, so will you be selling yourself for a specific job. The automobile may be used only as a pleasure car, in which case appearance, ease of control, comfort, and safety may be the first considerations. It may also be used for hauling a trailer, for fast cross-country driving, for heavy-duty hauling, or for riding the range. Always the car's particular adaptability for the job concerned must be taken into account.

Give or get? Many applicants put their entire concentration on "getting something." They think very little about what they have to offer. They are absorbed with "best chances," "future," "salary," and "raises." Their attitude is subjective instead of objective. Such an attitude might make it necessary for the employer to convince the applicant of his suitability for the position in question. The irony of this assumption is that an employer does *not* find it necessary, as a general rule, to do this. His problem is one simply of selection.

Before you begin figuring what you can GET, think about what you can GIVE! A businessman was once approached by an applicant who said his ambition in life was to make a million dollars and retire at an early age. He was told that if he would bring in twenty-five million dollars worth of business to the firm, he could expect to be paid a million dollars for his effort. This was a disappointment because he knew he did not have the ability nor the ambition to do the kind and amount of work necessary to complete such a bargain. There are probably many firms that would be willing to make a similar contract with you. However, if you are modest enough to admit that one thousand dollars a year is a fair beginning salary, you must consider your potentialities of being worth sufficiently more than one thousand dollars to warrant the employer's keeping you around.

There is a great misconception about this GET matter. Business is not a lottery from which you may take more than you give. Even the most superficial study of successful business careers will prove that the man who draws a good salary is the one who has the ability to earn something beyond the amount of that salary. This fact ought to be foremost in the mind of every person who seeks a job. Remember that "the wise men came BEARING gifts, not SEEKING them."

With that idea in mind, one ought to think about *selling* what he has, instead of "looking for a job." Make a list of prospective customers, study their needs, wants, and desires, determine how you satisfy the requirements, and, as a salesman, prepare the sort of campaign that will have the best chance of securing the sale.

Company analysis

There are at least two good reasons for finding out as much as possible about the company to which you are to apply. In the first place, you will want to know certain details of the company's organization and management to determine if it is the type of company with which you wish to be affiliated. Secondly, knowledge of the company will enable you to adapt your letter of application effectively and will give you a big advantage during the interview.

It is wise for applicants to apply only to companies in which they could be happily employed, in which they will be satisfied employees. If you wait until after you are employed to discover that opportunities for advancement are limited, that permanent employment is uncertain, and that the management is unsympathetic, you will not be able to maintain an attitude conducive to efficiency.　Furthermore, you increase the possibilities of short-term employment, an item which will always be a point of question in future applications.

Complete and accurate information will enable you to plan a more effective selling campaign.　Star salesmen always make a systematic and careful pre-analysis of their prospect in order to adapt their sales technique more effectively.　Fear of the unknown is one of the chief weaknesses of applicants.　If you know enough about the company to carry on an intelligent conversation concerning it and to ask leading questions, you will assure greater ease and naturalness during the interview.　Experience indicates that employment managers are frequently resentful toward applicants who obviously have made no effort to seek information before the interview.　A common question asked is, "Why do you wish to be employed in this organization?"　You should be prepared to make a thoughtful answer.

What to know.　The following general items may serve as the basis for your company analysis:

1. *History.*　How old is the company?　What has been the chief factor in its development?　What is its operating capital?　How has it increased?

2. *Location.*　Where are the main offices?　Where are the subdivisions?　Where do its supplies come from?

3. *Organization.*　What are the divisions of its organization?　How extensive is it?　Who are the chief executives?

4. *Product.*　What products does it handle?　Are there by-products?　How extensively are these products used?　Is there stiff competition from other companies?　How does the quality of the product measure up with the product of other companies?

5. *Personnel.*　How large a force does it employ?　What are the divisions of employment?　Does the company make provisions for retirement?　Are promotions made from within the ranks?　What kind of training school does it maintain?

6. *Special.*　There may be special considerations involved because of the peculiarities of the product.　What are they?　In short, find out everything you possibly can.

Where to find information.　The applicant who desires to insure his chance of being employed will be able to gather pertinent information concerning the company of his choice regardless of the difficulties involved or the effort required. One or all of these suggested methods may be used:

1. *Libraries.* Trade journals and magazines, business and industrial guides, special published reports, and convention publications are all to be found in the well-equipped library. Solicit the aid of the librarians if necessary.

2. *Direct correspondence.* Most large organizations maintain public relations or customer service departments. By writing directly to the company you may receive answers to your questions or specially prepared booklets that contain useful information for the applicant.

3. *Interviews.* Interviews with employees of the company often result in the gaining of more specific information than can be secured in any other manner. One should be careful that the employee interviewed is in good standing and in a position to give accurate and unprejudiced opinion and fact.

4. *Current news.* Careful attention to newspaper and radio reports of financial conditions and expansion plans may enable you to get information that is of primary importance at the moment of your application.

5. *Plant inspection.* In some instances it is possible to take a tour of inspection through the premises of the company. One college student, wishing a position in the accounting division of a large retail store, spent two days studying the lay-out of departments. He visited every section of the store, found out what was sold, how large it was, and how accounts were handled. He had something to talk about during the interview, and was hired.

Sample company analysis. The following analysis was made by a college student in preparation for a classroom practice interview. Information was obtained primarily through free advertising matter distributed by the company.

An Analysis of the Armstrong Cork

History

The Armstrong Cork Company was organized over eighty years ago when, in 1860, John Glass and Thomas Armstrong formed a partnership to manufacture cork stoppers in one small room in Pittsburgh. Upon the death of Glass, Robert Armstrong succeeded him, and with his brother founded the present company. The Company started expanding at that point and expansion has continued down through the years. In 1938, for instance, the Armstrong Cork Company purchased the assets of two glass-container companies.

Location

The original plant of the Company was located in Pittsburgh, Pennsylvania. As the Company expanded, plants were acquired or built in Beaver

Falls, Pennsylvania; Camden, Gloucester, and Millville, New Jersey; Fulton, New York; South Braintree, Massachusetts; Pensacola, Florida; Philadelphia and Lancaster, Pennsylvania; South Gate, California; and Dunkirk, Indiana. The largest plant of the Company, as well as its general offices, is located in Lancaster.

Since cork, originally an important raw material, comes only from Mediterranean countries, the Company early entered foreign markets and now operates plants in such places as Spain, Algeria, Morocco, England, and Canada and also distributes its products abroad in a large number of countries through the sales staff of its Export Department and foreign plants. With the growth and diversification of the Company, cork has assumed less importance.

Product

As of February 1, 1941, the Company manufactured a total of 350 types of products. This list includes such things as linoleum, felt base rugs, asphalt tile, rubber tile, glass containers, closures, insulating materials, fire brick and numerous specialities. The entire list of 350 classifications is related as follows:

1. The products are made wholly or in part of cork.
2. Each product serves the same purpose as that for which cork is, or at one time was, used.
3. The products are required in the application or installation of major products.
4. The product is desirable or necessary from the standpoint of marketing other products already included in the Company's line.

Organization

The business is organized around four main sales divisions:
1. Building Materials
2. Floor
3. Glass and Closure
4. Industrial

Each division, together with two smaller sales departments—Corkwood and Export—is operated almost as a separate business having its own sales and administrative staffs, products, and merchandising policies. In addition to the sales divisions, there are the usual operating or staff departments, Production, Research, Engineering, Controllers, Treasurer's, Secretary's, Purchasing, Personnel, Advertising, and so on located in the general offices in Lancaster. These departments serve to co-ordinate operations of the sales divisions.

Personnel

The Company prides itself on the opportunities it offers young men. As proof of this, it points to the fact that the average age of all executives is just forty-seven. Turnover of personnel is extremely low owing to rigorous selective programs.

When a man is finally selected, the division in which he will eventually be placed is assigned to him. He then moves into "Armstrong Manor," a large house on the outskirts of Lancaster—built like a fraternity. Here he lives with about thirty other trainees for a period of eight months while he receives training in theoretical and practical manufacturing and selling. At the end of this period, he is sent to a retail store for two weeks where he is given selling experience on the floor (this description is for salesmen of the Floor Covering Division). After this task of retail sales, he returns to Lancaster and after completing the training course, is finally assigned to a branch sales office in the field from which he operates with a territory of his own. His progress, thereafter, up through the sales and administrative organization depends upon his own proven abilities. This training program is estimated to cost the Company about $5,000 for each student, which is an indication of the thoroughness of its personnel training.

Job Analysis

The day is gone when a young man could present himself to the owner of a business and ask for "just a chance to work." Today you usually must be prepared for a particular job that requires a specialized skill or knowledge. Modern education, increased competition, and mass production have done that for us. There just is not time in modern business to employ a "general roustabout" and allow him to remain underfoot while learning "what it is all about." And it follows that employers are not interested in talking to applicants who present themselves for "just anything."

Applying for a specific job is, in itself, an indication that the applicant has some ability and, more important, that he has a definite notion of what he is worth to the company. To announce to your interviewer that you want a definite type of job aids considerably in creating an effective first impression.

Furthermore, it must be realized that application for a specific job does not necessarily close all doors to other types of work. Although you should not apply for "just anything," there may be times when you are willing to do anything for the sake of a job or because you feel you have the ability to grow into the kind of job you really desire. Even in this case make your application strong for some particular kind of job. If, for some reason, you cannot be hired, you have at least made a good impression. Your name may be filed in an "active" list of candidates or, better still, you may be employed in some other way until *your* particular job shows up.

In any event, your chances of securing a job will increase if the application is definite. Your ability to convince the employer of your worth will increase if you have a speaking acquaintance with the job and its requirements. Most important of all, from the speech standpoint, if you have made a complete analysis of the job, you can approach your interview with much more self-confidence.

What to know.   With these factors in mind, find the answers to the following questions about the job for which you wish to present yourself as a candidate:

1. What special educational requirements are necessary?
2. What special aptitudes are required?
3. How important is experience?
4. What kind of experience is helpful?
5. Is personal appearance an important factor in this type of position?
6. What traits of personality may be considered essential to success in this position?
7. What are the duties of a man in this position?
8. Are there special company requirements in this position not found in the general run of similar positions?
9. What is the salary range for such positions in this company?

Where to find information.   A satisfactorily completed company analysis may also reveal a considerable quantity of information about specific jobs.   In addition, one of the following means may prove valuable:

1. *Libraries.*   Scores of books have recently been published that describe various types of positions commonly found in business and in the professions.   Pamphlets, describing the duties, advantages, and disadvantages of various occupations, may be obtained by addressing the National Occupational Conference, 60 East 42nd Street, New York City.   These pamphlets sell for ten cents a copy.
2. *Interviews.*   Talking to a man who is actually engaged in the type of work you are interested in is the best means of finding out about the difficulties encountered and the specific duties involved. College students will find it profitable to discuss their plans with a professor in their major field.   Personnel offices are usually happy to speak to students about their occupational ambitions and often have specific tests ready to measure one's theoretical chances for success in a particular job.

Sample job analysis.   This sample job analysis was made by the same student who prepared the company analysis shown on a preceding page.   The analysis was an outgrowth of the student's study of pamphlets published by the company.

Job Analysis for a Position
as Salesman with the Armstrong Cork Company

The applicant must be a college graduate and must rank high in his class both in scholarship and outside activities. For the Floor Division, courses in merchandising, salesmanship, advertising, credit, and speech are of value though not essential. An engineering degree is required for certain sales training positions in the Building Materials and Industrial Sales Divisions.

Special Aptitudes Required

Excellent vision, compatibility with people, and an ambitious nature, evidence of administrative ability.

Experience

Importance is attached to the candidate's having made constructive use of spare time during his college course and in this sense, a record of part-time work while in college and during summer vacations is regarded as desirable.

Appearance

The applicant need not be handsome, but his appearance must be such that it will attract attention and aid in making a good first impression. He must be neat and clean, and dress quietly and in good taste.

Personality

It is essential that the applicant possess an above-the-average pleasing personality. This means that he must be able to meet people well and easily, and he must be able to carry on an effective conversation with little help from a second person. He must be forceful, but courteous and tactful; he must be talkative, but not obtrusively so.

Duties

The applicant's duties will be somewhat as follows:

1. Study of the product and merchandising and installation methods for eight months at Lancaster, learning, in this time, every phase of its manufacture and methods of selling it.

2. A short period in instructive retail selling of products acting as floor salesman in some large department store (this applies to the Floor Division).

3. Assignment upon completion of the course to the sales organization as a full-fledged salesman operating in his own territory from a branch sales office.

4. Travel and contact customers, usually dealers, or wholesalers. Advise customers on merchandising methods, assist in the training of their sales representatives, assist in the promotion of their sales efforts. Through (postgraduate) courses at Lancaster, learn increasingly effective sales methods and develop his abilities to assume eventual administrative responsibilities.

Salary

All salesmen are employed on a salary basis. The starting salary during the period of training is in line with that generally commanded by a college graduate.

Interviewer analysis

There are two ways of getting around in the dark. One method involves the use of an artificial light or some previous experience with the terrain in order to protect yourself from falling into holes, bumping into trees, or having the life frightened out of you by strange noises. This method, while still not as satisfactory as moving in daylight, does give you some assurance of success. The other method is to rush in blindly and progress by trial and error. Seldom does one use this latter method without receiving the worst of the deal, oftentimes skinned shins, blackened eyes, and shattered nerves.

You can get through an interview with an employer without knowing anything about him before the appointed hour, but the chances are against you. How long will it take you to "size him up"? How can you know his special interests? Must you discover that he has no sense of humor by making a fool of yourself with witty remarks that he does not appreciate? What kind of qualities does he expect in his employees? How will you reach common ground during the interview?

These questions and many more you will want to have answered before you gamble with your future. So much can depend on a slip of the tongue or a reference to a touchy subject that it behooves you to make an adequate investigation of the likes and dislikes of your conferee before you take the plunge.

Successful salesmen will tell you that only by "knowing your man" can you prepare an effective sales campaign. They will tell you that real salesmanship is the art of pleasing the customer and that the art is practiced by a thorough knowledge of the medium in which you work. Any resort to shortcuts inevitably leads to shoddiness and makes the game of selling little more than ordinary peddling. If you are anxious enough to secure a certain job, you will prepare a sales campaign. You will protect yourself by knowing as much as possible about the conferee in order that you may adapt yourself successfully during the interview. Applying for a job is the highest form of the art of salesmanship. You have the opportunity to sign the greatest order of your life—your future, your life itself.

Follows plan of conference speaker. In Chapter V are suggestions to the conference speaker for preparing a pre-analysis of the conferee. These suggestions should be followed as closely as possible by the job applicant. It may not always be easy to secure pre-analysis information, but it *can* be done, and if success seems important enough to the applicant, it *will* be done.

Arranging conferences with the employer's friends and business associates is a particularly valuable source of information. Such a conference may be of double-edged value. You may not only accomplish your purpose of securing information that will provide a satisfactory motivation for a business conference but you may also make a good impression on the conferee, who may, in turn, put in a good word for you. If he says nothing, you have still had the chance of making another contact and thus advertising the fact that you are available. Needless to say, the rules of effective conference speaking should be followed. Have your purpose clearly determined and your questions ready. Do not waste your conferee's time. One student, failing to heed this injunction in a classroom exercise in job applications, approached a friend of the "employer" with, "Can you give me any dope on this guy Jones?" His exit from the office more resembled the lamb than the lion.

Your Application on Paper

The letter

The application letter is simply a persuasive appeal to the employer to grant you a personal interview. Since there are usually many applications for one position and since an employer obviously cannot spend fifteen minutes with everyone who applies, utmost care and judgment must be used in the preparation of the letter to insure your chance of selling yourself in the interview itself.

Appearance. Perhaps there are 100 applicants for the one position in which you are interested. That means that 100 letters will pass through the reader's hands. "Pass through" is the right expression, for about 75 will be immediately discarded because the applicant was careless in arrangement and spelling, because he failed to make a good analysis of the job and of the man who had the power to hire him, or because he did not realize the purpose of the letter. The reader may discard an application before he breaks the seal on the envelope containing the letter. If the address is poorly written or the name misspelled, this, in itself, may be enough to suggest to the reader that the writer holds little stock in the qualities of thoroughness and care.

Even if the envelope is opened, the letter proper may receive no further attention if its typography is unattractive at first glance. Perhaps the letter appears crowded. The margins may be too wide or too narrow. The type may be light and faded or uneven. All these little mechanical deficiencies may be magnified by the man who reads 100 letters a day.

The reader's attention will next be drawn to the grammatical construction of the sentences. He will appreciate simple, straightforward sentences that express their meaning without ambiguity. Long, labored, complex writing is difficult to read and invariably results in a negative suggestion to the businessman. Do not attempt to impress your reader by the use of unnatural language or studied cleverness. Too many applicants make a fetish out of the supposed requirement of originality. If you have to struggle to be original and clever, you will be much safer to write a simple, straight-from-the-shoulder statement of fact.

It will be helpful if you think of the application letter as identical in form with that used in presenting a persuasive speech. In both cases a careful analysis of the audience is necessary to achieve the desired response. Also, presentation and delivery can mean the difference between success and failure. In addition, each must have a good attention-getting *introduction,* a complete and coherent *body,* and a final appeal for action in the form of a *conclusion.*

Introduction. The introductory sentences should serve to arouse the interest of the reader and compel him to read further. For this reason you may need to spend some time in preparing these few sentences. A commonly used introduction mentions the name of some mutual friend. This establishes common ground. However, avoid the trite expression, "Mr. R. S. Tripe has informed me that you have an opening in your bookkeeping department." "Has informed me" is probably the most overused phrase in application letter writing. Try a variation such as, "Mr. R. S. Tripe, in advising me about my future in the field of accounting, suggested that I apply to you for my first position."

Here are a few introductory sentences that have been effective:

Four years ago I left your organization to complete my college education. I am now ready to return to more efficient employment in your company.

For the past four years I have been interested in the field of credit management and would now like to apply my education in a practical way.

Last July I came to your office and made an application for a job as surveyor on one of your geophysical crews. Upon learning that I lacked only one year of school to receive my degree in geology, you urged me to finish. I have now graduated from the University of Blank and still want the surveying job with your company.

The current building program, revolving around the national defense movement, should greatly increase the activity of your company. This undoubtedly will mean that you will be faced with a labor shortage.

In your search for young salesmen to develop new territories, please consider my application.

Body. The body of the letter must present your qualifications for the job in a persuasive manner. A simple and direct statement of your case will receive a better response than the ornate and wordy letter.

If a data sheet accompanies your letter (and there is a growing preference among businessmen for the separate data sheet), you need not list all the details of your life in the letter. A letter accompanied by a data sheet should reveal something of the personality of the applicant. It gives you an opportunity to emphasize what you consider to be your outstanding qualifications for the job. As you write about yourself, write specifically. Avoid the tendency to make broad generalizations such as, "I am a young man with ambition" or "I firmly believe that I have the qualifications for this job." Such statements mean less than nothing to the reader. Tell him specifically what you have done and let him conclude that you are "a young man with ambition."

If you are not sure of your ability to write an effective letter, you will profit by a serious study of some good book on business letter writing, for the ability to write a good one will mean "dollars and cents" profit to you.

When you have finished your letter, ask a few of your friends to read it for you and comment on the reactions they have. Or, better still, take it to a disinterested businessman and ask his advice. They will see things you never thought about.

Conclusion. An application letter should contain the same type of conclusion as that used in a sales letter. It must call for action. If the letter has already attracted attention, secured interest, and created a desire, the appeal for action should bring results. Avoid the use of negative suggestion. This sentence was used by an applicant who was not granted an interview: "I know you are a very busy man and you must be just run to death by applicants, but if you will see me I know you will be pleased."

Consider the following as examples of a good close:

I will telephone your secretary in a few days to learn at what hour it will be convenient for you to see me.

I will be free to see you at any time you suggest. A self-addressed and stamped envelope is enclosed for your convenience.

The following letter was used by a graduate of a midwestern university. It was sent to seventeen employers; sixteen of them replied, five granted interviews, and two offered jobs without an interview.

Dear Mr. Jones:

Doctor Lawrence Wills of the College of Commerce office has suggested to me that I write you concerning a position upon my graduation in February. Doctor Wills mentioned that you have openings for capable young men who are willing and want to give their best in service to your organization.

When I receive my degree from the College of Commerce, I will have had specialized training in Banking and Finance as well as in Accountancy. My chief field of interest is cost accounting, in which I have had all the undergraduate courses offered by the College of Commerce, but I am interested in any branch of industrial accounting and would be glad to work in any division in which you think I would best fit. My general work has included not only the usual Economics and Accountancy courses but also such courses as Industrial Management, Business Law, and Business Letter Writing—all of which should help me give better service to you.

Last summer I gained some valuable experience which has given me a slant into the practical side of business. As assistant timekeeper and paymaster of approximately a $75,000 payroll for the California Packing Corporation, I not only had to learn to deal with people but also to realize the importance of accuracy as well as speed, neatness, and thoroughness in handling different business records.

This position along with my work in cost accounting at the Weiser Print Shop during the past school year has given me a chance to see what will be expected of me under actual business conditions.

May I come to your office to talk with you on any day you suggest? A letter will reach me at my campus address any time.

Very truly yours,

Stunt letters. Occasionally, when an applicant is seeking a position that requires peculiar creative or imaginative ability, a stunt letter may be used. The stunt letter is an attempt to secure attention and interest by resort to unusual lay-out, originality, or cleverness. There is a great danger, however, that such a letter may prove offensive to the reader by being more silly than clever. A certain personnel manager of a large retail department store cherishes a stunt letter that represents the maximum in lack of discretion. The applicant reversed the entire form of the letter, putting the salutation where the complimentary close and signature should be and vice versa. He also wrote alternate lines upside down making it necessary for the reader to invert the page for each line. This letter was most successful in receiving attention and interest, but, needless to say, the applicant was not employed.

The data sheet

Most established organizations furnish application forms to applicants for positions. The forms are prepared to supply answers that apply definitely to the type of employment offered. When you fill out the blanks make sure that your answers are honest and specific. Consideration is often deferred because the applicant fails to complete the form according to instructions. Employers read many hundreds of these applications in the course of a year and with such experience are inclined to be hypercritical in their examination. You must use the utmost care that your completed application is accurate, complete, and neat. Write with a good pen in longhand, unless otherwise specified.

If a company form is not furnished, you may prepare your own. Some persons, when campaigning for a job, have their data sheets printed or mimeographed for inclusion with each letter. The data sheet should include, in outline form: personal data, educational record, avocation interests, business experience, and a list of references who can and will write accurately of your abilities. Everything pertinent to your ability to hold a job should be included. There will be some overlapping with the information in your letter, but this is not harmful.

The data sheet on pages 178 and 179 is a simplified composite of some fifty representative business application forms. The infor-

This form should be filled out in the APPLICANT'S HANDWRITING. All information given will be treated as confidential.

Name in full _____ Date _____

Home Address _____ Telephone _____

Campus Address _____ Telephone _____

Date of Birth _____ Height _____ Weight _____
　　　　　　　　Mo.　　　　　Day　　　　Year

Nationality or Lineage (American, Scottish, Jewish, etc.) _____

What language do you speak other than English? _____

Marital status _____ Dependents: Children _____ Adults _____

Religious affiliation _____

For what position are you applying? _____

Why do you wish to work in this organization? _____

_____

_____

_____

_____

_____

What do you do for recreation? _____

Do you have a hobby? What? _____

Of what clubs or societies are you a member? _____

_____

_____

_____

_____

Outline your education: _____

_____

_____

_____

_____

Describe in detail the type of work that you are best qualified to do by reason of education and previous employment and why you feel qualified for the position for which you are applying: _____

_____

_____

_____

_____

What is the outstanding accomplishment of your business or professional career? _____

_____

_____

What is your definite aim in life? _____

_____

Character and Business References

Name	Address

mation asked for here is that most often required. Use it for your class assignment in application interview.

The Interview

The interview is the climax of the long and detailed preparation that you have been urged to make. If you follow the preparation-plan scheme, you will be on the road to making your interview participation, if not wholly successful, at least satisfying to yourself and your conferee, for a job well done IS a satisfaction whether the results are to your liking or not. An application interview is a *speech* situation and should be conducted as one. An "interview expert" can no more prepare you for your application than can a "speech expert" teach an inexperienced speaker to prepare and deliver an effective speech within the space of a few days. That is the reason we ask you not to be deceived by the "easy method" or the short cut to job finding.

If by our definition you are an ABLE MAN or if you are doing something about becoming one, and in addition if you have something to say and possess the skill to say it effectively, the major obstacles to successful interviewing have been passed. These three things determine whether your interview will bring you a job or not. One cannot substitute or short-cut such matters as these at the zero hour. This implies—and we mean it to do so— that there are many candidates (some employers say 90 per cent of all who apply) whose chances of finding the job to which they aspire are as improbable as the discovery of a glacier in the middle of the Sahara Desert. One might, for example, preach the value of appearance to Joe College until he is blue in the face. Perhaps Joe could be persuaded to wear garters, press his trousers, wear a necktie, and polish his shoes, but what can you do about his close-cropped hair, his nicotine-stained fingers, and that look in his eye that earned him the nickname of "Droopy" among his fraternity brothers? What can be done for "Blundering Benny," who is consistently tactless and impolite? Ask him to follow rules for fifteen minutes and he will freeze up completely. Or who will teach "Mouthy," who has not used a complete sentence in ten years, to do an acceptable job of expressing himself during his fifteen-minute bid for fame?

This could work itself into a very dismal picture and, perhaps, provide an answer for those who wonder why they never "get the breaks." Suffice it to say that the ABLE MAN again has the advantage.

After you have prepared your several analyses, written an effective letter, and as a result been granted an interview, your problem is simply one of gaining confidence in your ability to handle a face-to-face speech situation. If you follow the dictates of good business conference in a natural and unaffected manner, you should have little difficulty.

Common methods used by interviewers

You should be prepared to adapt yourself to any of the following interview methods used by the experienced employers:

Applicant talks. Some employers attempt to "lead into" the candidate by provocative questions and statements to encourage him to do all the talking. You can learn more about a person in fifteen minutes of listening than in an hour of conversation. This is a commonly accepted theory among business employers. Self-expression means just what it says—expression of the self. What will you talk about for fifteen minutes? Do you know enough about your field to speak specifically about some phase of it for that amount of time? Do you keep up on current events and recent business trends to the extent that you can talk about them effectively? If you cannot, you can only hope and pray that you draw a conferee who does most of the talking—or resolve by dint of effort and application to prepare yourself before you find it necessary to seek a job.

Employer talks. A second method of interviewing sometimes used is almost continuous talking by the conferee. Occasionally a man will do this without reason, being motivated by the pleasant sound of his own voice. But, more often, the conferee has a definite purpose in mind—to observe your reactions to what he says. This is another illustration of the fact that it is almost impossible to dissemble sincerity. The interviewer will be watching your eyes, your facial expression, and the covert action of your muscles to reach his decision about your qualifications. You will need to be an alert, eager, and honest listener to appeal to this conferee. Take an active part in the conversation by apt use of receptive silence. If you agree or disagree during the interview, make your vocalizations articulate and clear. He may be attempting to test your submission to dominance. If you sink completely under his control, you may indicate a lack of initiative and will. If you resent the dominance too forcefully, it may reveal impoliteness, conceit, and lack of willingness to be directed.

Question and answer. The method most often used is the question and answer technique. The questions may be "stock" questions that the employer uses on nearly all of the people whom he interviews. Some conferees may disregard the subject of the applicant and the job and question you about totally unrelated subjects. The only rule to follow is honesty. If you are asked questions you cannot answer intelligently, tell him you cannot or that you have not given the matter enough thought. There is no shame in "I don't know," unless the subject is something which you should know. The employer is likely to lead you on in order to give you a chance to air your prejudices or blast away at pet-peeves and thus reveal your weaknesses. Many applicants have succumbed to the method and talked themselves right out of a job.

The following excerpt from a typical application interview reveals a dishonest and weak candidate:

Employer: Well Mr. Jones, do you think a business can justify adding advertising costs to the product sold?

Jones: Yes.

Employer: How?

Jones: (With hand on chin and revealing mental blankness) Well, I, er—er, if . . . uh, there are lots of reasons.

Employer: What are they?

Jones: I don't remember.

Employer: Why do you want to go into the advertising business if you can't answer a simple question like that?

Jones: Well, I know that business is justified because I took a course in college and I distinctly remember that the instructor explained that one day.

One experienced personnel manager, who has held more than 50,000 interviews, says that 90 per cent of the people he has turned down were rejected by their own fumbling attempt to carry on an intelligent conversation. Think before you speak and avoid vague, confused answers.

Don't be dismayed by nervousness. You may expect to be

highly nervous, but the conferee has had much experience with nervous candidates. He is trained to recognize it and its causes. If your nervousness is not due to complete inadequacy, he may try some method of putting you at your ease, such as leaving the office for a few minutes or simply saying a kind word to you about it.

Trick methods. Often there are good reasons for an employer to use some sort of trick method to select the right person for a job. Some industrial companies that receive a large number of applicants for every job must use a method of interviewing that will dispose of the unsuitable ones quickly. In some offices the interviewer sits at a high desk where the applicant passes by without being seated. Only a few words are exchanged and the interviewer may make a decision in less than a minute. In such a situation, the value of "first impression" is paramount.

In some positions aggressiveness is an important consideration. One interviewer for such positions employs the following technique:

He says that if an applicant who lacks punch and sales ability comes to him, he turns him away promptly. In the first interview, especially with college men, he is as discouraging as he can be. He says that if a man comes back a second time, he knows he has good quality. On the second call, the interviewer is again somewhat discouraging, but gives the applicant a little more time. If the applicant comes back a third time, the interviewer feels he is a first class prospect.[1]

Many interviewers recognize the danger of being "taken in" by a candidate with a pleasing personality and little else. To guard against the selection of such a person, the interviewer may ask very difficult and specific questions about material with which the applicant is supposed to be familiar. This usually reveals the bluffer in a short time.

A college graduate who was a candidate for a minor executive position reported an unusual experience with his interviewer. He was asked to come to the interviewer's hotel room at a certain hour. When he arrived the man was not in. He was forced to wait for two hours. During this time another company representative had been observing the applicant, following him around, and attempting to hear any remarks that might be made. Later

---

[1] *Business Ideas for Increasing Profits*, Prentice-Hall, Inc. 5035.

it was revealed that the interviewer wished to learn how the applicant would react to this rather difficult situation.

While such trick methods are the exception in interviewing, it is wise to prepare for whatever may happen.

"Do's" and "don't's" for the applicant

Since an applicant has little opportunity to know just how a particular interview may be conducted, he will find it impossible to prepare for everything that may be encountered. His conduct must be adapted to whatever situation he meets. The following *Do's* and *Don't's* should be observed in all cases:

Do's AND Don't's OF APPLICATION INTERVIEWS [2]

Do's

1. Do watch time—be prompt for the appointment and sense when to leave.

2. Do sit up in the chair and be attentive. Don't act as if you were conferring a favor on the company by appearing.

3. Do make a survey of the company before the interview so that you can ask and answer questions from an adequate background.

4. Do prepare your sales presentation carefully, even though the occasion may not permit you to give it in its entirety.

5. Do be prepared to ask some intelligent questions about the company, its personnel, and the nature of the work. It shows interest, as well as knowledge of your field and of the company.

6. Do look at the man occasionally—but not through him. You'll have no luck trying to hypnotize him.

7. Do remember that English and speech may be as important as your technical qualifications.

8. Do know fundamentals and be prepared to discuss them—which may include knowledge of competitor's product.

9. Do be prepared on the latest trends in your field. You will not be expected to have much experience, but you will be expected to know theory, trends, etc.

10. Do be careful of your voice qualities.

11. Do be familiar with application blanks and fill them out neatly.

12. Do look pleasant and smile.

13. Do be a good listener.

14. Do make it clear, though perhaps indirectly, that you have something of value to offer.

Don't's

1. Don't appear in rough, dirty clothes. That he-man myth has been exploded. But don't overdress.

---

[2] Anderson, C. R., *The Technograph*, April, 1934. Used by permission of the author.

2. Don't forget the interviewer hires for many positions and may not remember you, even though you saw him yesterday. Identify yourself promptly, giving name, job wanted, or the particular ad that you are answering—thus saving time and needless questions.

3. Don't try to avoid naming your home town by saying that you "live in the northern part of the state" or "ten miles from Springfield."

4. Don't give a "four cold wiener" handshake or try to show enthusiasm with a "bone crusher."

5. Don't read mail on the desk.

6. Don't smoke unless the interviewer suggests it.

7. Don't distract attention with mannerisms. Look and act alert, but not like a humming bird.

8. Don't sell a hard luck story or waste time with irrelevant talk, such as what you did in high school, but condense and stick to the point under discussion.

9. Don't act as though you expected a $5,000 job.

10. Don't just ask for a job—ask to do something in which you are vitally interested.

11. Don't take friends with you.

12. Don't sit without an invitation.

13. Don't punctuate with "See?" "Understand me?" "You will agree—."

14. Don't put hat and coat on a man's desk.

Rehearsing the interview

The best way to learn is by doing, but failure to find a job is an expensive way to educate yourself. The next best method is to hold a few practice interviews. Ask your friends to help you. Let them assume the role of the conferee. Give them a desk and an office and allow yourself to be ushered in. Do everything just as you plan to in the real situation. If something goes wrong or if a difficult question is asked, do the best you can. Under no circumstance should you "break character." Make the interview complete to the exit. Then ask your friend to give you his unvarnished reaction to your application. Don't permit him to flatter and compliment your effort. Seek constructive criticism. Don't depend on just one friend. Repeat the game with as many as are willing.

It is wise to reverse the roles a few times. Assume the part of conferee yourself and let the friend be the applicant. It is good practice for both of you and gives you the chance to see a candidate from the "desk side." You will learn much about the use of the "you attitude."

The following lists of questions can be used as the basic core for your rehearsal. They are the result of considerable investigation.   Active professional interviewers have contributed to the list.   Take time now to study them and formulate satisfactory and specific answers.   Let the questions in the second list control your conduct.

Questions You Should Be Prepared to Answer During the Application Interview:

1. Why have you made application to us?
2. Have you been refused positions by other companies?   Why?
3. What are your ambitions in life?
4. What has been your greatest achievement in life?
5. What is the largest salary you have ever earned?
6. How much salary do you expect here?
7. What do you consider your strongest qualification for this particular job?
8. What other jobs are you able to do?
9. What are your hobbies?
10. Do you prefer working with people or with things?
11. What is your marital status?
12. From what sort of environment have you come?
13. What is your father's occupation?
14. How deep in debt are you?
15. Have you ever been fired from a job?   For what reasons?
16. Give an example of a particularly successful job you have done.
17. What kind of treatment did you get from previous employers?
18. How does your education fit in with the work of this organization?
19. Are you economically independent?
20. Did you earn any part of your college expenses?
21. Are you willing to start at the bottom in this organization?
22. Where do you go for amusement and recreation?
23. Do you appreciate criticism?
24. What kind of people do you like to be with?
25. What would you do if you discovered dishonesty or unfairness among your fellow employees?
26. How long do you plan to stay in this position?
27. What is your feeling about labor unions?
28. What do you consider reasonable working hours for this type of position?
29. Are you interested in making a lot of money?
30. What kind of reading do you do now?   What have you read in the past three months?

Questions to Which the Interviewer Will Seek an Answer Without Asking You Outright:

1. Does this man seem sincerely eager to succeed?

2. Does this man seem to have a clear idea of his value to this company?

3. Does he show evidences of being aggressive?

4. Is he frank in his answers to my questions?

5. Is his personality such as to insure his getting along with his fellow workers?

6. Does he express himself clearly?

7. Is he open-minded to new ideas?

8. Does he show signs of being observant?

9. Has he good common sense?

10. Is he a team worker or a lone-wolf type?

11. Is he capable of sustained concentration?

12. Is he a clock-puncher or a job-doer?

13. Does he have a satisfactory working use of the English language?

14. Is his appearance pleasing on first glance?

15. Does his stock go up or down as the interview continues?

16. Is he careful in money matters?

17. Does he make good use of his leisure time?

18. Does he have many friends?

19. Does he belong to a church, social organization, or civic group?

20. Is he a capable organizer of his work?

21. Has he sufficient initiative to work with a minimum of supervision?

22. Is he tactful?

23. Does he have a sense of humor?

24. Will he work best with things or with people?

25. Is he the type of person who would make a dependable employee?

These and many other questions will be going through the mind of the man who interviews you. Everything you say or do may help in determining his final decision on any of these points.

Closing the interview

You have heard the old story about the man who came to dinner and stayed to become a permanent guest. Why do people have so much trouble going when their visit or task is finished? A small fortune is awaiting the man who can write a popular book entitled *How to Say Goodbye*. Until that book is published, remember this: when you sense that the conferee has finished, speak your exit line and go. To linger overtime is to destroy all the advantages you may have gained up to that time. Or if you do not wish to rely on your "sense," limit your interview to fifteen minutes and at the end of that time suggest that you have probably taken enough of his time. If he wants you to stay, he will say so and you can breathe more easily. If the conferee begins to finger papers on his desk, to clean out his desk drawers, or to look at the door and your hat, it is past your bedtime—get out! If he has to rise, hand you your papers and hat, reach for the door, and lead you to it, you might just as well begin another campaign. You have lost that one. But do not be discouraged. You should be wise enough to learn by experience.

Interview check lists

Some companies use prepared check lists or rating forms that are filled out by the interviewer during the interview. These lists constitute a permanent record of the impression made by the applicant and are often used to recall certain applicants when new vacancies appear in the company. If your interviewer fills out such a list during your interview, do not let it bother you. He is trained to do two things at once, and be assured he is not neglecting you.

There is a wide variance in the questions included in the check lists. Some companies find that certain qualities merit more consideration than others for the particular type of positions they offer. However, it has been found, after a study of several check lists used by reputable companies, that a composite of them all would include the major items of the speech triad, namely, ABLE MAN qualifications, knowledge, and effectiveness of expression. These are often concealed under such terminology as personal appearance, general health, honesty and sincerity, understanding, aggressiveness, attitude, experience, voice quality, clarity of speech, expression of ideas, and suitability, all of which are expressed through effective or ineffective speaking.

The check list on page 189 is patterned after the personal balance sheet on pages 28 and 29 in Chapter II. It will serve as a good measuring device to be used in rehearsing your interview. Other things being equal, if you can receive a high rating on this form, you may expect no difficulty in any interview you have.

The Follow-up

The follow-up to an application is an effort to consolidate and improve the impression made in your interview. In instances

Composite Check List
(Check One)

	Very Poor	Inferior	Average	Good	Excellent
IMPRESSIVENESS					
OBSERVATION					
INITIATIVE					
THOROUGHNESS					
DECISIVENESS					
ADAPTATION					
LEADERSHIP					
ORGANIZING ABILITY					
CONCENTRATION					
IMAGINATION					
SPECIAL KNOWLEDGE					
GENERAL KNOWLEDGE					
VOCABULARY					
PRONUNCIATION					
ARTICULATION					
EXPRESSION OF IDEAS					
VOCAL QUALITY					
ANIMATION					
DIRECTNESS					
SELF-CONFIDENCE					
SINCERITY					

RESULT OF INTERVIEW

Not employed ( ) Active file ( ) Employed ( )

Interviewer's comment:

where the interviewer suggests a possibility of your being considered for the position, the follow-up, wisely executed, may result in a final favorable decision.

The follow-up letter

Unless the conferee tells you outright that he has no place for you, it is sometimes effective to write a follow-up letter. If he concludes the interview with, "We'll keep your application on file" or "We may have some openings later," this is a lead. Wait a few days and then write a brief note. Remind him of your recent interview (he may not remember you), thank him for it, add any part of your credentials not included in your first letter or interview, and mention briefly your continued interest in the position. In some cases it may be useful to write more than one follow-up letter, adequately spaced in time, of course.

Although they very rarely receive them, most personnel men admit that they appreciate a thank-you note from applicants who have been given some consideration. If the interviewer has taken his time to talk with you or to give you information or valuable advice, it is only common courtesy for you to show your appreciation.

The follow-up interview

Often the interviewer will request that the applicant "Come back in a few days" or "Keep in touch with us." Usually this means that an attempt is being made to fit the applicant into a position. Following such a lead with a second interview is the most effective means of follow-up. A telephone call or a letter would have less chance of making a good impression and maintaining the goodwill already established.

Our previous example of the interviewer who put a premium on aggressiveness suggests that for some types of positions a follow-up interview may be necessary even though little hope is given during the first one. The applicant must use his own discretion to determine what course of action, if any, he should use.

A Final Word

Because it may influence your success more than anything else in your chosen occupation, a job application should be approached with the utmost seriousness and preparation. When you consider that an organization such as R. H. Macy and Company, New York's largest department store, receives an average of 750,000 applications a year, and that only a very small number of these applicants are employed, you can realize the emphasis that must be put on excellence in all the techniques of job application. The ABLE MAN with adequate knowledge and skill in expression will not be bothered long by the bogy of unemployment.

QUESTIONS

1. Why is the job application interview essentially a sales interview?

2. Why should you make a self-analysis before seeking an application interview?

3. Should you have a "give" or "get" attitude in applying for a position? Why?

4. What kind of information should be gathered in making a company analysis? Why?

5. What kind of information should be gathered in making a job analysis? Why?

6. From what sources can the material in a company and job analysis be secured?

7. Why is it important to analyze your prospective employer before holding your application interview?

8. What are the requirements of a good application letter?

9. What can be said in regard to using "stunt" application letters?

10. What can be said of the data sheet that accompanies your letter of application?

11. What rules and practices should be followed in the job interview conference?

12. What are the "do's" and "don't's" for the applicant in the job interview?

13. Should you rehearse your job application conference? Explain.

14. What questions will you be expected to answer in the average job interview?

15. How can the job applicant determine the correct time for terminating the interview?

16. What can be said of the "follow-up letter" and the "follow-up interview"?

EXERCISES

1. If you were a personnel manager, what factors would you consider most important in making your decisions regarding applicants? Why? Write a 500 word paper in which you discuss this matter.

2. Hold a few practice interviews with some friend who is also interested in the application interview. Alternate in the position of employer and applicant. Offer constructive criticism of each other's attempts.

3. Short practice interviews may be held during the class hour with students acting as employers and applicants. A brief class discussion should follow each interview.

4. *Realistic interview assignment.* The purpose of the following assignment is to give you the most practical experience in application possible under a class situation. A member of the faculty will be selected by your instructor to act as your "interviewer."

(a) Assume that the faculty member selected is the personnel manager of the company to which you will apply.

(b) Make a complete company analysis, job analysis, and analysis of your "interviewer."

(c) Write a letter of application to your "interviewer" and include a data sheet. If the letter and data sheet are effective you will be granted an appointment for an "interview."

(d) The "interview" will be held in the office of the faculty member (15 minutes maximum).

(e) The "interviewer" may use a check list that will indicate the effectiveness of your application.

(f) If any sort of follow-up is indicated you must use your own judgment as to what method would be most suitable. The assignment is not complete until you have received a definite decision from the "interviewer."

SELECTED READINGS

Boynton, Paul W., *Six Ways to Get a Job,* Harper and Bros., New York, 1940.

Edlund, S. W., and Edlund, M. G., *Pick Your Job—And Land It!,* Prentice-Hall, Inc., New York, 1941.

Gardiner, Glenn L., *How You Can Get a Job,* Harper and Bros., New York, 1938.

Hepner, Harry W., *Psychology Applied to Life and Work,* Prentice-Hall, Inc., New York, 1941.

Hoving, Walter, *Your Career in Business,* Duell, Sloan and Pierce, Chicago, 1940.

Laird, Donald A., *The Psychology of Selecting Employees,* McGraw-Hill Book Co., New York, 1937.

Lyons, George J., and Martin, Harmon C., *The Strategy of Job Finding,* Prentice-Hall, Inc., New York, 1940.

MacGibbon, Elizabeth Gregg, *Fitting Yourself for Business,* McGraw-Hill Book Co., New York, 1941.

Maule, Francis, *Men Wanted,* Funk and Wagnalls Company, New York, 1937.

Part III

PUBLIC SPEAKING

Building the Public Speech

I. PRELIMINARY CONSIDERATIONS
   Study of audience
   Selection of a topic
   Formulation of a specific purpose

II. GATHERING SPEECH MATERIAL
   Personal experience
   Interviews
   Correspondence
   Books, magazines, and newspapers
   Radio broadcasts

III. THE USE OF INTEREST AND BELIEF MATERIAL
   Illustrations
   Specific language
   Slogans
   Visual aids
   Factual data and statistics
   Testimony
   Repetition

IV. ANALYSIS OF MATERIAL
   Outlining the material
      Introduction
      Discussion
      Conclusion

V. MAKING USE OF THE OUTLINE
   Writing from the outline
   Speaking from the outline
   Reading and memorizing the speech
   Using a critic

Building the Public Speech

VERY FEW persons are able to give an acceptable speech on the spur of the moment. Speech-making demands much preparation. It is true we know some men who can speak rather effectively if they are called upon unexpectedly, but they do so only because they have met the same situation many times before or because they feel so strongly about their subject that their remarks spring from full and true inspiration. But these cases are rare. The average speaker knows that speaking is a responsibility that must be discharged with care and preparation. Would a contractor build a house without a blueprint? Most of them would not. Occasionally they may try, but the result is always a house full of imperfections and inconveniences.

The preparation of a speech is like an insurance policy for the speaker. It protects him against worry, rambling, nervousness, and ineffective speaking. When a speech has been carefully prepared a speaker can face his audience with confidence and some degree of surety that his purpose will be attained.

Preliminary Considerations

Let us assume that you have received an invitation to speak before a certain group. Although they may tell you that you are being allotted twenty minutes on the program they usually will not select your topic. That is as it should be. Accepting such an invitation is an easy and pleasant thing to do, but there is more to it than first meets the eye. It will do you no good to think and worry about the speech for a couple of weeks. That will only intensify your nervousness. Your only chance to justify your accepting the invitation is to start a well-regulated routine of preparation for it.   The following steps are fundamental and sound; they are the working basis of successful speech organization:

1. Study your prospective audience.
2. Select a topic.
3. Formulate a specific purpose.
4. Collect material and information for the speech.
5. Analyze the material and eliminate all that is irrelevant to your specific purpose.
6. Organize material by rough outline.
7. Prepare a speaking outline.

Study of your audience

What is the nature of this group to which you are to speak? What are its interests?   Answer these questions before you go any further.   Take into account any and all characteristics of the audience that may affect your speech.   Are you in similar businesses?   Do you live in the same community?   What problems do you have in common?

If you can determine what they might like to have discussed, consider this question: Would they like to hear this subject discussed by you?   Do they regard you as an authority on this particular subject?   If they do not, they are likely to be antagonistic toward you.   A doctor may speak on *Cancer Therapy*, but you should not, unless you are qualified.

Perhaps the occasion will suggest something to you.   Is it a special celebration of some kind?   If so, what?   People gathered together for a particular reason rightfully expect a speaker to take that reason into consideration.

What things are of common interest to all persons?   Self-preservation, self-esteem, or one of the other desires may be taken as your cue.   All persons will be interested in knowing how they may identify quality and values in food merchandise.   They may be interested in knowing how various canned foods are prepared or anything that pertains directly to their vital interest of self-preservation.

If it is your intention to speak on a highly controversial subject, you must determine what resistance, if any, the audience may have either to you personally or to your proposed subject.   In such an instance you will be under the necessity of first establishing personal prestige for yourself, and secondly, of gaining the attention of the audience through approach on common ground interests.

Remember that it is your duty as a speaker to return, in full, adequate dividends for the investment of time that the audience makes in listening to you. Consider that audience in the selection of your speech topic and, indeed, throughout the entire process of preparation. If you speak over the radio and the speech does not satisfy the hearer, he may turn the dial and thus cut you off. In the auditorium the audience has no such advantage. If they dislike you and your speech, they must sit in suffering silence while their anger and opposition intensify. Protect yourself against this possibility by considering your audience first.

Selection of a topic

After you have analyzed your audience and have determined what their interests are, you may begin the process of selecting a subject. Find something on which you are well informed or something that you can learn about through investigation. It is unreasonable to think that any person can speak on any subject. He may lack the necessary background. The subject may be so complex that no one besides an expert could hope to give it an intelligent discussion. Do not overlook your own personal experiences. The richest and most desirable source of speech material springs from one's own background of knowledge and experience. If you are observant, your daily reading will suggest speech topics to you.

Formulation of the specific purpose

The speech topic only suggests the general area about which you are to speak. Topics are usually broad and general and might well stand as the title of a year's study. For instance, the subject *Goodwill in Business* is sufficiently broad to cover the whole realm of industry. If you limit the subject no further, you would have to speak for days in order to scratch the surface. Many speakers fail to be effective because they never clearly establish the point that they wish to leave with the audience. Write on a piece of paper the exact response you wish to achieve. For the subject *Goodwill in Business,* your specific purpose might be, "I wish my audience to understand what the grocer does, in the way of service, to establish goodwill." You might formulate it thus, "I wish to show my audience what it costs to keep goodwill in the grocery business." If you are speaking to an audience of fellow grocery men or even a group of merchants in other lines, your specific purpose might be, "I wish my audience to believe that goodwill in business is the only way to keep business." In any case, you will help guarantee your success if you use this method. It helps to limit your subject. It gives you something to work for. It eases your problem of finding material for the speech.

Have you ever listened to a speaker talk for an hour and still not say anything? What he said may have sounded good. He may have said many interesting things. At the end of his speech you might even remark that he was a "good" speaker. But when your friend asks you what he said or what he asked his audience to do, you recall that there was nothing very tangible in the entire speech. The speaker who just talks, no matter how well, and never reaches a conclusion is like a merry-go-round. You may ride a merry-go-round for hours and enjoy the ride and the music, but when it is all over you will be right where you started.

If you make a business trip from New York to Los Angeles you will not go by way of Birmingham, St. Paul, Kansas City, and Seattle. Your desire is to get there by the most efficient route possible. Neither do you board a west-bound train simply for the ride. You travel only when you have some definite place to go, and you invariably select the most satisfactory means of getting you there. So it is with public speaking. Never appear before an audience unless you have a specific purpose in mind, a desire to achieve a definite response from your audience.

As you well know, the aimless and undirected speaker is all too common. He rambles from point to point, letting one idea suggest another with seeming disregard for the endurance of his hearers. Perhaps he likes the sound of his own voice or perhaps it flatters his ego to stand before an audience; whatever his motivation, of one thing we may be sure, his audience will rapidly lose all respect for such a man and will not be anxious to hear him again.

But the purposeful speaker is in a different situation. He knows that audiences are difficult to please and that they are seldom receptive to the idle wanderings of an aimless speaker. With this in mind the speaker studies his prospective audience, selects a topic of mutual interest, determines the reaction he desires, finds the speech material that is pertinent to his topic, arranges it in proper order, and proceeds to give the audience a clear and concise understanding of the subject under discussion.

Gathering Speech Material

Before you begin the job of gathering material for your speech, resolve to create some system for tabulating the things you find. Experience will prove that your memory cannot be trusted. Keep notes of your discoveries in black and white. Probably the easiest way of doing this is to use small filing cards. Four by six inch cards are the most convenient. Every time you run across a significant item jot it down on a card for future reference. Indicate also the source of the item in case you wish to refer to it again.

Look for anything that might help you develop an idea. After reading an article, write down a brief summary of what the author said. Include also a notation of your reactions to the article. If you find an illustration or an example that appeals to you, do not try to remember it—you may not be able to; write it on a card. Statistics, quotations by authorities, facts, unusual ideas, effective slogans, and anything else that might be used to support one of your own ideas, should be recorded.

Personal experience

Personal experience offers the richest source of material for speech making. It brings a familiarity into your talk that is appealing. Your most effective stories and illustrations spring directly from your own experience. The elderly lady customer who yesterday was sure her purchases came to eighty-eight cents instead of eighty-nine cents offers a good example. Instead of arguing with her, although you knew you were right, you admitted an error and totaled the order at eighty-eight cents. Goodwill cannot be achieved without some expenditure. In this case you invested one cent in goodwill. Use this story when speaking on *The Cost of Goodwill in Business.*

Every day something that is fresh and pertinent as speech mate·

rial happens right under your nose. The older one becomes, the wiser he should be, although many people reach old age without being aware of the richness of their experiences. Develop an observing attitude. Look for the little things. If one hundred customers walk into your store each day, you have one hundred chances to study human nature, one hundred sources of speech material.

Interviews

Casual conferences, daily conversations, or arranged interviews give you an opportunity to get the "other fellow's" ideas. Two minds are better than one. It is a waste of time to spend days solving a problem that has already been solved by someone else.

Correspondence

Do not overlook the advantages of obtaining information by correspondence. Personal letters of inquiry often bring valuable results. Make use of public service organizations. Colleges and universities are usually glad to answer your questions. Their trained faculties can often give you the desired information or tell you where you can get it. Some universities maintain bureaus of business research whose purpose, in part, is to supply facts to businessmen.

Books, magazines, and newspapers

The local library will be glad to furnish material for you. Trained librarians can locate information on any subject in just a few minutes. There is almost no limit to the amount of information to be found in a library. But, strange as it seems, only a very small percentage of a community's population ever make use of it. In the library you may consult newspapers, magazines, professional and trade journals, yearbooks, encyclopedias, special documents and reports, books on specific subjects, biographies of famous men, and general literature, all of which may give you ideas that will make your speech worth while.

Radio broadcasts

Often the latest news of happenings in business is broadcast by some well-known radio commentator. These speeches are made by men who are on the ground floor of current business trends. The facts that they present usually can be trusted, and their comments and interpretations of those facts should be utilized as a source of speech material.

The Use of Interest and Belief Material

Perhaps you have heard speeches similar to the lecture given by a certain college professor. After the lecture, a student who had been absent asked one of his classmates, "What did the prof talk about?" The reply was, "I don't know; he didn't say."

Or maybe you have listened to a speaker who talked on and on in unfamiliar words, assuming that his audience had the same background that he possessed. At the conclusion of his speech you may have been aware that the speaker really had something to say and that he knew what he was saying, but that he had certainly been unable to communicate those ideas to his audience.

So we must look for means of interesting an audience and clarifying and supporting ideas that might otherwise be lost in a maze of abstract discussion. For this purpose we may use illustrations, specific language, slogans, visual aids, factual data and statistics, repetition, and testimony. These are the things that add "flesh and blood" to a speech. The speaker who ignores them merely puts one more barrier between himself and successful speaking.

Illustrations

The word illustration, as used in this discussion, includes analogies, figures of speech, stories, and jokes. Each of these is used by the speaker to clarify an unfamiliar reference or to make an abstract statement concrete and down to earth.

Illustrations are usually considered as means of interesting the audience or of resting them during intervals between heavier parts of the speech. Although they do serve this purpose, their most useful function is to clarify. The average audience is not capable of attending to sustained reasoning and therefore needs constant translation to everyday, familiar experiences.

Because illustrations are so potent an aid in speaking, one often hears them misused. Never try to "work in" an illustration simply because you think it is clever or will "get a laugh." Remember that an illustration cannot stand alone. It is valuable only if it adds to a point or idea that you wish to impress upon your audience. It is always distressing to hear a speaker, led away from the subject by an entertaining story, try to get back by using a sickly expression such as, "Now, let's see, where was I?" or "But to get back to the speech . . ."

One must also consider his audience when choosing an illustration. If it is a mixed audience the choice must be one that will interest all and offend none. Make sure that your illustrations arouse desirable associations. A foreign-born person likes a good story about his people only if it does no injury to the dignity or pride of himself or his fellows.

You can make a valuable and fascinating hobby by taking a little time occasionally to jot down illustrations on small filing cards, as already suggested. You will be surprised at the number of really good things you can find in the course of a day, if you look for them. If your notes are filed, you will have little trouble, when you are ready to prepare a speech, in selecting those illustrations that will be pertinent to your subject.

Specific language

What do you think of the person who says, "My gastronomic satiety admonishes me that I have arrived at the ultimate state of deglutition consistent with dietetic integrity," when he simply means that he has had enough to eat? You probably want to tell him to "get off his high horse." Many speakers, feeling the importance of the speech situation, try to impress their hearers with language too formal or too pompous. They are fooling no one but themselves, for audiences much prefer the simple word to the unfamiliar, polysyllabic one.

EFFECTIVE	INEFFECTIVE
buy	procure
trade	exchange
money	capital
pay	reimbursement
poor	destitute
cut	discount
try	endeavor
hasten	expedite
secretly	surreptitiously

Also wherever possible the specific word should be used. The word *building* is a general word. Do not use it when you mean *church, house, store, factory, shop, garage,* or *warehouse.* Words should call up an image of the object referred to. If you say *building* and you mean *store,* your audience will not have an exact picture of what you mean.

Why do some speakers insist upon using the abstract? The reason is clear. It takes clear thinking and complete understanding to use the specific word. The abstract and general term covers up the deficiencies of thought and preparation.

Slogans

Nearly everyone recognizes the value of a slogan that is original and fresh. Slogans are short and concise, "pack a lot of punch," and are remembered for a long time. Advertisers are constantly on the outlook for good slogans that can be used to sell merchandise. Some firms offer thousands of dollars for the one that hits the right spot. A speaker is somewhat in the same situation as the advertiser. He has something to sell and the use of a slogan is one way to do it. Sometimes slogans can be used as the title of the speech and constantly repeated during the speech until the audience associates it with the one idea that needs to be remembered. Examples of good slogans are: "Independence Made America—Trade Independent," "Service with a Smile," "The American Way," "Strength in Unity," and "Remember Pearl Harbor."

Visual aids

Sketches, diagrams, charts, and maps may be used to clarify the material of an informative speech. Their use is probably greater and more effective in this type of speech than in any other. The speaker should be careful in using material of this kind to stand well to one side in order to avoid obstructing the view. Visual aids add much to the clearness of a speech, especially when the talk consists of showing progress over a period of time or when it is necessary to make comparisons between figures.

Factual data and statistics

Closely allied to visual aids are factual data and statistics. They present a total and complete picture of the situation and have their uses in every form of speaking and writing. Grand totals, percentages, comparisons between periods, and the like may be shown. A speaker may gain immediate attention from his audience if he lays down a barrage of facts and statistics in the introduction of his speech. The facts should be simple statements of the situation. Unless absolute accuracy is necessary, round numbers should be substituted for the exact figure; they are easier to remember and do not require too much thinking on the part of the audience.

The following introduction illustrates how factual data and statistics may be used:

> The food and grocery industry is the biggest business in America. The government tells us that the United States food bill amounts to more than 20,000,000,000 dollars a year; in other words, the housewives spend approximately 63,000,000 dollars for food every day.
> The retail food and grocery business of the country is handled by 445,000 grocery and combination stores, with more than 1,250,000 men and women employed. This group of employers and employees is one-third as great as the army mobilized by the United States for service during the World War.
> The food industry is not only the largest industry in the country, but the most indispensable and the most progressive. Anyone who doubts its progressiveness should compare the modern food emporium, with its emphasis on service, efficiency, and cleanliness, with the store of a generation ago.

Testimony

Testimony is invoking the authority of others to support your own statement. The wide use of testimonials in printed advertising attests the value of calling upon well-known persons for their opinion. The effect of testimony is corroboration. It brings before the audience another man who says, in effect, "I'm back of your speaker. What he says is true. I agree." It may be used in any type of speech but is particularly useful in the persuasive speech. Sometimes we will not believe regardless of how much good sense and reasoning is presented, but if someone who has our respect believes in something, we are inclined to go along with him.

Testimony should always be carefully considered before using it. Select the words of men who are acknowledged by your audience as being honest, unprejudiced, and in a position to know the facts.

Repetition

Constant repetition of an idea is sometimes an effective means of arriving at a final response. Slogans are effective because they are short and catchy and can stand constant repeating with the result that they imbed ideas in the hearer's mind as being true. But the value of repetition can also be achieved, and less obviously, by repeating the same idea in other words, or translating a statement into an illustration. This procedure adds color and force to what is said. Repetition is also valuable in summing up main ideas at the end of the speech. The main ideas are the things that carry the final impression. If they are lost in a maze of detail and explanation, the audience may experience difficulty in thinking back to the major points you set out originally to establish.

Analysis of Material

As you gather the various materials for your speech, you will be aware that certain main ideas are taking shape. You will find that several pieces of information already support one general and important idea. Your next step is to determine these main ideas. You have your specific purpose, which is the one broad response you seek. Let us say, for instance, that your specific purpose is, "I want my audience to contribute to the Community Chest fund." Perhaps you will find three good reasons why they should contribute:

1. The Community Chest provides for the less fortunate members of our community.
2. The Community Chest is the most efficient charity organization.
3. Every employed citizen, as a matter of civic pride and self-protection, should contribute freely.

These three ideas, if impressed upon your audience, will carry the weight of your argument for action. But each of these must be supported by the facts, illustrations, testimony, and other materials if they are to induce the belief you seek.

Any material that does not support one of your main ideas must be eliminated. No matter how clever or how persuasive you think it is, leave it out! Construct your speech according to a plan that drives directly toward the specific purpose. If, for instance, in the Community Chest speech, you use a bit of material not applicable to the specific purpose or in support of a main idea, you detract the attention of the audience from your desired response. When you finally get back on the right track, it will take your audience some time to catch up with you. Consequently this rambling will cause misunderstanding. The audience will look for the connection between your declared purpose and the unrelated material just used. By the time they discover that there was no connection, you may have passed over a pertinent point.

It is in the choice of main ideas that the speaker proves his ability to analyze. If the main ideas chosen do not carry the best available appeals, you can expect the speech to fall short of its objective. Before you finally select these ideas, check and recheck through the material that you have accumulated in order to reassure yourself of its relevance. Ask yourself again and again, "Are these the few important ideas that will promote my specific purpose?"

Outlining the material

Experienced speakers usually develop a method of recording the material that they wish to use in their speech. William Jennings Bryan used to jot down suggestive words and phrases on a small slip of paper that he carried to the platform with him. However, for the inexperienced speaker, mere suggestive notations prove to be totally inadequate. One of the best methods of tabulating the plan of your speech is by the use of a complete sentence outline.

(Main Idea) I. Advertising is a method of increasing sales.
    A. The most successful businesses have spent thousands of dollars for advertising.
        1. The Carter Dept. Store increased business 65 per cent in three months by well-planned advertising.
          (a) This was all organized within the store.
          (b) The advertising was done chiefly by radio.
          (c) Slogan contests were sponsored to increase listener interest.

B. It is certain that customers are affected by good advertising.

    1. . . . .

        (a) . . . .

        (b) . . . .

        (c) etc.. . . . .

II. Second main idea . . . .

    A. etc.

Notice the use of symbols in the above outline. The main idea (I) is supported by two subideas (A and B), which in turn are supported by sub-subideas (1), etc. This kind of organization gives the whole speech a coherence and order that makes it easy to follow. Ordinarily the main ideas should be restricted to as small a number as possible. There is no limit except time to the number of subideas that may be used.

A speech will naturally fall into three distinct divisions, introduction, discussion, and conclusion. Each of these divisions has its own peculiar purpose that cannot easily be ignored.

The introduction. The introduction of the speech has two chief functions, to create an interest in the subject and to suggest along what lines the subject will be developed.

The first few minutes of a speech are the hardest. During that time the speaker is trying to adjust himself to the speech situation and the audience is becoming adjusted to the speaker and his purpose. It is necessary to "crack the ice" in those first few moments. The audience may not be antagonistic toward the speaker, but at any rate they are probably only passively interested. They may be thinking about their own problems or about the speaker who just finished. How can you turn their attention to you and your subject immediately? Obviously, you must say something that will arouse their interest, something that will make them listen.

By all means, avoid beginning with the well-known, "unaccustomed as I am to public speaking," or, "I don't pretend to be a public speaker, but . . ." Why tell them you are an inexperienced speaker? Why suggest that your speech will not be good? That is really what you do when you begin in this way. A speaker is under no necessity to apologize to his audience. If you are ineffective they will find out soon enough, and your apology will not ease their suffering. If you are a good speaker but lack confidence, your audience will never know about your lack of experience unless you tell them.

Begin the speech with something that will catch their attention immediately. A startling fact or an interesting observation will do the trick. A speaker once opened his speech with the statement, "Within a week some member of this audience will die, leaving behind him a family whose grief will be unmeasurable." That struck a vital interest. The audience immediately perked up and listened. Then by clever choice of ideas the speaker brought their attention around to his purpose, which was to persuade them to join a health insurance group.

Plan carefully what you will say in the introduction. First impressions are the strongest and a speaker is usually in need of creating a good first impression. Select something original for the opening. Do not rely on old stories or old, overused bromides.

Richard C. Borden, in an unusual and interesting book called, *Public Speaking—As Listeners Like It,* says this about the introduction:

Smokers do not like matches that fail to light with the first scratch. Listeners do not like speakers who fail to "light" with the first sentence.

When you rise to make a speech, do not picture your audience as waiting with eager eyes and bated breath to catch your message.

Picture it instead, as definitely bored—and distinctly suspicious that you are going to make this situation worse.

Picture your listeners as looking uneasily at their watches, stifling yawns and giving vent to a unanimous "HO HUM."

The first sentence of your speech, like the three red-skins who bit the dust in the opening sentence of the Western thriller, must crash through your audience's initial apathy.

Don't open your speech on Safety First by saying: "The subject which has been assigned me is the reduction of traffic accidents." Say instead: "Four hundred and fifty shiny new coffins were delivered in this city last Thursday."

Don't open your attack on installment buying with the sentence: "I would like to invite your attention tonight to the grave consequences which may follow continuance of the installment plan psychology in buying." Say, instead: "Some of the people in this room suffer from a deadly disease —the disease of future chasing." [1]

---

[1] Bordon, Richard C., *Public Speaking—As Listeners Like It!,* Harper & Brothers, 1935, pp. 4–5.

As soon as you have the attention of the audience focused on you and your speech, you must indicate what the general plan of your speech is. Give them a few hints as to what general things you are to discuss. This will help clarify your position and enable the listeners to follow more easily your trend of thought. It gives them something to look forward to. They will become mentally and emotionally set and prepared for whatever you have in store for them. After this attitude is once achieved, let nothing take you from it.

Dr. Little of Arthur D. Little, Inc. gave this splendid introduction to a speech entitled, "Impending Changes in our Use of Fuels":

When one observes a growing plant for an hour, it seems a fixed and static thing. Such progressive change as may be taking place proceeds too slowly to make impression. When, however, the development, which may have taken months for its fulfillment, is crowded into the few minutes required to run off a motion-picture reel, we gain an altogether new appreciation of the dynamic power and driving force behind that evolution in which green shoots are followed by stem and branches, leaves, bursting buds, and flowers.

It is much the same when we survey a specific industry. We may realize that changes are in progress, but the general impression we receive is one of established equilibrium. We need, therefore, to review quickly the development that has already taken place, in order that we may gain a true appreciation of the forces which urge it forward and that we may sense the direction of its trend.

The discussion. This is the main body of your speech. Its purpose, of course, is to carry the weight of your specific purpose. Here you present your main ideas and the material which supports those main ideas. All that has been said about material and the psychology of winning response applies to the discussion.

The conclusion. A definite conclusion is necessary. In some cases it will amount to nothing more than a very brief summary of what you have said in the discussion. In those instances the purpose is to clarify and impress again the main ideas. Imagine that your audience did not hear your speech at all and that you wish them to take away at least a skeleton idea of what you have said. It will not be needless repetition. In fact, the listeners will appreciate your attempt to impress further the important points. It gives them something tangible to grasp.

In the persuasive speech the conclusion should be a climax to the discussion, a final appeal for belief or action. You have spent the preceding time loading the gun, finding the target, aiming at the target, and finally drawing a perfect bead on it. Now, pull the trigger. Everything is set; all you need to do is strike at the springs of action.

Remember Patrick Henry's famous "Liberty or Death" speech. His conclusion is a classic example of appeal for action:

> The next gale that sweeps from the north will bring to our ears the clash of resounding arms! Our brethren are already in the field! Why stand we here idle? What is it that the gentlemen wish? What would they have? Is life so dear, or peace so sweet, as to be purchased at the price of chains and slavery? Forbid it, Almighty God! I know not what course others may take; but as for me, give me liberty, or give me death!

It is highly emotional. It is the climax of a rather lengthy and persuasive discussion. Imagine yourself in that audience. Would you not be moved to action by these final words?

Definite rules for organization of speeches cannot be set down with any finality. The method differs for the individual speaker, the topic, and the speech situation. It is a complex and variable problem. The serious student of speech will study many speeches to observe methods of organization. He will read several authorities on the subject and will constantly seek to develop his ability to analyze material and arrange it for the most efficient and effective means of gaining his desired response.

Making Use of the Outline

For best results, prepare an outline well in advance of the speaking date. Go over it carefully several times to make sure that you have selected the proper ideas and material to support your specific purpose. When you have satisfied yourself on that point you are ready to prepare the speech for delivery.

Writing from the outline

Some speakers find it helpful to use their outline as a guide in writing the speech out in full. Writing is one of the best methods of learning. If you choose this method, write the speech completely, following the outline in every detail. When it is complete, stand and read it aloud once or twice. Make no effort to memorize it. Indeed, you will be much wiser to destroy the written copy after a couple of readings. It will already have served its purpose of impressing upon your mind the general gist and order of the speech.

Speaking from the outline

Another method of preparation, and probably the best, is to use your outline as a guide. Before you go to the platform, practice the speech aloud several times. Go over it again and again, always aloud and always standing! This method will accustom you to the sound of your own voice and to the feeling of speaking before an audience. Imagine that your audience is before you. Do nothing in this practice session that you would not do were you actually facing a real audience. You will find that each time you practice, new ideas and better phrasing of sentences will occur to you. As you continue, you will sense this constant improvement. You may even discover that some ideas you thought of while writing the outline seem absolutely out of place when you speak them. If so, they should be eliminated, rearranged, or altered.

This oral preparation is the best thing you can do to insure effective delivery. Do not depend on the inspiration of the moment. Many speakers have found, all too late, that the inspiration did not come, much to their personal distress and the disgust of the audience. As you stand, practicing your speech, you will feel impulses to gesture, to emphasize certain words and thoughts. Do not resist these impulses. They are good! They are the roots of effective delivery.

Reading and memorizing the speech

Probably the one factor, more than any other, that makes speech effective is the sincerity and sense of communication that the speaker suggests in his delivery. Even though you have written the speech yourself, your constant attention to the reading of the words will lose for you all the desirable illusion of spontaneity. You are very likely to slip into a "reading tone" that is dull and monotonous. Often on the radio we hear a politician or businessman speaking. Although we cannot see him, we know that he is reading his speech. We lose the necessary personal element. We become aware of the reading and this attracts our attention away from the thoughts he is trying to present to us. However, if reading a speech is ever justified, it is in the radio studio. Here the contact with the audience is seemingly decreased. You cannot see them and they cannot see you. The microphone offers little sign of reaction. This condition causes even the most experienced speakers to falter. One well-known speaker, while speaking over the radio for the first time, stopped abruptly in the middle of his speech and said, "I'm sorry, I cannot go on. How can anyone speak to an audience he cannot see?"

Read your speech only when it is impossible for you to do otherwise; in which case, double your effort in oral preparation.

Some of the things characteristic of reading a speech are also true of memorizing it. It takes an expert to give a memorized speech and make it sound as if he were speaking it for the first time. Too many of us know that our memory cannot be trusted. When we memorize, we worry constantly about our next sentence, wondering if we will remember it when we come to it. Our concentration is therefore drawn away from our thoughts and to the words themselves. This makes for a mechanical and monotonous speaking of words. Again, the audience will sense your method of preparation, and in this instance they will turn their attention to worrying about whether you are going to be able to finish without forgetting. This, too, destroys the sense of communication. Only the well-trained speaker can speak from memory with real effectiveness.

The inexperienced speaker, with adequate preparation, will always be a more effective speaker when he speaks extemporaneously.

Using a critic

Some speakers like to try out their speeches first on some friend or associate. This is often a satisfactory way of discovering mistakes that you yourself would not notice. However, choose as a critic someone who will be truthful and candid with you. Tell your critic that you want him to tell the whole truth about the speech and the speaker and to spare nothing! Would you not rather have one person tell you you were off the track than to have an audience of several hundred go away thinking you were completely ineffective?

Wives and husbands often make good critics because they are anxious for their mates to make a good impression. Employees and business friends, under most circumstances, do not make good critics. They may be too anxious to keep your goodwill to risk telling you the truth. If your criticism is motivated by the critic's desire to keep on your "good side," you will be much better off to speak to an old chair or a bridge lamp.

But whether you use a critic or not, satisfy yourself that what you have to say and the manner in which you say it will be acceptable to your prospective audience.

QUESTIONS

1. What routine step should be taken in the preparation of a public speech?

2. What factors should govern the selection of a topic for a speech?

3. What rules should govern the selection of a topic for a speech?

4. What is the object of selecting a specific purpose for a speech?

5. From what sources may the material for a speech be selected?

6. What rules should be followed in recording the material?

7. What rules should govern the type of material selected?

8. What rules should govern the selection and use of language in a speech?

9. What are "main ideas" in a speech? What rules should govern their selection and use?

10. What rules should govern the outlining of a speech?

11. What are the functions of the conclusion to a speech?

12. What are the two chief functions of the introduction to a speech?

13. How should the speech outline be used in practicing delivery of the speech?

14. Under what circumstances should a speech be read from manuscript?

15. As a general rule should a speech be presented from memory or should it be presented extemporaneously? Why?

16. What advantages may be gained by practicing the presentation of your speech before a critic?

EXERCISES

1. Select three different types of audiences before whom you might be asked to speak. Outline in not less than two pages an analysis of each of the three audiences.

2. Select three topics that would be suitable for speeches before each of the three audiences analyzed above.

3. Write out the specific purpose for each of the nine speeches suggested above.

4. Select material for one of the above suggested speeches. Gather this material from at least ten different sources. Record the material and identify each source.

5. Write out in complete sentence form the main ideas for three of the above suggested speeches.

6. Outline in not less than two pages two of the above suggested speeches.

7. Write out in not more than 150 words the introductions to the two speeches outlined.

8. Write out in not more than 150 words the conclusion to the two speeches outlined.

9. Practice presenting one of the two speeches outlined before three different critics. Write in not more than 500 words their suggestions for improving the speech.

10. Select two speeches found in print and study them to determine the type of organization followed by the speaker. Write a brief constructive criticism of each speech.

SELECTED READINGS

Monroe, Allan H., *Principles and Types of Speech,* Scott, Foresman and Co., New York, 1939. (Chapters V, VI, VII, VIII, IX, X, XII, and XIII.)

Sandford, William P., and Yeager, Willard Hayes, *Practical Business Speaking,* McGraw-Hill Book Co., New York, 1937. (Chapters IV and VI.)

Sarett, Lew, and Foster, William T., *Basic Principles of Speech,* Houghton Mifflin Co., New York, 1936. (Chapters VIII, XIV, and XV.)

Wheeler, Elmer, *Tested Public Speaking,* Prentice-Hall, Inc., New York, 1939.

Delivery of the Public Speech

I. STAGEFRIGHT
   Causes of stagefright
      Feeling of responsibility
      Feeling of inferiority
      Lack of preparation
   Reducing stagefright
      Relaxation
      Experience
      Attitude
      Preparation and plan
II. FROM OFFICE TO PLATFORM
   Delivery defined
      A problem of adaptation
III. PERSONALITY IN DELIVERY
IV. THE VOICE
   Relaxation
   Proper breathing
   Quality
   Overcoming monotony
      Rate
      Force
      Pitch
      Pauses
V. BODILY ACTION
   Value of bodily action
      Means of communication
      Increases attention
      Stimulation to the speaker
   Posture
   Gestures
      Gestures to clarify
      Gestures to emphasize
      Overt and covert action
VI. POLARIZATION
   Sincerity
   Directness
   Animation

Delivery of the Public Speech

ALTHOUGH IT may not be generally admitted, the actual delivery of a speech probably keeps more men off the platform than any of the other problems of public speaking. There are many intelligent people who can analyze a subject, organize it, and even find the elements of audience interest; yet only a few ever reach the platform and face an audience. This may explain why some persons are inclined to deride speaking as a highly developed art by saying, "Anyone with a lick of sense can gather material and put it into understandable language." But they reckon without the realistic situation of walking out before the piercing eyes of a waiting audience. That is when your material becomes a speech! It is even a little curious that we should read speeches or that scholars should undertake to study the speeches made by great orators long since dead. A speech is a living and audible utterance made by a living and animated speaker.

It is also quite common to hear men who do other things successfully declare that they cannot "make a speech." They seem to think that the ability to speak before an audience is a "gift" with which they are not endowed. They may listen to a good speaker and then confess that it looks so easy or that they have the same ideas that the speaker presented. Yet *they* never talk.

Well, what is it? Are they self-conscious? Do they feel awkward? Do they think the audience will laugh? Are they afraid that no words will come? Do they worry about their appearance, their big nose, cumbersome hands, missing hair, or gold teeth? Perhaps. These and other equally silly reasons keep many people silent when they might speak with more than average authority.

The most important factor in all speaking is the MAN, the real inside, the complete individual, the integrated personality. An ABLE MAN will be attended to by any audience. Violation of all the rules and techniques of effective delivery, however essential for polished speaking, will not ruin the speech of an ABLE MAN who has something to say. Faulty delivery does result in distraction, but if the speaker and his message are sufficiently attractive, the chance for such distraction is lessened. Again, it is a matter of compensation.

Stagefright

The first thing a beginning speaker wants to talk about is stagefright, and even after he has given a thousand speeches and has become a "professional," a speaker will continue to talk about it. Let us say this right now: if a speaker approaches the platform without being the least bit nervous, there is something wrong. His lack of nervousness probably reveals his feeling that the situation is not important enough to get worried about. Many students in college speech classes show no understanding of the speech situation by being completely nonchalant and naive in their classroom recitations. A good teacher will immediately become suspicious of such people.

The causes of stagefright

While there may be a multitude of minor reasons which contribute to the total experience of stagefright, the large majority of these may be grouped into one of the following causes: (1) a feeling of responsibility, (2) a feeling of inferiority, (3) a lack of preparation.

Feeling of responsibility. The fact that you are to consume the collective time of your audience is sufficient reason for you to be concerned. If you are to speak to 1,000 people for 30 minutes you will be using 500 hours of the world's time. In other words, your 30-minute speech amounts to a consumption of 62½ working days. You had better have something to say! This feeling of responsibility to your job as a speaker is the only commendable cause for nervousness. It is a healthy condition, for it tunes your whole mind and body to the situation. Your audience may even sense the motivation and respect you for it. As Richard C. Borden says, it "is the penalty you pay for being a race horse instead of a cow."

Feeling of inferiority. Many people when required to make a speech have a feeling of inferiority or of incompetence in meeting the speech situation. They may feel that they are inferior to the members of the audience or that what they have to say is not important. The trouble is usually a warped sense of values. Students in a speech class have a great advantage not possessed by businessmen who have to make a speech. The student can make errors in class without losing more than a percentage of a daily grade, and he will profit by receiving understanding and competent criticism. The businessman, on the other hand, in an actual speech situation, may lose a percentage of his salary or of his company's profit and gain nothing but an increased feeling of inferiority. The best cure is to "forget it," but that is not always so easy to do. You need to straighten out your sense of values. Talking it over with a wise and experienced friend may help. You may also set about the task of making yourself a completely superior person in regard to the subject of your speech. If you are to give a speech on *Income Tax* and you study the subject until you know more about it than any member of your audience, you can approach the platform with a decided advantage.

Lack of preparation. Probably the most common cause of stagefright is the result of pure and unadulterated laziness. One should never attempt to speak at all unless he is sufficiently imbued with a desire to communicate some worth-while idea and is willing to spend the necessary time to develop himself as an authority on the subject. There is no excuse for lack of preparation, and if you suffer for this reason, then we say may your suffering be long and severe!

Reducing stagefright

It is probably impossible and unwise to lose all feeling of nervousness while speaking. It is only important that you be able to control your nervousness so that it will not interfere with effective speaking. If you suffer, that is unfortunate; but if your audience suffers, that is intolerable. Rattling papers, quaking hands and knees, nervous mannerisms, and shifty eyes may prove to be such a distraction that they occupy the center of attention while your speech is forgotten.

Relaxation. Most distractions are the result of too much muscle tension. Nervousness and muscle tension work in a vicious circle. As you become more and more nervous your muscles become tighter and tighter. Hold your arm straight out from your body and slowly tense every muscle from the shoulder down to the tips of the fingers. Soon the fingers will begin to quiver and then the whole arm will begin to tremble. If this tension is distributed throughout the whole body, it is only natural that the knees should buckle and that you should lose control over your body. The obvious cure is relaxation. You may have to practice the art of relaxation as you practice your speech for delivery. Many speech books include a series of exercises designed to help the speaker overcome this tension.

You may help to overcome the tension during the speech by making a special effort to use the body. Free and abandoned gestures and walking will help release the body muscles and decrease the nervousness. If you are in a class, you may take extraordinary liberties with this method. A very nervous student was advised to keep walking around the room during his speech. The instructor led him on the first round. Round and round he went, several times, talking all the while. Needless to say, the hearers did not get much from his speech, but soon he decided that walking so much was unnecessary. The tension had been somewhat lessened. He confined his pacing to the platform and gradually centered himself in one position but continued using gestures and bodily movement to emphasize his remarks. Before long he was perfectly relaxed and standing in an effective and commanding posture with his nervousness under control.

Experience. Experience continues to be the best teacher, although her methods are often cruel and heartbreaking. Many appearances soon give a speaker a feeling of self-confidence. Professional speakers, singers, and actors seldom reveal nervousness, although most of them will freely confess that it continues, regardless of the number of times they have appeared. Through experience they have learned to relax and control the distracting results of stagefright.

Attitude. The beginning speaker may compensate for his lack of experience by adopting the correct attitude toward the speech situation. By analyzing the causes of his nervousness he may put himself in a mental state that will increase his confidence. He may conclude that his position is as good as, or perhaps better than, that of the average member of the audience. He will know that no harm will come to him. He will feel that what he has to say will be worth listening to. Put yourself in the position of the audience. What do you think of speakers? What do you notice? What things draw your attention away from ideas? You may be able to think of very few times when you found yourself being unduly critical. Audiences come to hear, not to condemn.

Think through the situation very carefully. Adopt an attitude of "I must tell my audience what I believe; this thing means life and death to me; I will fight for it." If your purpose is firmly fixed and your desire to communicate is strong, the chances of difficulties owing to nervousness will be greatly diminished.

Preparation and plan. The possibility that you may forget or that ideas will fail to come to you is certainly enough to worry anyone into a bad case of stagefright. Let us reiterate that there is no substitute for preparation and plan. If one can feel that he is saturated with his subject, that he is really an authority by virtue of his experience or his study, and that he has a good plan for presenting his material, he need have little fear about forgetting. But one cannot be satisfied with meager preparation—two or three days' thought during spare moments, a stray quotation picked at random from current reading, and a few notes jotted down on a scrap of paper. Preparation is a matter of degree and quality. If the thought of stagefright is sufficiently alarming to you, you may well afford the time and effort it takes to follow a rigid system of gathering material, making a brief, analyzing the material in terms of audience interest and experience, formulating a speaking outline, and practicing orally before a mirror until the speech becomes a part of you.

From Office to Platform

Delivery defined

Delivery is the speaker's means of communication. It has but one purpose, to project speech material to an audience through the physical means of voice and body. The effective speaker offers a minimum of distractions to the idea. He loses himself in his material. Every gesture, action, or inflection of the voice adds to communication because it is motivated by a desire to clarify or emphasize an idea. Attention is not focused for even a second on anything outside the realm of the speaker's message.

A problem of adaptation. We have pointed out that the everyday conference situation is effectively carried on by an ABLE MAN who speaks with sincerity and authority. The public speech differs only in that you will not be interrupted, that you must enlarge your speech delivery so that all can hear and see, and that you will adapt your manner and material to the occasion and the general interests of the audience. You will retain, however, all the qualities of directness, sincerity, authority, and animation that make conference speaking effective.

Suppose you have an idea about how your company might increase its sales of a certain commodity. As you ride down the elevator on your way to lunch you meet the sales manager and, in order to pass the time, you begin to tell him about this idea of yours. He is immediately interested and suggests that you take your lunch with him. While eating, you continue the discussion. Your earnestness makes him listen. He asks questions and you answer. While you are talking, the vice-president comes up and joins you. He is also interested and begs you to go on with your exposition. Soon another joins the group, and another, and another. Soon fifteen or twenty men are gathered around your table. Someone suggests that this is something every man on the sales staff ought to hear. A secretary calls each on the telephone. When they arrive it is decided that the meeting should be held in a private room. Here they want you to stand up so that they can all see you. Here is an audience of one hundred men. You are standing before them—speaking. Public speaking? Yes. If your speech now has the same qualities it had while you were eating lunch plus adaptation to the larger group, you will be giving an effective public speech.

Where is the line of demarcation? When does conversation end and public speaking begin? If you can figure that out, you might also get to work on the egg-and-chicken priority question. Delivery remains the speaker's means of communication and it must be adapted to the audience whether that audience is made up of one person or one thousand.

Personality in Delivery

Personality is an overused and much abused word in our language. Its definitions are myriad. Yet it must be employed here because there are some aspects of personal acceptance and sociability that cannot be explained without recourse to that word. You like a person or you do not like him. Why? If you know him you may be able to find several reasons. However, one often merely sees or hears another person and concludes that he is either good or bad. What is personality? For our purpose let us define personality as the outward manifestations of the individual's real intrinsic worth or character. Personality is what the audience *sees* or *senses* in a speaker. It is, in a way, the "front" presented to the world. This "front" is not always a true indication of the real value of the man behind it, but it is usually used as a basis for opinion. Many fine people indulge in harmful mannerisms and attitudes that are in conflict with their best interests.

Let us examine a few specific cases of speakers whose personality works for or against them. These illustrations are drawn from an average list of persons who have sought for advice on how to become more effective speakers.

Neil Prather is an intelligent individual, and, after you have associated with him for some time, you begin to like him a great deal. But Prather carries himself in the stiff armor of pomposity. He works hard to make an impression on friends and acquaintances. He seems to think that the heavy, studied, aloof manner is necessary to make people appreciate his intellect. When he speaks in conversation he is dogmatic and overbearing. He rolls off words as though they were coming straight from on high. Needless to say, Prather offends many people. They talk about him behind his back and criticize him for his lack of humanity. When he speaks publicly, the attention of the audience is drawn immediately to his manner, and, though a few may respect him for his command of the English language and for his keen analysis of the subject, there are few indeed who give him open-minded attention.

Mary Snook is a typical college co-ed type. She is sweet, pretty, and physically attractive. As a student, she is lucky to get by on average grades. Her interests center on shades of finger-nail polish instead of public opinion polls. Yet she is pleasant, has a nice sense of humor, recognizes her lack of keenness, and admits that she would rather spend six hours on the dance floor than six minutes listening to daily news broadcasts. Mary has many friends. But Mary as a speaker is definitely "skim milk." Audiences like her for what she is, but they do not respect her opinion on any serious subject. If she is ever to be effective, it will be necessary for her to acquire more information and an authoritative manner to go with it.

Art Howard is a successful businessman in a small town. He never went to college and never had any lucky breaks. What he lacks in education and opportunity he has made up for with hard work and friendliness. Howard is understanding, kind, and sympathetic. He is what most of us would like to think of as Mr. Average Citizen. Howard makes many speeches as president of the local Chamber of Commerce, and though he is not a polished speaker, he never fails to hold attention or to draw the commendation of his audience. Sincerity, vigor, honesty, and earnestness are the qualities that put him on top. People immediately sense these things in him and respect him for them.

John Masters was graduated from college and began work as a partner in his father's paper mill. The fact that he was graduated from an accredited college means absolutely nothing; the only thing he got was a diploma plus four years of the most hilarious fun he had ever had. He dresses tastefully, is well-mannered, and looks like the partner of a successful business; and he is, through no effort of his own. But John is shallow. He talks "big," but it is all bluff. Exposure to training in public speaking classes has given him a certain facility with words and the outward signs of an effective speaker. When he speaks he does a good technical job of presentation, but still he falls short of being successful. Audiences sense immediately his mental inadequacy and take him for a nice, well-to-do young man who would be better off as a listener than as a speaker.

Personality is manifested in two ways, through the voice and through the use of the body. These are the two chief factors to be considered in delivery. As you improve your skill in the use of your voice and body in delivery, you simultaneously improve your personality. It follows that the person who learns to deliver a speech effectively will also be more effective as an individual.

The Voice

How often have you listened to a speaker on the radio and made a comment such as, "I'll bet he is a typical Mr. Milquetoast" or, "How would you like to hear that voice in the dark on some lonely road?" Voices serve as a very strong index to human characteristics. The weak and apologetic sounding voice denotes similar qualities in the character of the speaker. The loud, harsh, boisterous, bellowing voice makes you think the speaker is either a bully or a pompous bluff. Audiences respond to the sound of voices. Monotony puts them to sleep. High, shrill, rasping or nasal voices make them squirm. More than that, the voice reveals personality.

If you would hold the attention of your audience and keep them listening to your speech, your voice must be free of all distracting, unpleasant sounds. It must be sufficiently strong to be easily heard, it must be pleasant, and it must possess enough variety in pitch, force, and rate to indicate a lively sense of communication as you speak.

Relaxation

Very few persons have anything organically wrong with their vocal mechanism, but many do not use correctly what they do have. Some speakers tighten up their throats so much that sounds are literally squeezed out, resulting in a variety of unpleasant sounds. The throat must be relaxed in order to get the greatest efficiency from the vocal chords. Within a space of one or two inches around the vocal chords there are nearly thirty pairs of muscles that control the action of the voice box. If you tighten your throat and assume a "bull dog neck" attitude, you put a strain on these muscles that prevents them from functioning properly. The result will be an unpleasant tone. Relax the throat before speaking. Allow all the strength to leave the throat suddenly. Let the head fall to the chest, then roll it from side to side, using only enough tension to control its direction. As you approach the platform maintain this feeling of relaxation using only the minimum of strength necessary to keep the head erect. Occasionally, during your speech, attempt to recapture this feeling of relaxation.

Proper breathing

It is not necessary for a speaker to have "iron lungs" or to have a great lung capacity. The essential requisite is that the speaker have control over his breathing and sufficient breath to support a full, rich voice. It takes very little breath to vocalize. Use no more than is absolutely necessary. The breath, of course, is the motivating force that causes sound in the voice box. If that breath is short and choppy, it follows that the sounds will be equally unpleasant. Speak with an economy of breath. Practice deep rhythmical breathing and work to control a steady stream of air on exhalation. Vocalize a pleasantly-toned "ah" and see how long you can prolong the sound without its becoming unsteady or changing quality. You should be able to sustain such a sound for fifteen seconds. Trumpet players can double and even triple that time.

Quality

A voice that may be said to have good quality is one that is supported by a strong and steady column of air, one that is vocalized in a relaxed throat, and one that is enlarged and amplified by resonance. Vocal resonance is achieved when the sound produced by the vocal chords is enriched and intensified by being reflected off the interior walls of the throat and head. A pure sound is colorless and unpleasant. Every musical instrument, for instance, has its resonators that are designed to amplify the fundamental notes produced on the string or mouthpiece. The same principle applies to speech sounds. Fundamental vibrations from the vocal chords should be allowed to enter the nasal passages so that a nice balance between nasality and flatness may be maintained. While humming a strong *mmmmmm* sound one can feel the amplification in the nasal passage. As you open the lips the quality of the *mmmmmm* will change. Allow it to glide into an open *ah (mmmmmmmm-ahhhh)* maintaining a sufficient portion of nasal resonance to make the sound full and rich. While speaking, one should give all sounds the same balance accorded the *ah* sound, varying it only as emotional content dictates.

The necessity of having a pleasant vocal quality is of enough importance for any serious speaker to spend time in developing the best quality he is capable of producing. Persons whose vocal quality is very unpleasant would do well to seek individual instruction from a competent voice teacher; others may improve their quality by self-study.

Overcoming monotony

Monotony is the technique used by hypnotists to put their subjects to sleep. It is often used by speakers with similar results. In order to hold the attention of the audience a speaker must constantly use variety in his speech. In the composition of a speech we use illustrations, examples, and other factors of interest to keep the listener alert. In the voice there should be constant change or variety by judicious use of rate, force, pitch, and pause.

Rate. By using change of rate a speaker is able to identify for his audience those parts of his speech that are most important. Main ideas and thought groups should ordinarily be spoken slowly and deliberately. Unimportant transitions, connective phrases, and modifying phrases should be spoken rapidly so that they will be subordinated to the thought-carrying groups. Constant change in rate is utilized by all effective actors and speakers; listen to a few and follow their example.

Force. Change in vocal force means varying the loudness or volume. Here again the use of variety is twofold, to hold attention and to emphasize important words and ideas. A well-known speaker once appeared on a lecture program before a group of college students. He had a good strong voice that made audibility no problem for the audience. During the speech, however, he noticed that his audience was becoming restless and turning its attention to other things. He dropped his usual vocal force and began to speak in a very soft and quiet tone; he almost whispered. Those members of the audience who were being inattentive were aware of the change and leaned forward to hear. The drop in force drew their attention back to the speaker.

Nearly every sentence contains a word or two that needs special emphasis. One means of making such words stand out from the rest of the group is either by speaking them with increased force or by speaking them more softly than the rest. If a speaker has a keen sense of communication, he will have little difficulty in selecting the words which deserve such treatment.

Pitch. Changes in pitch are called inflections. The effective speaker uses constant change of inflection. His thoughts and

feelings regulate the changes.   Try speaking this sentence to convey the indicated meanings:

We must do this. (the others will not)
We *must* do this. (it is imperative)
We must do *this*. (but not the other)
We must do this. (so they say)
We must do this? (why can't they?)
We must do this. (we failed on the other)

In each case the inflection is governed by the meaning you wish
to imply.   Of course, changes in force and rate naturally accompany the inflection.   Often a person may have the entire meaning
of his words misinterpreted by such a criticism as, "I know you
said that, but I thought, by the way you said it, you did not mean
it."   Inflection is necessary to communicate accurate meaning
and feeling to the listeners.

An interesting game, which illustrates the importance of vocal
variety, is played by having one member of a group deliver a
speech using only the letters of the alphabet for his words.   He
may use gestures of all kinds to accompany his recitation of the
alphabet.   The important thing is that he have a definite thought
to communicate.   Other members of the group attempt to guess
what that thought was.

The game is similar to the situation that might exist if you
found it necessary to communicate with some person who spoke
another language.   Both of you might be partially understood
through the inflections and changes in the voice.   The word
"slimey" can be understood whether it is pronounced as "slimey,"
"krausnia," "akyaka," or "shlooey."

Pauses.   The pause is the speaker's method of punctuation, and
accurate punctuation is as necessary in speech as it is in writing.
A pause is a stop in vocalization, not an opportunity to use a
series of "and-uh's" and "er's."   Such vocal crutches annoy listeners, and you may be sure they will remember them longer than
the ideas that were squeezed in between.

Pauses may also be used effectively as a method of emphasis.
A sentence spoken forcefully and followed by a pause gives the
listener in the audience a chance to digest the thought.   It permits him to mull the idea over in his own mind for a moment

before he is forced to turn his attention back to the speaker. Audiences need many such pauses, if they are to get much out of a speech.   A reader has a chance to regulate pauses, during which time he can crystallize the preceding ideas; the speaker must perform this task for the audience.

You can do much for your voice by adopting a critical attitude toward your own and other voices that you hear every day.   Try to analyze what you consider the good qualities in the voices of the people you talk to in conversation.   Why are some pleasant and others unpleasant to hear?   Listen critically to your own voice or ask friends to give you frank opinions about how your voice affects them.   If it is at all possible, it will be well worth your while to have a recording of your voice made by a competent voice recorder.   This is the surest method of identifying your own faults.

For one who cannot afford the time or the money to take speech lessons from a good teacher the next best method is to do a great deal of reading aloud.   Reading the daily newspaper or a magazine article may offer you a real opportunity to experiment with and improve the voice.   Oral reading of poetry is particularly helpful because poetry puts more demand on vocal variety and quality.   Monotonously spoken prose is bad enough, but poetry spoken without regard to feeling and meaning is little short of deadly.

Bodily Action

Value of bodily action

One of the common remarks made by beginning students in speech is, "Gestures are unnatural to me because I never use them."   The only answer is that the student is unnatural if he never uses gesture or bodily action.   A speaker who never moves a muscle during a speech will soon find himself talking to empty seats.

Bodily action, including gesture, facial expression, walking, posture, and change of bodily tension, has at least three prime values in public speaking.   It is an effective means of communication, it compels an audience to be attentive, and it stimulates the speaker.

Means of communication. Primitive man used sign language entirely. Even today, if you are in a foreign land you can make yourself understood by using descriptive gestures and postures. But action is not limited to such situations. Observe yourself in any conversation with a friend. Do you not use gestures, facial expression, and bodily movement to emphasize your words? Such action is important primarily because people catch impressions through the eyes more readily than they do through hearing. Try to direct a stranger to a point several blocks away without using gestures to indicate the direction. He will be confused, and you will experience difficulty in choosing words to express your meaning.

Increases attention. Besides helping you to communicate ideas and feelings, bodily action will help in holding the attention of your audience. Most of us respond more easily to action than to sounds. We carefully attend to any moving thing. Take a lesson from the quail, which is hunted in the fields every fall. Sometimes you can almost step on the bird before you see it. The bird exercises a natural instinct to remain perfectly still, blended in the background, in order to escape notice. As a speaker, you will fail to be noticed, if you do not engage in some bodily action.

Action is contagious. Watch a prize fight and observe yourself striking blows and absorbing them with the fighters. Glance at the other spectators; they will have their fists doubled and may even "swing a few." This tendency for audiences to imitate the action that they see is called empathy. It is an unconscious affinity between audiences and effective speakers.

It has been said that a well-dressed man is one so faultless in his attire that no one ever notices what he has on. In other words there is nothing distracting about his attire. The same thought might be applied to the bodily behavior of the speaker. It is as necessary for him to use some bodily action as it is imperative that he wear some clothing; yet neither action nor clothing should divert attention from the man and his subject.

Stimulation to the speaker. Bodily action also has a beneficial effect on the speaker himself. As he increases his use of bodily action he becomes freer and more animated and therefore is able to do a better job of communication.

Try walking about in a slow lethargic manner for a few minutes. Let the shoulders droop and the hands swing uselessly at the side. Relax so completely all over that the very job of staying on your feet is an effort. Does not this make you feel dull and tired? Imagine that you have discovered a fire in your room. Will you walk slowly to the top of the stairs and stand still while you say to your friends, "Fire, fire—there's a fire in my room. Everyone come and help me put it out! Bring the extinguishers and buckets of water!"? Of course not! In all probability you will move about quickly, shouting your orders, waving your arms in the air, and speaking with great force and animation.

But you will not always use such force in your speaking. If you used the bodily action suitable to the fire situation to say simply to your friend, "Do you want to go downtown with me this afternoon?", he would probably advise you to consult your doctor. Use gestures for a specific purpose and "suit the action to the word." As you speak with animation you will find that you are increasingly stimulated by your own action, for it is useful for both audience and speaker.

Posture

In the days of elocution, speakers were given exact angles at which to place their feet and specific directions about how to hold the body erect. The result was usually a stiff and unnatural position. Such rules tended to make a speaker self-conscious and proved distracting to the audience.

It may be sufficient to say one should stand in a comfortable position that offers him the greatest possibility for the use of the body as a medium of communication. That means on both feet and ready to act. He should avoid postures that are as obvious as a yellow tie on a red shirt.

These are some of the common errors in posture to be avoided:

Debutante Slouch. The weight rests on one leg, the other leg being relaxed and bent slightly at the knee. Such a posture throws the whole body out of line. It is weak and "wishy-washy."

Shy Rabbit. The weight of the body is back on the heels, the head drooping and hands flopping, plus a blank-looking face. It is enough to prompt any audience to get up and leave.

Drunken Sailor. Some speakers plant their feet 12 to 18 inches apart and begin to sway from side to side. They roll rhythmically from port to starboard and back again.

Sonja Henie. This is a skating posture. With hands behind the back the speaker shifts weight continuously from one foot to the other, each time drawing back the relaxed foot and leg. He consumes a great deal of effort going nowhere.

Barrel-chested Bruiser. A few speakers antagonize their audience by standing as though they were waiting for the bell to ring sounding the start of the fight. They push out their chests, rub their hands, and stand ready for the first taker.

These are only a few of the types of posture that definitely distract attention. They do so because they are not motivated. Let your posture help show your eagerness to put your message across and keep it consistent.

Gestures

Gesture is a frightening word. It has connotations that have tainted the original meaning. Comedians speak of giving a speech "with gestures," as if any good speech were ever given without them. Students ask, "Do I have to make gestures in this speech?" Of course you do, if the thought calls for it. Any kind of bodily action springs from an impulse to clarify or help in the communication of ideas. Can you possibly convey the idea that the fish caught last summer was the biggest fish in the lake without using some kind of descriptive gesture or action? You may try, but the story is never as good.

Movement should be spontaneous. It should not be planned but should result from the immediate desire to emphasize or clarify meaning and feeling. No one can give an effective speech until he is able to break down inhibitions and allow his body to work for him instead of against him.

There are two general types of gesture that may be employed, gestures to clarify and gestures to emphasize.

Gestures to clarify. The gesture to clarify is motivated by a desire to supplement oral exposition. It is used to point out definitely a thing referred to in a speech or to suggest size, number, place, or other physical aspects. The following sentences provide motivation for clarifying gestures:

There was the mountain up on one side, and down below was the most beautiful lake I've ever seen.

Mr. Jones stormed into the room, threw down his books, and plopped into a chair.

Take this road straight ahead for about six blocks, then turn right at the traffic light; go three blocks up the hill, and you'll find the house set back from the road right across the street from the old flour mill.

As you speak these sentences you will feel an impulse to point the finger or move the body in the direction indicated by the words. Obey the impulse and make a full, strong gesture out of it.

Gestures to emphasize. The gesture to emphasize strengthens the mood or feeling expressed vocally. The gesture may be little more than the tightening of the fist or an outstretched hand as though pleading for some cause. The words will not suggest the movement, but the speaker's feeling about them will. Patrick Henry would have looked a bit queer if he had remained perfectly still while finishing his famous speech with: "Forbid it, Almighty God! I know not what course others may take; but, as for me, give me liberty, or give me death!" Try speaking the following lines with real sincerity and see if you will not be moved to use some bodily action:

As one who is honored to be in the service of the government I say to the industrial leaders of America, "What a challenge comes to you! You have never failed; you won't fail now."

It is no longer a question of change or continuity. Change is inevitable. It is now a question of revolution by consent, in peace, wrought by intelligent and patriotic men, or the terrible and senseless upheaval of masses with hatred in their hearts.

Here, among all the serenity of God's world, was a hopeless, cringing bit of humanity being slowly eaten away.

It is silly to say that any one kind of gesture should be used to accompany a particular thought. Different speakers will achieve good results with a variety of gestures. The chief thing to remember is that action must be spontaneous and motivated. If a gesture has these two qualities, it will probably be helpful and effective.

Only a few talented speakers are able to command attention without much action. An effective speaker who uses very little movement of any kind usually has many other qualities, mental, vocal, or spiritual, to compensate for lack of movement. For the beginning speaker it is sometimes good advice to use many gestures, even random ones, instead of remaining apathetic. The gesture will at least attract attention to the speaker. Random movements and gestures for the novice will develop into motivated ones as he gains more and more experience in speaking.

As you use movement in conversation, so should you use it in public speaking; you must, of course, enlarge it to enable every member of the audience to see.

Overt and covert action. *Overt* action is any obvious movement. It is what the psychologists call explicit action. Reaching for another helping of potatoes is overt action. But suppose you used the same gesture to accompany the thought, "I dare you to step across this line." Do you think you would cause anyone to hesitate? Nothing in the movement would suggest the earnestness behind it. *Covert* action is the unseen, but readily sensed, muscle tone or tension that should accompany every overt action. Covert action is the product of sincerity. When it is missing, an audience will know the speaker is not sincere.

Suppose you meet another person for the first time. As you exchange greetings and shake hands, you feel that that individual really does not care whether he knows you or not. Why? He smiles and shakes your hand with seeming eagerness, but something is lacking.

You hear a businessman say, "I'll quit my job and go back to selling can openers before I'll see this new policy adopted." He speaks loudly and uses profuse gestures to emphasize his remark, but you instantly know he does not mean what he says. Why?

A school boy reciting in a contest says, "The communistic elements in our government must be smashed!" and he strikes the speaker's stand with his clenched fist. You feel like breaking into laughter. Something is missing. The overt gesture is there, but the face is blank, the body is relaxed, and the arm and fist used in the gesture come down in a studied and planned manner. He is not sincere, and you know it because you fail to sense the covert action.

The unfortunate part about bodily action and gesture is that while it is possible to use planned overt gestures and bodily activity, it is impossible to "put on" covert action. You must be sincerely earnest in your belief and feeling and in your desire to communicate to the audience. Only in this way can all the aspects of effective delivery be integrated and made to satisfy. Mere words will not go very far. One can stay at home and read words at his leisure. Audiences want words plus flesh and blood, when they listen to a speaker. "I love you" is weak oratory on the printed page. "I love you" spoken as an exercise or practice to a broom sounds too flat to be convincing. But "I love you" spoken by a young swain to the familiar receptive audience carries all the persuasive techniques known to man.

Polarization

Audiences are made up of individuals, each with specific and varying interests. In order for the speaker to be effective, he must force every individual into a homogeneous pattern. This is called polarization.

Let us consider an average audience of businessmen gathered in the main ballroom of a convention hotel. They are here to listen to a purchasing agent talk on *The Robinson-Patman Anti-Discrimination Act*. The men in this audience are away from home and away from the office. They have been meeting old friends, talking serious business, getting new ideas, having a few drinks, and, in general, enjoying the whole experience. These things are on their minds as they sit down. Manke and Swanson come in together; they have not seen each other since the "good old days on the road." They have lots to talk about. Brown is trying to work out a way of presenting a new retirement plan to the "boss." Grunwald is cooking up some sort of trick to play on that pretty waitress down in the coffee shop, and Filer has been trying to decide what sort of gift he can take back to his wife. In short, each member of the audience has at least one important idea occupying the center of his attention. These things are uppermost in their minds.

The speaker's problem is to capture these centers of attention for himself and his subject, and then to hold that attention for the duration of his speech. A minister usually includes group singing of a hymn before he begins his sermon, and this mutual participation by members of the congregation induces polarization. When the minister begins his sermon he speaks to an attentive and unified audience, but the public speaker rarely begins with this advantage.   He will have to be alert and effective to preserve attention once gained, for distracting ideas are waiting in the fringes of attention.

Sincerity

Audiences are never won over by insincere speakers; in fact, sincerity might be called the first rule of effective speaking. There must be sincerity in composition and in delivery, and, though there are no rules for achieving sincerity, you can be sure that an audience will recognize the lack of it.   In delivery sincerity is revealed primarily through vocal qualities, directness, and animation.

Directness

From your own experience, you know that you like a speaker who seems to include you in the speech.   You see him look directly at you at times and you somehow have the feeling that what he says is entirely for your benefit.   People are vain creatures and they resent being ignored.

There are two kinds of directness, namely *physical* directness and *mental* directness.   Physical directness implies that the speaker sees every member of his audience; his eyes do not wander to the floor, the ceiling, the walls, his hands, or to one particular section of persons.   Richard C. Borden's rules for directness are: " (1) Look at your listeners, (2) Look at your listeners all the time, (3) Look at all your listeners, and (4) Actually see your listeners." [1]

You have, perhaps, noticed while speaking with another person, that although he was physically direct there seemed to be a "faraway look in his eye."   He was looking at you and seeing you, but his mind was somewhere else.   Mental directness requires that the speaker have a real sense of communication and that his mind work in terms of "Now listen, Murphy" or "I know what you're thinking, but . . ."

If you wish to keep your audience polarized you will create

---

[1] Borden, Richard C., *Public Speaking—As Listeners Like It!*   Harper & Brothers, 1935, Chapter IV.

such a strong feeling of directness that your audience would feel embarrassed to think of anything but what you are saying.

Animation

Animation means more than general bodily action. It implies more than routine movement. The pendulum on grandfather's clock seems to be alive, but as you watch it beat out its monotonous hours you feel that it is using its maximum energy on each swing. It has nothing in reserve. A speaker should use bodily action, facial expression, and gestures that are properly motivated by feeling and content, but he ought also to evidence an "emergency supply" of energy that he is not using. That "emergency supply" serves as an attention-holding device; for as long as there seems to be a possibility of greater things to come an audience will remain undistracted and on the watch.

If speakers would only be sincere, direct, and animated, they would not need to worry too much about the minor errors they commit in delivery. At least they could keep their audiences polarized, and though they might not win prizes as great orators, they would gain respect for themselves and their cause.

QUESTIONS

1. Why do so many people feel unqualified to present a public speech?
2. What is stagefright? What are the causes?
3. How can a speaker overcome stagefright?
4. Why is the delivery of a public speech primarily a problem of adaptation of the skills developed in good conversation and conference speaking?
5. To what extent does the personality of the speaker influence the effectiveness of his delivery? Discuss.
6. To what extent does the voice of the speaker influence the effectiveness of his delivery? Discuss.
7. What is proper breathing in speaking?
8. How may a speaker overcome monotony in the presentation of his speech?
9. What is the value of bodily action in delivery?
10. What rules should be followed in regard to posture and gestures?
11. What is meant by polarizing the audience?
12. What must a speaker do to polarize his audience?

EXERCISES

1. Listen to two speakers and prepare an analysis and a comparison of their delivery. In what ways were they effective? In what ways were they ineffective? Did they command attention? What aspects of voice, bodily action, personality, and so on, tended to distract attention? To what extent did their delivery improve the effectiveness of their speech material?

2. Deliver a two-minute speech to the class using letters of the alphabet instead of words. (A B C D E F G? O S A R. X Y Z, L M N O S, P D Q! etc.) It is not necessary to have a real thought in mind, but assume at various times the manner used in simple exposition, telling a funny story, exclamation, pleading, and so on. Show sincerity, directness, and animation, and make use of changes in rate, force, pitch, and pause.

3. Prepare and deliver a persuasive speech on some controversial subject—racial equality, socialism, communism, government control of business, taxation, and so on. Pick your subject out of a real conviction. Fight for a cause. Instruct the class to be noisy and ill-mannered; allow them to interrupt with questions or to make brief comments during the speech. Your problem is to win the argument, but in order to do so you will have to command respect and attention.

4. Memorize one of the following selections or choose a short passage from one of the sample speeches in Chapter XIII, and deliver it as though it were your own:

The first people who went into the Rocky Mountain section of the United States were gold seekers. But in the great rushes to the Western Eldorados all of the people who traveled in prairie schooners, or on mule back, or who pushed carts across the plains were not miners. The merchant, the shoemaker, the lawyer, the doctor, went along to follow their chosen lines, and perhaps as many as sought for gold came from the farms of the East and the Middle West.

The only trees which they found outside of the pine and its relatives were strings of willows and cottonwoods along the banks of occasional western streams. A short distance from running water the land seemed able to support only the prairie dog, the rattlesnake, the bison, the coyote, the cactus plant and the sage-brush. But there were traditions of irrigated farms on the Rio Grande below El Paso, and sporadic attempts at irrigation had been recorded in various parts of the West. The farmers who followed the booms ploughed the land and diverted water upon it. They proved that the soil of the semi-arid West, when properly irrigated, produced worthwhile crops. The mining states of yesteryear are agricultural sections today.

—From "Federal Encroachment Through Regional Authorities," by Ralph L. Carr, Governor of Colorado.

The American businessman of yesterday conquered a continent, laid the foundations upon which an industrial system of free enterprise was erected, and developed the most efficient productive machine the world has known.

The American businessman of tomorrow, in cooperation with the American worker, must create a society in which men and not things shall be the goal of social endeavor, in which the ideals of democracy shall be translated into economic realities, and in which economic practices shall be judged by ethical criteria.

If by "business as usual", business men mean the continuance of an economic life motivated by self-interest and the desire to acquire, organized upon autocratic principles, and grounded in a philosophy of materialism, it is quite certain that business tomorrow will not be as usual. The business man of tomorrow is called upon to re-base and re-motivate the economic life. In the new order, the impulses to creative action and service will be stronger than the acquisitive impulses. The democratic principle must be extended to the work-life of men, both for purposes of justice and the efficiency that emerges from cooperation. Materialism must give way to a humanitarianism that sees all work in terms of its spiritual significance, as making possible fullness of life for all men everywhere and which regards the industrial order as an instrument to produce that which is necessary or useful or beautiful. This means that engineer, executive, economist and ethical idealist must enter partnership.

One of the fundamental weaknesses of the American industrial order lies in the conflict of interests at its heart. Unfortunately, American business at first sought to block the organization of labor and, later, to sabotage it. Instead of working out an intelligent cooperation between organized workers and organized employers, the refusal to recognize the right of the worker to organize led to conflict. The result was that labor, forced to fight for the right to organize, developed leaders qualified to do battle.

—From "The Business Man of Tomorrow,"
by Bishop B. Bromley Oxnam.

What we need today more than anything else in our American life is education for freedom. We need to know what freedom is and what it is not. We need to know the extent to which it depends on law and the extent to which it depends upon sound public opinion. We need to know the four foundation walls on which representative democratic government and liberty alike must be erected. Let me enumerate them, and as I do will you ask yourselves how many people in the United States understand these four foundation walls of democratic government and liberty as they should? The first is the relation of our nation to other nations. It involves not only military problems of national defense but diplomatic and commercial relations the world over. The second is the maintenance of peace and order within our country. This involves the work of the militia and of the police and of our criminal and civil courts. Every kind of state must protect itself from external dangers and must maintain internal peace and order if it is to survive, but a democracy to survive and maintain freedom must do more. Accordingly, our third foundation wall is honest elections. The sanctity of the ballot is essential to the continued existence of liberty. The fourth foundation wall in a democracy is popular education. An illiterate electorate will sound the death knell of liberty. On these four foundation walls of sound international relations, of domestic peace and order, of honest elections, and of adequate popular education the structure of freedom must be built. Of late years we have tended to ignore these fundamental considerations in our interest in the newer functions of government. These newer functions all center around two problems: What is the state to do for the citizen and where will it get the money to do it? These problems are important, but with all deference I submit that they are subordinate to the others if freedom as we have known it is to survive.

—From "American Freedoms,"
by Arthur T. Vanderbilt.

And then for the first time, as the richest nation in the world, with the highest standard of living that ever had been accomplished in the universe, we moved back into the Old World. For the first time we turned our backs on our own march of liberty and moved back into the bitternesses of the century-old struggles of Europe. I understand that it was a challenge. They said it was a war to make the world safe for our kind of understanding; it was a war to end all war. That seemed worthy of America's contribution. America had always contributed before. Out of God's blessing we had reached back into the Old World in its every difficulty; whether it be flood or famine, earthquake or war, wherever distressed people sent up their cry to a God-fearing people for help, America had extended her hand. But now we were asked to extend more—our blood, our force, our prayers. And we did. And we turned to with everything we had, believing, as the chaplain told me as a common soldier, that God was on our side. The German soldier of that day had printed on his belt, "Gott mitt uns," and his chaplain told him the same thing. But he came from a different government; he came from a government of centralized power with an individual with lust for power and the arrogance that goes with power—and it always will go with power, whether it is centralized in Germany, Italy, France, or America. The lust for power causes men to die. We felt that we were wiping it out. And when the Armistice was signed we were glad, for our President spoke that day and said, "All that America has fought for has been accomplished." And the bells rang, the whistles blew, and old men and little children rejoiced in the streets.

—From "America,"
by C. Wayland Brooks, Senator from Illinois.

SELECTED READINGS

Barnes, Harry G., *Speech Handbook,* Prentice-Hall, Inc., New York, 1941.

Borden, Richard C., *Public Speaking—As Listeners Like It!* Harper and Brothers, New York, 1935. Read Chapter IV.

O'Neill, James M., *Foundations of Speech,* Prentice-Hall, Inc., New York, 1941.

Sandford, W. P., and Yeager, W. H., *Practical Business Speaking,* McGraw-Hill Book Company, New York, 1937. Read Chapter VII.

Sarett, Lew, and Foster, William Trufant, *Basic Principles of Speech,* Houghton Mifflin Company, New York, 1936. Read Chapters IV, V, VI, and VII.

Tucker, Marion S., *Public Speaking for Technical Men,* McGraw-Hill Book Company, New York, 1939. Read Chapters V, XIII, and XIV.

Types of Business and Professional Public Speeches

I. EXPOSITORY TYPES
    Explanation and instruction
        Suggested titles for speeches of explanation and instruction
        Sample instructional speech
    Goodwill
        Suggested titles for goodwill speeches
        Sample goodwill speech
    Oral report
        Suggested titles for oral reports
        Sample oral report
II. PERSUASIVE TYPES
    Question of policy
        Suggested titles for policy-determining speeches
        Sample policy-confirming speech
    Promotional
        Suggested titles for promotional speeches
        Sample promotional speech
    Inspirational
        Suggested titles for inspirational speeches
        Sample inspirational speech

Types of Business and Professional Public Speeches

Expository Types

Explanation and instruction

SPEECHES OF explanation and instruction demand the most careful attention to the rules of exposition. The test for such speeches is their clarity. The material and organization of the public expository speech follows the same pattern as outlined for the expositional conference.

In general, the only distinction between instruction and explanation is that the speech of instruction is given in answer to the question "How?", while the explanatory speech is in answer to "What?"

SUGGESTED TITLES FOR SPEECHES OF EXPLANATION AND INSTRUCTION

Instructional

1. How to take care of an automobile
2. How to set up an accounting system
3. How to grow hybrid corn
4. How to manufacture cloth from wool
5. How to draw up a real estate contract
6. How to perform the operations in electric wiring
7. How to play football
8. How to keep a library card catalogue
9. How to set up space in a newspaper
10. How to extract a tooth

Explanatory

1. What is hybrid corn?
2. What is a coulee?
3. What is banking?
4. What is the difference between bookkeeping and accounting?
5. What is badminton?

6. What is Poole's Index?
7. What is 300,000 pounds per square inch?
8. What instruments are used in the "Nutcracker Suite?"
9. What is retail marketing?
10. What is a light year?

Sample Instructional Speech

The following instructional speech was given by Edwin A. Boss at the 33rd annual convention of the Southern Hotel Association, June, 1941.

How to Modernize and Manage a Hotel [1]

I have come a long ways to talk to you today but I know that this fact alone does not give me any reason for talking a long time, to the extent that I become tiresome.   I am mindful of the advice that the Deacon of the Church gave the new Minister, when after giving him numerous instructions, said to him, "Now, Parson, about your preaching—you can talk as long as you please but remember after twenty minutes go by, you might as well quit and save your breath, as after that time, there won't be anyone paying any attention to what you are saying anyway."

In trying to assemble something worth-while to say to you, I have decided that perhaps if I say in my own words. many of the things I said at the Toledo Convention, even though it be repetition, it might be in keeping and perhaps helpful to a few of you.

Having hotels, many of which are small, in fact some of them with only fifty rooms, I am often asked, "Why did you decide to buy small hotels?"

Well, when you start out in business for yourself on your 25th birthday with $800 to your name, which you managed to save by frugal living and denial, between leaving high school and that age, you just don't buy big hotels for $800—or do you?

How He Started

The purchase price of that first 38-room hotel was $5,000 in cash.   The bank furnished the difference of $4,200 on my promissory note.

I believe that as Steward on a dining car—that my showing personal interest instead of a mechanical interest in this banker, as well as in other guests, which I know did not go unnoticed by him, proved to be the open sesame or the opportunity that knocked to make it possible to borrow the money that purchased that first hotel.

So that was the start.   Repaying the loan in a little over a year put me in a position to ask for a renewal, when I bought a nearby county seat hotel of 50 rooms for $10,000.

I was shortly afterwards called to the Army as the World War was on, so I sold one hotel and kept the other.   Upon returning, after fourteen months'

---

[1] Reprinted by special permission of the American Hotel Association.   The speech as reprinted here is not complete.

service, it has been another hotel every now and then as it was possible to buy them.

That is enough to give you an idea of the step by step progress that has taken me 25 years to acquire 21 hotels.

As most of these hotels are between 50 and 100 rooms, it is mainly to operators of hotels of this size that I am directing my remarks. I am certainly not egotist enough even to believe I could say anything of interest to operators and managers of large hotels.

The Winning of a Strike

If asked what I would be most proud of in those 25 years, I would tell you it was my coming out victorious in a 3-week labor strike in Des Moines which occurred at the time they were happening to all hotels over the country and this one had the usual momentum back of it—with pickets walking in front and all deliveries stopped. After some negotiating and claims made, an arrangement was agreed to by both parties that we would leave the result to a secret vote of our employes as to whether I should sign a Union contract or not. The result was that 71 employes voted that I should not sign and only two voted that I should.

You say that was easy as my organization was with me, and I say that is the reason for my pride in the victory. All of our organizations have been with us once; the trick is not to lose them. Of course, your group meetings help, especially if you are there yourself and do not leave it to Elmer. Also, I stress the importance of daily greetings to employes, both on the street and within my hotel with a friendliness that is unmistakable, as that is helpful too.

I have worked for others long enough to know that not all managers and owners have that human understanding.

Courtesy to Employes

Surely it is worth a lot to you for new employes to hear from old employes just what kind of a fellow you are and they do ask and it does help if they are able to say you are a pretty fine fellow to work for. You know by being pleasant and courteous to employes we encourage them to be pleasant and courteous to our guests.

Remember they evaluate us as we evaluate them. All of this reminds me of a great speech I once heard, and since labor worries and guest satisfaction are such a large part of our day's work, I believe it is worth referring to now. The subject matter was, "If I were to resign could I be re-elected?" Probably the speaker would have made this apply to hotels by asking: "Would the landlord of the hotel you operate feel relieved if you were to sell out and move on, or, would he want you to stay and continue to operate his hotel?" That is, if you left, would he want you back?

Would your Board of Directors be glad if you resigned as manager of their hotel and relieved them of telling you the bad news, or would they regret your leaving and insist that you stay?

Would your guests feel gratified if you were to resign as manager or would they want you to be re-elected—that is to stay?

Would your own employes want you re-elected? As a manager, working with other local hotel managers in your city, would they think enough of you to want you to stay and continue to be one of them? If you left, would they be glad if you returned, to be re-elected as we may put it?

Ownership Is Desirable

But to get back to the hotels, I have title to ten hotel buildings, the rest are on lease. We struggled through the depression without a calamity but owning several of the hotel buildings helped us greatly to do this. I say to you, don't be afraid to buy hotel buildings. I found that the rent I was paying three different widows, owning three different properties, was the sole support and sole remaining asset of what were once good sized estates, the rest having been liquidated and lost. But the hotel buildings were still, month by month, the old age security check for them.

So, I decided, since I am going to be an old man some day, and might even leave a widow, that based on this actual experience, to which I was a party, leaving a hotel building would be one of the best assets I could leave my estate. Some hotel men are so unthinking they boast—"I wouldn't own a hotel building." Well you are probably buying one for someone else with your monthly rent check and while the landlord is loafing in Florida, you are putting in long hours working for him.

Some Too Large to Buy

Some buildings, though, are too large an investment to buy. If you can't ever really own it, don't contract to buy it. I often think of the Stevens hotel in Chicago. If Mr. Binns, its manager, was offered his hotel, with nothing down, and at ⅓ its original cost, it would be about $7,000,000. Even as young as he is, he probably could never live long enough to own it as the highly profitable years, intermixed with the bad years, the increasing competition and the big city obsolescence, to say nothing of his own advancing age, while he is going on with the struggle, would, I believe, make it impossible to ever own it. So score one for the small hotel which one can really own and leave to his estate.

Every hotel man here has been confronted with the making of an important decision in the early years of his life. Some have made the decision of going into business for themselves in a small hotel and have continued to stay in business for themselves, steadily improving their position and adding a hotel now and then, or, selling out and buying a larger one. Nothing unusual about that. Scores of hotel men have done it. But some of you have chosen to continue as a hotel manager, and perhaps because you have always worked in big hotels and big cities, you would give no consideration to buying a small but leading hotel in a small city.

You have by training and circumstances, which perhaps were uncontrollable, built yourself up to where operating a small hotel would look like a let-down to both your pride and your ability.

Young Men Must Choose

Our sons, our Cornell and Michigan graduates, are going to be face to face with this important decision that you have already made. Whether to start in a small way with a personal ownership or to start off with a bang as a big city Assistant Manager or Manager? Each course is a hazardous one, each has its own reward.

Will this youngster, after advancing age, regret some day the circumstances that lured him to marble walls, glamorous lights, luxurious surroundings that seemed to offer more, and especially the chance to live well and to meet important people?

Or, will he some day wish—that he had his own leading hotel in a small city? Will he wish for more independence and security, to call his working time and leisure time pretty much his own? Will he wish that he was an important citizen in a small city instead of a comparatively unimportant citizen in a large city?

Or, will he do as so many others have done; start in business for himself, go stale—forget to work without a master over him and finally—be neither an owner nor a desirable manager?

But you are the men who made your decisions years ago. You are now either highly successful hotel owners or highly successful hotel managers, and to you I will relate my plans that I intend to follow, so that I may continue to make additional progress in the small hotel field for many years to come.

Know Food

First, I am going to continue to study and learn more about food. Too many hotel men in smaller hotels know too little, and pay too little attention to food. As a chain operator, who has to depend on managers, I am handicapped by the fact that out of every twenty applicants, one or two will have any worthwhile food experience.

Of course, you men being successful hotel operators, do know food, and yet, traveling from one of your hotels to another, I'll gamble I would find a wide variation in food, both in quality and service and in the very food room itself, not only in design but in working arrangement.

My food criticism of the smaller hotels is this: Food preparation is not given enough personal attention by the manager or owner.

If you happen to have a good chef you look great—like a big town operator. If you have a very mediocre chef, or a poor average chef, too often you look like a mediocre manager. How often is a hotel manager only as good as his chef, as far as his food department is concerned?

Think that statement over. If you had a few inexperienced managers working for you, you would concur in the proof of that statement.

Or, if you see yourself as others see you, you would know your food department needs more intelligent application.

While trying to find a good chef, one must supply his food department with that necessary additional personal attention and headwork, to keep the quality so close to par that the lapse will be unnoticed by the guests. They say it takes a heap of living to make a home. Well, it also takes a heap of attention to operate a successful food department as it should be operated.

I don't know but what you do have to be a chain operator to realize how hard it is to get a hotel manager to give proper attention to his food department, and when he won't do it working for someone, naturally he will also be lax about it when he goes into business for himself.

What a Manager Should Do

I am continually encouraging each manager to—*spend more time in his food department*—promising him that the very minute he begins to go into his coffee shop, help seat the guests, help give menus, help fill water glasses and butter plates, and, if he will, on particular orders go into the kitchen to be sure that the food leaves in proper order, instead of waiting until it is served in the dining room, and then apologizing for it if something is wrong, as 11 out of 12 hotel men will wait and do; that as a manager, he will immediately be marked for a raise of several thousands of dollars a year, even in our organization.

I say this because that kind of a manager in a hotel of 125 rooms or less cannot be stopped from being a success.

The public will acclaim him one because he is such a rare bird that the public will react favorably. He will be noticed and appraised by the public as an exceptional owner or manager.

If you think that is an ordinary qualification, check up on yourself, check up on your manager and see if either of you work that way. You ask why is that so important, that the head waiter can do that? But here is how the owner or manager elevates himself far above the head waiter: a manager or owner works that way only *when he has an intense interest and enthusiasm and is determined to make his hotel go places,* an enthusiasm that will reflect itself in every department and every employe.

He will read, he will study, he will be the man who will put your menu in his pocket when he comes to your restaurant and will compare it with his. No matter where he eats, or what convention he goes to, he will come back to his own food department with some worthwhile suggestions to his chef. Haven't you seen good chefs become just ordinary chefs, working for some hotel men?

Haven't you seen some average chefs become good chefs, working under a good food man—one that knows how?

Read the Hotel Magazines

You owners and managers read more hotel magazines. You get around the country and see things, while the chef has his face stuck over the range, and you should tear out or noticeably mark these items or pages in hotel trade papers that pertain to food, or grab the phone, if otherwise too busy, and tell the chef in your own words of a dish or salad you were served last night, and ask him to try it right away, while the appearance is still fresh in your memory.

I think marking items for him is a better coaching method to improve your chef than simply to see that the chef is furnished with trade papers, which may or may not be read for the sake of improvement.

It may be presumptuous of me to talk to you that way, yet about two months ago I ate the poorest piece of apple pie in one of the leading Chicago hotels that I ever hope to eat. In fact, I have often thought the bigger the hotel, the poorer the apple pie, and often order it at the end of the meal because usually I am feeling ashamed of my own ability as a food man when it is dessert time, so order a piece of apple pie to counteract my diminishing faith in myself.

Double Size of Pudding Servings

While talking of dessert items, returning from last year's Hotel Association convention in Seattle, I spent two hours with the chef of the Davenport hotel while in Spokane. I was surprised to find the chef's great pride was his puddings, and the large number he sold, mainly, I believe, because of the extra large portions he served for an order. Since coming home, we have doubled and tripled the size of servings of puddings, as I saw at once that we, like most hotels, were serving a large piece of pie but only a couple of tablespoons of a pudding. The guest value-balance hasn't been there.

You know, my speaking of that apple pie is confidential, because that manager would never hear it from me direct, and that is what is wrong with so many food departments. Isn't it a fact that the manager doesn't get to know just how poor his food is, because no matter how cold and unseasoned the vegetable, how poorly prepared or tasteless the entree, nor how much crabbing you have been doing about everything, when he comes around and asks you, "How's the food?" you always say, "Fine, it's just grand, everything okay"? So, no complaints are not any positive indication that you are a good food man. It is that repeat business, that doing a little more business every year, that tells the story, as a guest too often doesn't complain; he just doesn't come back.

Poor Breakfast Menus

Most hotels of 125 rooms or less have poor breakfast menus. Some large hotels too. We never seem to give them anything but stepchild attention. It is amazing that there can be so many poor breakfast menus. Look at your own when you get back home. Perhaps it still has some fruits on it, like sliced oranges, for example that have been carried over from one menu to the other for years, and unless these states are different from Iowa, you don't serve an order of sliced oranges more than once every six months.

Too often club breakfasts are simply copies from one print job to another or else they are the collection put out by a cereal house that gives you some free menus for putting cereal on each club breakfast.

Do you and your chef realize that you usually have only two breakfast fruits to prepare? For instance—right now, it would be rhubarb and prunes in every state. Nature has taken care of the rest for you so that they don't have to be prepared. So, surely, having only two to be prepared, they can be correctly prepared, but how often is this accomplished?

Luncheon Menus

On luncheon menus I think there are too many soup to dessert inclusive luncheons. No doubt it's all right to feature a complete luncheon but if that is all you have, it isn't a good menu in my opinion.

I think you should have some specials for the men who don't care about soup or dessert, and, these specials should be priced less the price of soup and dessert and not priced as much as the regular luncheons, as so often the specials are priced so that in self-defense, the guest finally says, "Oh Hell! I might as well eat the full luncheon, they both cost the same" and then afterwards he complains of feeling stuffed and wishes he hadn't eaten so much.

Dinner menus are usually better set up than the other menus but quality often lags on this meal, as some of the food may be left over from lunch and steam-tabled out or left out until cold and reheated.

In Between Menus

The between-meal menus and night menus are another stepchild in most hotels, objects of too little study and attention. Pretend you are a guest and look yours over the next time you are eating in your coffee shop. Just personally, I think it should list only a few selective, well chosen dishes, set out in large, bold type. I am continually pounding away to our managers that we have so many food items that are 90% to 100% saleable, and that we have so many others, 75, 60 and 50% saleable. Why not prepare the 90% to 100% items as far as you can? Why do you have so many 40, 50 and 60% items on your menu?

The Haberdasher certainly doesn't try to fill his store with 50% saleable items. You say you must have them for variety's sake, and I answer, the millionaires that have been made, and are being made today, in the food business, are the ones that sold and still sell only a few items 100% saleable, and 100% well prepared.

Remodel Your Eating Rooms

I hope that every small city hotel man, if he has not already done so, will remodel his eating rooms. Get them up to date. This food business can be greatly increased—it is a proven fact.

It seems that there is becoming year after year a more definite market for a well-planned food room. You say there is too much competition now in your town. Well, who is the chief competitor in this food business? I will tell you; it is the home. Why? Because the home is now the source of the largest amount of present and future tangible food business that we have. Once again, why? Because it is the trend of the time for industries to take over many of the services formerly performed in the home.

For instance—who bakes their own bread? Who does their own sewing —even things they can do cheaper? Laundry—more and more is going to commercial laundries.

Here are the four other good reasons why we should have a better eating room.

1. Families are getting smaller, even our homes are built with less space being allotted to dining room and kitchen.

2. More women are in industry and even after marriage they stay in industry. They have increased earnings, shorter working hours, consequently more time to spend over a meal in a restaurant.

3. Automobiles tend to increase the sale of food. People are out riding and do not want to prepare a meal so they eat in the restaurant.

4. The fourth is the reason that there are so few good servants to be had today and they are harder to secure each year, so families naturally turn to the restaurant rather than struggle with the problem.

Modernization

Now, I want to talk on something I know I have got to keep doing in order to keep progressing, and that is to keep *Modernizing*.

You know the more one analyzes the subject of modernization, and what it really is, the quicker he comes to the conclusion that the biggest factor is *Buying:* what to buy, and—Is the Cost Worth It? As, after all the *objective of modernization is Profit.* Without it why spend the time and money?

Yet, many of us have learned that when we thought the cost too high; when we thought, instead of going ahead with a modernizing program today that it could just as well be delayed a couple of years, that we paid for that passive attitude, and delay in lost profit, just as much as if we had gone ahead and spent the money, as we lost the equivalent in possible profit. We lost because we were not making a profit when our competitor was; our guestroom average was not getting any higher, and his was; people com plained more about prices, and ate less in our Coffee Shop; they had one drink in our bars, and then rushed away, instead of lounging around and spending more money.

So, many times when you say you can't afford to pay for modernization, you are going to pay for it whether you modernize or not. The guest will see to that, whether he is a room customer, a food customer, or a bar customer.

It is an age-old axiom, still working, that you cannot stand still. You either go forward or backward with the times, with your hotel, and with your bank account.

For fear you will hesitate to accept my word for it, that Buying is the biggest factor in Modernization, I will explain further what I mean.

It is self-evident that as quickly as you decide to modernize, you start considering *buying something,* and the very minute you start buying, you start making some mistakes. In the first place, if you start from scratch and buy a hotel, and let's concede that you make a good buy financially, so far as profit, lease, etc., are concerned, it is still possible you bought other mistakes when you bought this hotel. Just plenty of them, and, while you are looking at me now, I'm telling you that sometimes I think I have bought every mistake in the world. Every hotel I have bought has been filled with mistakes. Some, architects made.

Architects' mistakes have made it much tougher for many of us in the operation of our hotels. They have added thousands of dollars to the operation costs of Southern hotels alone, to say nothing of the inconvenience and worry that they have caused us, as well as the lack of good atmosphere in our lobbies and public rooms, which they have left us to try to overcome.

Employ an Architect

Yet, your first step in Modernization is employing an Architect. Try to do without him, and you will lose every time. I have almost reached the point where I would not even buy window screens without consulting an Architect. I have found it pays big dividends; many times he has saved much of the Modernization cost in the ideas he has given me, but the secret is in *having the right Architect.* Just any Architect will not do. Get one who understands hotel problems. Notice the write-ups on Chicago hotels, and you will notice that usually the same architectural firms lay out the public rooms, the night rooms, etc.

In Des Moines, two architects have done most all the work. I mention this because I think any small hotel man is a chump if he tries to do his own layout and architectural work, and he is still a bigger chump if he does not employ an architect who knows hotel layouts, and there is only a handful of them in this section of the country that I would have any confidence in for hotel remodeling.

Perhaps I am emphasizing this more than some of you think is necessary, but if I have anything in this paper today worthwhile to you, it is to tell you to *quit being your own architects,* and I know! I've tried to be my own, and I've made some horrible mistakes, and so will you and it is because I want to see the small hotel have more of the respect of its guests and its local community that I am so earnestly pleading for you to take your problems to a good hotel architect as you will save money, regardless of his fee; and you will definitely have made progress toward being a better hotel man.

Knowing How to Buy

And now, for the buying of materials and supplies, of all kinds, required for modernizing. You may hesitate again to believe me when I say that only one salesman out of five from whom you buy or have ever bought anything from, is qualified to sell you. Think that over! I am bitter when I think that I have bought wrong, item after item, because I followed the salesman's advice. They do not know, and if you don't know, your manager doesn't know, and your wife doesn't know, then you are just out of luck, and 80% of the time that is what happens and that is why I have bought some horrible mistakes myself in many individual items, and, take my word for it, when I bought these 21 hotels I bought plenty of mistakes with them—mistakes that my predecessor made, and I emphasize again that he made 80% of them because he followed the advice of some salesman who did not understand his problems, or else just didn't care what happened, so long as he got his sales commission.

So again I repeat, a good job of Modernization, in a small hotel, depends upon your ability to buy intelligently. Most of the time the salesman is honest with you, but he just doesn't know, and, unlike the doctor who has buried his mistakes, you will still have to live and worry day after day with the salesman's mistakes.

Buying Too Cheaply

Again, most of us buy too cheaply. Then we buy again to correct that mistake, so we spend more money than we would have if we had bought quality in the first place for a small amount more.

For example, I have thrown away hundreds of bed-springs, where, if the hotel man before me had spent four or five dollars more, they would have been just as good today. And think of the additional comfort the guests would have had all these years, but, no, the salesman probably decided he could sell the Old-way Sagless for $5, but would lose the sale if he would try to sell him the $9 coil of a few years ago, so the Old-way Sagless was bought, or a very poor-cheap, coil spring, and now, it goes on the junk pile.

Room Redecoration

And when you redecorate a room, of course, you must choose between wall paper or paint. Hair oil is a deadly enemy today of wall paper, even though we have costly, so-called washable, wall papers that do not seem to be able to resist hair oil, and which has increased our decorating expenses tremendously.

In Des Moines, we have canvassed and painted our rooms, or else used only Imported Salubra papers. Some managers say, with much justification, that often employes are more destructive of the guest rooms wall papers than the guests. I often see the evidence of this in the dustcloth line where the maid has wiped the desk and where she has wiped the top of the dresser.

Also, their not thinking to turn off radiation quickly soils the wall covering, whatever it may be. Be sure you take the old telephone off the wall and replace it with a new cradle desk phone, and it might be well to move down that old bottle opener, as most openers have been installed as high as your head, so that the ginger ale will fall all the way down the wall, when an opener should be only about thirty inches high, like the bar-tender wants it at the bar.

Remodeling Bathrooms

Progress in plumbing is such that I am sure a lot of money will have to be spent in taking out the old leg bathtubs, if you still have them. We are doing it, as it will cost us money in lost business if we do not, perhaps just as much as it will cost us to change them over now. Many shower-heads are entirely too high and must be lowered if you expect the showers to be used. Electric razor outlets have to be supplied, but the modern, overmirror light fixtures take care of that cheaply enough.

Speaking of imitation tiles for your bathrooms, I prefer the metal tile called "Duratile." I have used rubber, linowall, veostile and marsh tile made in Ohio, but prefer the Duratile to the others.

Guest Rooms

The room numbers must be modernized so guests can read them. Many country hotels are lax in this detail. The room numbers placed on the inside of doors are also a great guest convenience and cost very little. The inside chain and bolt is rapidly becoming a necessity to give privacy, and perhaps a little more ventilation. The public is insisting upon better lighting in the rooms, and we must provide it. Chrome refinishing is going to make hotels look brighter; toilet hinges that look unsanitary and tarnished should be rechromed during your dull season. Worn-looking faucets can also be made to look like new, as Chrome is a real boon to hotel keepers.

The cuspidors are either out, or on their way out rapidly, and we small hotel keepers should follow suit and leave them out of the guest rooms.

Air Cooling

Fans must be provided for summer, and over the long pull, I think the ceiling fans are the cheapest to buy. The new pedestal fans are also becoming a popular number, and have the advantage of being portable. Insulation of the attic space is also a means adopted by many hotels in keeping summer heat out, and it is very effective. It will also save money on the winter fuel bill.

Ask ten women what they consider the nicest little extra convenience a hotel room can have, and nine out of ten will say—a wash cloth. Are you supplying one? The Kleenex holder is not a necessary item but an appreciated adjunct to the bathroom, in the higher priced rooms. Have you felt of your pillows lately?

Can you lift one without straining the muscles in your right arm? This is not an exaggeration in some hotels—we know—we have had them.

I have felt some sand bags in other hotels too.

In the fall, we order several hundred pounds of ungraded down, which we can buy only at Thanksgiving time from poultry houses, as that is the big goose picking season. They make a very soft pillow, softer I think than a fifty percent white goose feathers and a 50 percent down, which is the usual stock in trade pillow. These three pound pillows cost us $3.50 a pair made up, but are worth every cent of it in guest satisfaction.

Get the Clerks Upstairs

And here is one that hits you right in the mid-section. President Moore told the Greeters at their recent National Greeters convention at Houston —"Hotel business is the only place where the customer buys something without seeing it, and where the room clerk, all too often, has never seen it either."

We can't do anything about the first part of his statement, but shame on us for the last part of this statement and more shame on us if we don't go home and do something about getting our clerks upstairs to thoroughly inspect a certain number of rooms daily, or weekly, so that they are familiar with the rooms they are trying to sell.

Accounting

I would be lax indeed if I did not say something about modernizing your accounting methods. I am sure that today the guest likes the registration card better, and we should be modern enough to give it to him, and to throw away the out-moded register sheet. The transcript sheet should be used to make your clerks fitted to handle a better job, and to make you a better hotel man.

Inventories

If no food-cost control system is used, then I am sure a food-inventory taken every two weeks, to my knowledge, is the next best way to handle it.

You should be interested enough in your hotel to take a food inventory on the 15th, and the last day of the month. It will probably pay big dividends for you to do this, even though you do your own buying and are around the Coffee Shop much of the time, as many of you will use this as an argument, or an excuse, for not doing so.

A bar-room inventory cannot wait for two weeks. We all know that money disappears quicker in a bar than in any other department, because it just doesn't seem to be considered stealing, to "knock down" in a bar.

The same employe, who would hurry to you if he found a $5 bill on the floor, would not let his conscience bother him, if he "knocked down" this amount in the liquor room. So, we believe, a bar inventory should be taken, and the percentage of cost figured, at least every week. Cigars and cigarettes should be inventoried also, once a month at least, and even though you do this, you will be surprised to find, you are usually short from $3 to $10 a month, so, if you never take an inventory, you can gamble on it—you are short at least two or three times that amount each month, regardless of your good opinion of the ones handling the cigar and cigarette cash.

I know the individual, small-hotel owner, hates to make out his monthly hotel report or financial statement, and too often he takes the course of least resistance, and simply figures out that what he has left over, after all his bills are paid, is profit. It may be, but there is surely a more modern way of doing it.

How to Compete

In conclusion, let me say that your best chance today to win in the race against tourist camps is that you have good food, priced right and served right, that you have good rooms that are a full step ahead, and not a step behind a tourist motel in comfort, convenience and cleanliness.

You must have better personnel, more of pleasing personnel and less tip-conscious personnel. You must use better judgment in pricing your rooms to families, to make your guests leave in a happy frame of mind. In traveling, that is what you would want. That is all any, able-to-pay traveler wants.

We are blessed with many splendid hotel trade papers. Their progressiveness has made us progressive. We, who have been successful, have become so because we read them and keep up with the modern tempo they set for us, and just as long as we continue to read and study and observe, just so long will we continue to go forward, leaving the world a little better than we found it.

Goodwill

Increased competition and changing economic conditions have necessitated various changes in the methods of conducting successful business. One of the most significant changes is found in the increased activities of public relations and public service departments. If a company or organization is to continue efficient operation, it is often forced to render the public some free service or information. Nearly every large organization maintains an extensive library of informational pamphlets which may be obtained simply by asking for them. The petroleum industry offers travel information and maps; some organizations produce traveling exhibits. Many other services are rendered, all in the name of goodwill.

The small businessman, of course, is not able to provide this type of expensive service to his customers. He has, however, a very effective method at his disposal that he can use on many occasions and in innumerable ways. The goodwill speech is the small businessman's device for rendering a public service. Its effectiveness is proved by the fact that the larger organizations employ high-salaried speakers for this very purpose.

Anyone engaged in business or professional activities is familiar with the many demands made upon him for speeches at the usual public gatherings or civic luncheon clubs. To many this is a distasteful duty, but, actually, it is a rare opportunity for creating goodwill. Alert businessmen will welcome all such chances to speak.

The goodwill speech is essentially a type of exposition. Its purpose is to inform or clarify. But it is double-edged. If you give a dollar bill to the newsboy on the corner, you will have his goodwill. If you help a motorist by towing his car to a garage, you may earn a life-long friend. If you are able to give valuable information to your neighbor that may save him considerable unnecessary expense, he will probably wish to reciprocate, or at least he will be more tolerant of ashes that blow across his back porch from your ash heap. The businessman who gives interesting or valuable information in a luncheon speech may gain many new friends and customers and thus create goodwill for himself and his business.

Nearly everyone is a specialist or expert in some particular field, and the goodwill speaker should talk as an expert. His speech must present facts and information in an interesting manner. He must be particularly careful to speak within the realm of the experience of his audience. One new idea presented and clarified by the use of a dozen familiar examples is better than a dozen new ideas half-way explained. In a goodwill speech the speaker may take greater liberty with the use of interest material. Picturesque exposition, humorous examples, and illustrations may all be used in greater quantity than is advisable in other types of exposition, for if the speaker proves to be dull and ineffective his chances of creating goodwill are lost.

The ABLE MAN qualities of the speaker will again be recognized as an essential part of the speech. The most valuable information or service given by one who is unattractive in personality is never appreciated as much as when it is given with a "smile." Individual qualities are so important that goodwill for an organization is often created simply because we know a representative or an employee and like him.

Suggested Titles for Goodwill Speeches

1. Accountant—The Accountant and Your Profit
2. Minister—The Church in a Troubled World
3. Engineer—Defense Construction
4. Artist—Design in the Home
5. Farmer—The Farm Is Modernized
6. Lawyer—Income Tax Reports
7. Journalist—Yellow Sheets

Sample Goodwill Speech

The following goodwill speech was presented by Paul G. Hoffman, President of The Studebaker Corporation, to the National Farm Institute held at Des Moines, February, 1939. Notice that the content is essentially expository and abounds in interesting factual material. No attempt is made to sell or persuade.

Prices of Things Which Farmers Buy, Including So-Called Management of Prices by Industry [2]

I felt signally honored when Mr. Waymack invited me to speak at the National Farm Institute. I accepted with alacrity—too much alacrity, in fact, because I paid too little attention to the subject assigned to me. If I had given it the serious attention it deserved, I would have been compelled to decline in favor of someone better qualified than myself. When it comes to the prices of things which farmers buy, I can speak with knowledge only of automobile prices. When it comes to the so-called management of prices by industry, I plead complete ignorance. There has been no management of prices in the automobile field. I do feel that I have a pretty clear picture of what has happened to prices in the automobile industry, and why it has happened, because I have devoted my whole business life to selling, manufacturing and pricing motor vehicles. The only way open to me to discuss the subject assigned is to tell that story and leave you to make such general application of the ideas as you think justified. I recognize that agriculture faces many difficult problems peculiar to it and quite different from those confronting industry. Perhaps one contribution we can make is to insure more stable markets by the promotion of employ-

---

[2] Reprinted by special permission of the author.

ment at good wages and to institute industrial policies which will assure you the benefit of the lowest price possible on things you have to buy.

It is fair to say, I believe, that the automobile industry is the perfect example of the impact resulting from the completely free interplay of intensely competitive forces on those who make and sell the product. There has been a rather free interchange of patents among manufacturers but there have been no agreements aimed at softening or civilizing the force of competition. In the field of distribution, the NRA was operative for a short time, but aside from that it has been a free-for-all battle. The overall picture has been one of unfettered competition, with no attempt at price management from within the industry and no control or protection from government.

The effect of this highly competitive situation on manufacturers is revealed by the fatality figures. Of the more than 1,500 companies that have built cars at one time or another, only about 30 different name-plates remain today. There are no reliable figures available as to mortality among dealers but here again a high percentage have fallen by the wayside. It is a rather sad picture for those who did not make the grade, but those who did have been amply rewarded. Furthermore, it is quite typical of the whole system of free enterprise. Every man who invested a dollar in either manufacturing or selling motor cars did it of his own free will. It was up to him to appraise the risks and decide for himself whether he wished to make the investment.

The more important questions are: What has this fierce competition within the industry done for you, the customers? What have its effects been on labor? On these answers we should, in my opinion, base our verdict as to whether we should attempt to enlarge the area of our economy in which free competition prevails or should go in the opposite direction and substitute governmental controls of one kind or another.

Everyone in this audience is, of course, well aware of the fact that the quality of motor cars has steadily improved through the years and that the price of cars has just as steadily declined. But it has been a gradual process and perhaps you have forgotten the kind of cars we had thirty years ago. It is vivid in my mind because my father purchased our first family car in February of 1908. It was a 1905 Pope-Toledo, for which he paid approximately $1,500. Its price as a new car was about $3,000. We lived in a suburb fifteen miles west of Chicago. He purchased the car in Chicago but it couldn't be delivered until April because the roads were impassable.

During the winter months we had been planning for our first long trip which had as its destination Sycamore, Illinois, where my cousin, Henry Parke, who is quite well known in farm circles, resided. We had to wait for one week of sunshine to dry out the roads before starting our adventurous journey. As a consequence we got under way one Saturday morning about the middle of May. This delay gave us time to make proper preparations. We equipped the car with two extra casings, six extra inner tubes, and sufficient tools and equipment to outfit a small machine shop. Incidentally, those extra tires cost $75 each and the tubes were about $12 apiece, if I recall correctly.

I was the chauffeur, and my father, mother, grandfather and aunt were the passengers. Nothing much happened until we got to St. Charles, except two punctures. On the west bank of the St. Charles River, going up the hill I tried to shift from third to second. It was a difficult shift because the old Pope had a progressive type transmission. I didn't make the shift, which was unfortunate because the service brake on the car was located between the clutch and transmission. When you weren't in gear, you had no brakes. We started to roll backward. My aunt first threw our lunch overboard and then made a flying leap herself. Father kept cool and yelled at me to turn the car into a bank. This I did, and we finally came to a stop. We picked up my aunt and what was left of the lunch and proceeded again. Time will not permit telling all the details of that journey but suffice to say we were mired in a swamp six times and had to stay overnight in a farm house. While we were mired, the petcock at the bottom of the crankcase had broken and the oil had dripped out of the motor, with the result that we burned out all our bearings. In trying to get the car started again, my grandfather, who insisted on cranking downward, had the misfortune to have the crank slip. He hit his head upon the sharp radiator and I still recall vividly his standing in the middle of the road with blood all over his face, my mother crying, my aunt hysterical and my father and me trying to patch him up. We finally did get the car started, but headed for home and not for Sycamore.

When we got to St. Charles, my mother and aunt got out and took the train home. Father, grandfather and I headed for Aurora where the nearest garage was located. My grandfather enjoyed faultless command of one of the most richly diversified and dynamic lines of profanity in that section of Illinois. The motor would die unless I kept it going fairly fast and as a consequence I had to take all the "thank-you-marms" between St. Charles and Aurora at about thirty miles an hour. Grandfather almost went through the top each time we hit one of them and as a result the air was blue between those two towns and stayed blue for some weeks thereafter. The car was in the garage in Aurora for thirty days being overhauled. Cars were like that and motoring was like that thirty years ago.

But we don't have to go back thirty years to show the improvement in motor cars. In 1920 we built a Studebaker which weighed 2,900 pounds, had a 45-horsepower engine, and was four inches shorter than our present Commander. It delivered for $2,500. Our 1939 Commander weighs 3,160 pounds, has a 90-horsepower engine, and it delivers for $965. Each company could show a similar improvement in product and lowering of prices. The whole summation of the improvement of the motor car can be expressed in the phrase that you have been getting a better and better ride for less and less money. In the period from 1906 to 1916 automobile transportation cost on an average approximately $13\frac{1}{2}$¢ a mile; on a comparable basis, from 1917 to 1927, 5.6¢ per mile, and from 1928 to 1938, 2.7¢ per mile. It is interesting to note the rapid increase in the volume of automobile transportation as a better and better ride has been offered for less and less money. In 1908 there were approximately 140,000 cars in the United States. They covered 700,000,000 vehicle miles. In 1938 approximately 30,000,000 cars and trucks were registered. They accounted for 250,000,000,000 vehicle miles—ten times the combined mileage of all other forms of transportation. Automotive transportation has become America's biggest industry.

Now let's ask—how was all this accomplished and what brought it to pass?

The answer, of course, is "a number of things." Better roads have played a vital part. In 1908 we had no hard-surfaced highways—today we have more than 150,000 miles. Essential as this road development was to the automobile industry, it did not cast its benefits exclusively in our direction. It changed the pattern of both rural and city life. It brought economic benefits to all and it has added immeasurably to the joy of living.

As far as the car itself is concerned, the answer to what has been accomplished lies in the driving force of free and open competition. Your dollar has been king, and in fighting for it, we, the manufacturers, have waged the battle of the ages in the fields of engineering, mass production, selling and advertising. It has been an unceasing warfare. In the thirty years that I have been in the business the same relentless pressures have been constantly and inexorably at work. We bring out a new model and immediately thereafter set our engineers to work improving it, making it better, and, by smart designing, bringing down the cost. During the past two decades not less than $20,000,000 per year has been spent for engineering development and research. Our production executives have had the equally important job of constantly improving techniques so that cars can be manufactured to higher standards at lower costs. In each decade hundreds of millions of dollars have been invested in new machinery. Our sales executives have been charged with the responsibility of distributing our production with a constant lowering per car cost.

It is these continuing and relentless pressures that are responsible for the spectacular results that have been achieved. There has been no thirty-year plan nor even a five-year plan. Things have happened because they had to happen if we wanted to stay in business. We have not dared to pause because if we did, we would have passed out of the picture.

Our improved engineering, improved techniques, and lower selling cost do not alone account for the dramatically lower prices of motor cars today. A vital element has been the reduction in gross profits for both the manufacturer and dealer. I don't think that most people realize how big that reduction has been. Let me give you the facts. Twenty years ago—yes, even ten years ago—the average car manufacturer had a gross profit of about 30 per cent on each car he sold. Today his gross profit ranges from 12 to 15 per cent. I can quote you some exact figures from Studebaker as an example. In 1928 we had a gross margin of $300 on a car, the list price of which was $1,000. On a $1,000 car today our gross profit is about $120. In a big year such as 1937, when 5,000,000 cars were produced by the industry, net profits per car ranged from $25 to $60 in the low and medium priced fields.

As prices have come down, the per-car gross profit enjoyed by the automobile dealer has shrunk proportionately. His greatest problem, however, arises out of the fact that today he has to sell two used cars in order to dispose of one new car. In other words, he buys almost twice as many used cars from the general public as he does new cars from the manufacturer. There is plenty of evidence to indicate that you, the public, do a better job of selling your used cars to him than he does selling new cars to you. The more successful dealers who have developed a certain immunity against your persuasiveness, make net profits that range from $30 to $50 per new car.

Parts suppliers, tire manufacturers, and all those who provide various types of service to the automobile owner, have all come within the same competitive area as the manufacturers and dealers themselves. Results have been similar. Take tires for example: Those tires on that Old Pope-Toledo, which cost $75 each, were good for a maximum of 2,500 miles. Today a tire for the same weight car costs less than $20 and is good for as much as 25,000 miles. In other words, a dollar today will buy thirty times as much tire mileage as it did thirty years ago. The petroleum technologists have made their contribution to modern automotive transportation. Today's engines would not operate efficiently on the kind of gasoline we had thirty years ago. Similarly, high speed lubricants are absolutely essential to the efficient performance of the motor cars of today. Here again the quality of fuels has gone up while the cost has steadily declined.

How has labor fared while this rapid mechanization of industry has been carried forward? It may seem paradoxical, but while the industry has led in the adoption of the newest and most efficient production methods, *there has been no aggregate technological displacement of automobile labor in the factories.* Except for 1931 to 1933, the man-years of employment per hundred cars produced has varied only between 8.4 and 11.3 in the last fifteen years. In 1923 the man-years per hundred cars was 10 and in 1937, 10.8. This is the statistician's way of saying that it took eight more men to build each thousand cars in 1937 than it did in 1923.

The reasons for this sustained high level of employment per car are not hard to find. To begin with, many of the new machines were installed to make possible a better product rather than to increase production. Others were purchased to improve working conditions, others to reclaim by-products, and still others simply to increase capacity. The aggregate of all these installations resulted in a better dollar for dollar value for the customer, but did not displace labor. Some individual installations did reduce labor requirements in the manufacture of specific parts. In these instances, however, competition compelled the automobile makers to plow back most of the resultant savings into larger and better constructed vehicles to be sold at lower prices. This, in turn, brought additional new labor requirements. Actually the constant application of new machinery in automotive plants has tended to improve the position of the worker and increase employment at steadily increasing wages. Let me show you what has happened in the case of our own company since we embarked upon a program of mechanization.

In 1908 Studebaker was manufacturing automobiles but its principal business consisted of carriages, wagons and harnesses. Our total investment in plant facilities was $5,600,000, which was principally in buildings and workmen's benches. We had 3,000 employees so that each employee had behind him an investment of approximately $1,900. Our total sales volume was approximately $6,000,000, or an average just under $2,000 per employee. The work week was 60 hours, six days of 10 hours each. The average employee worked about 300 days in a year for a total compensation of $600. That seems very low but I ask you to recall that the annual sales per employee were under $2,000 and out of that amount had to come all material cost, selling expense, overhead, etc. Studebaker's profit per employee in 1908 was a small amount indeed.

In the thirty years that have followed we have invested more than $30,000,000 in machinery and mechanical equipment. Our average factory employment in the three years 1936, 1937 and 1938 was approximately 6,000 hourly workers. Each man had behind him an investment of approximately $5,000 in machinery. Our average annual sales for that three-year period were $61,000,000, or approximately $10,000 per employee. The average hourly rate for the three-year period was 90¢. Today it is 96¢. The average annual hours of employment during the period were 1,668, yielding an annual wage of approximately $1,500.00. Contrast this with the $600 received by the workman in 1908 for his 3,000 hours of work. In other words, the average employee has during the past three years received two and one-half times the pay for slightly more than one-half as many hours.

Now I want to pay my respects to two statements frequently made in reference to the employment situation in our industry: first, that machinery has made robots of men, and, secondly, that the pace is so fast that men wear out at an early age. Machinery is important in a modern automobile plant, but the men who operate those machines are more important.

They take just pride in their skill, and if anyone here believes that craftsmanship passed out of the picture when the machine came in, I invite you to visit our plants and talk to our workmen. We have a substantial number of men who were with us in the old wagon days and they can speak for themselves, but I assure you that there is no yearning on their part to return to the days of hand labor. As to the charge that men wear out at an early age, I will let the figures themselves tell the story. Fifty-six per cent of the workmen in our plant are over 40 years of age; 25 per cent are over 50 years of age, and we have a group of 350 men who are over 60 years of age.

Incidentally, yesterday, February 16, we celebrated our 87th birthday, and during all that time we have never had a strike in our plant. To sum it all up, it is my positive conviction that the machine has not enslaved men—it has freed them. It has not created unemployment—it has added to our employment. It has not made robots of working men but, on the contrary, it has made them better, more enlightened citizens who take, if anything, a greater pride in their workmanship than did the craftsmen of the by-gone day.

I have tried to paint for you as clear a picture as I could of the benefits that have come both to the public and to labor as a result of the free interplay of competitive forces upon those who make and sell motor cars. On the face of the record, those benefits cannot be challenged. They outweigh, in my opinion, the difficulties that beset those of us who have tried to make a living out of the industry. Speaking as the president of an independent company which has felt the full force of competition from the "Big Three," I have no complaints to register. They keep us on our toes, but we like to think that we keep them from getting too complacent.

It is up to us to give you, the public, a better motor car than they can offer, or we are not entitled to your money. Speaking as a dealer, and I happen to be a dealer as well as a manufacturer, I want no price-fixing agency controlling my transactions with my customers. I have found by experience that a successful business can be built, provided customers are offered good value and good service.

It seems to me, and I think I follow Mr. Davis, that the present ills of our national economy, insofar as industry and business are concerned, do not come out of free competitive enterprise but, on the contrary, proceed from restrictions that have been placed on free enterprise by business men themselves and, to an increasing extent, by the government, too often at the request of timid business men. It is my opinion that the great need is for an extension of the competitive pattern followed by our industry into a constantly widening area of our economy. Let me summarize that pattern for you. Competition has been tough but fair. The bigger companies have made no effort to drive the smaller producer out of business by resorting to secret rebates or concessions that were demanded by some big business men in the past generation. There have never been any price-fixing agreements of any kind or character. There has been a continuing policy of passing on to the public the benefits of technological advances in the form of better products and lower prices.

Unfortunately, the area in which free and open competition has been practiced has become narrower than wider. There has been an increasing inclination toward price-fixing with or without government sanction. It reached full bloom during the NRA, but even since the Supreme Court declared that set-up illegal we have had a little NRA in the coal industry, we have had the Miller-Tydings Act, the numerous State NRA's, and the Wages and Hour Act, all of which tend toward price fixing. I contend that business and government should join forces in attacking monopoly and monopolistic practices and thus start the tide flowing in the opposite direction. If we don't, more and more regimentation is certain, and in the end some form of fascist control of our economy is inevitable.

This whole idea of controlling prices and wages by government fiat is far from new. In fact, it started to fail thousands of years before the word "fascist" had ever crossed the mind of man.

Just within the last few weeks a savant of the Oriental Institute of the University of Chicago has announced results of a recent study of clay tablets on which the ancient Chaldeans, Assyrians and Babylonians left their records for posterity. From the end of the third millenium, even before the great Hamurabi, down to Ashurbanipal in the seventh century B. C., "benevolent kings and strong kings attempted to create prosperity for their people and a feeling of good will by announcing official prices and, at times, official wages." The results, this learned professor shows, were almost uniformly unsuccessful in bringing the promised abundance. "Business refused to be bound by artificial price levels," he says, "and often truthful contracts exhibit drastic variations from the promulgated official prices."

Rulers in the later Babylonian period, this savant says, made no attempt to control prices. Then he concludes: "It is significant that the picture of a prosperous Babylonian business life which has come to us from classical sources is the picture of this later age."

Price and wage controls didn't work for the Babylonians, and they have not worked for the benefit of business, labor or the consumer at any time since. The Roman Emperor Diocletean tried them in the fourth century; Colbert, the Minister to Louis XIV, tried them in the sixteenth century; and Hitler, Mussolini and Stalin are trying them today. The net result of these efforts on the part of the state to control the economy has been slavery for the workers, disaster for business and either subsistence or starvation for the masses.

There is, in my opinion, no easy way out of our present difficulties. We can't loaf our way out or legislate prosperity—we have got to work for it. We will start toward a real recovery in the United States only if and when business, labor and farmers cease their migrations to state capitols and Washington asking for special privilege, but, instead, go for one purpose, and one purpose only, and that is to see that free enterprise is kept free in America. Only by so doing can we hope to pass on to our children our heritage of liberty, under which America has become the greatest nation in the world.

Sample Goodwill Speech

The following address by Franklyn Bliss Snyder, President of Northwestern University, was presented to the 29th Annual Meeting of the Chamber of Commerce of the United States, May, 1941. Dr. Snyder's purpose is to create goodwill for education. He uses a great deal of interesting material and speaks as an expert and an authority.

AMERICAN YOUTH IN THE PRESENT EMERGENCY [3]

I take great personal pleasure and pride in the privilege that your committee has accorded me today of talking with you for a little while about the young men and young women whom I know best—the young men and women of college age who are looking out rather wistfully, through eyes as yet unclouded by age, upon the world that you and I have given them to live in.

I think the college men and women of America are a large enough group to be representative; I think they are typical of all classes of our society. I know they are a vocal group, and I believe and hope that they are and will be an influential group in our national life. I want to tell you what those young people seem to me to be like, and then very briefly to state what we in the American colleges and universities are trying to do for them.

What are they like, your sons and daughters in colleges from Maine to California? Well, the person who tries to answer that question finds himself confronted at once by a series of contradictions and paradoxes. When you say that the young American on a college campus is lazy, you have told the truth; but you must add that he is most unbelievably energetic. When you say that this young American and his sister are materialistic in their thinking, you have told the truth, for they are greatly concerned with such problems as: what good will this work I am doing now do me when I want to get a job; what value is there in this curriculum? They ask questions which my generation never asked, and they want them answered in terms of dollars and cents. Yet at the same time they are idealistic; and I know of no group anywhere that is more certain to be dreaming dreams and thinking long, long thoughts than the young people who, half an hour before, were saying, "What value is there in this particular job?"

When you say that the young American on college and university campuses

---

[3] Reprinted by special permission of the author.

is concerned with trivialities, you have told the truth; they get excited about the most ridiculous things. Yet I know no group by which you are more certain to be asked those probing questions that go down to the very depths of an individual's life, or of a nation's life, than the group of men and women whom I am thinking about today.

They are a curious crowd—lazy and energetic; materialistic and idealistic; greatly bothered about the nonsense of life, and seriously concerned with the fundamentals of individual and national happiness.

Some people say, "Are not these young people on college and university campuses unduly frank? Have they not discarded all the old reticences and drawn the veil back from some of the sacred things in life?" And I say, yes, they are frank. They are very frank. They are no longer to be put off with those evasive answers which my generation, when it was in college, accepted. They wish to know the truth about life, and they ask questions which admit no evasion. It was interesting to me to see on our own campus not long ago a group of seniors and juniors who said, "We think this institution is derelict in a significant respect. The one thing most of us will be sure to do will be to get married, and you are not giving us any practical advice on how to live happily after marriage. Will you please institute a course of lectures on the psychological, physiological, and anatomical aspects of marriage?" I confess I swallowed hard for a minute or two, because it seemed a rather large order. Yet there was no denying the request, and we said, "All right, we will look into it, and we will get some sort of action. You want, we suppose, one series of lectures for the women, and another for the men?"

"By no means. We are going to live together, and we want these lectures given to men and women at the same time."

Well, I think it is all to the good, ladies and gentlemen. It doesn't bother me at all, and the situation which I have just described on our campus is one that you will find duplicated on most American campuses.

Frank? Yes, very frank, but frank in a good way.

"But aren't they very critical? Aren't they too critical?" someone says; and I admit that the American man or woman on a college campus feels it his prerogative to criticize everything, and he takes full advantage of the privilege which he accords himself. A short time ago—oh, six or seven months, perhaps, but it seems only yesterday as I think of it—I found myself one afternoon looking into the faces of five men under the chairmanship of a lad whom I knew, whose first name was Jim. I said, "What is it, boys? What do you want?"

"We are the Committee of Investigation," said Jim.

"Well," I said, "that is fine. There is a lot around here that ought to be investigated, but where are you going to begin? What is it that you want to investigate?"

"The university."

I said, "That's a pretty large order. There were 23,000 students here last year and 1200 members of the faculty. Don't you think you had better narrow the problem just a little, focus your lens a bit more sharply?"

"All right," said Jim, "we will begin with the Board of Trustees. We think they are slipping something over on us."

I said, "They are. For every fifty cents worth of education that you pay for, they slip you an additional fifty cents worth that someone else has paid for; but that probably wasn't what you had in mind."

"No, no," said these lads. "We want to investigate the sociological and political backgrounds of the Board of Trustees."

Well, then I saw some fun ahead of me, and I said, "Now, go slow. There are forty-four of them, or thereabouts, and if you try to make a personal inquiry into the sociological and political backgrounds of all forty-four, you won't get very far in the course of this winter. Why not pick out one individual, a man who has had some experience here at home and is known across the country—a man who has been President of the National Chamber of Commerce and the American Golf Association. Here is the person you ought to begin with. If you take your committee down to his office, I will guarantee that he will give you a hearing, and that by the time the hearing is over, you will have learned quite a lot. I'll call him up now, if you wish."

Jim looked at me for a minute or two, and then said, "Mr. Snyder, are you kidding us?"

"Well," I said, "maybe I am just a little."

There was silence among the committeemen, and then the chairman broke out (I apologize to the ladies), "To hell with this investigation!"

Now, isn't that delightful?

Not more than four weeks ago I was visited by another committee, a committee to protest against certain action which the university had found it absolutely necessary to take; these people's rights, as they thought, had been infringed upon. We talked with them, my legal vice-president and I; we told them the story as fairly and honestly as we could, and they arose and left us. The next day I received a copy of their "minutes," as they called them, which read thus: "The committee waited on the president to protest the action concerning so-and-so. The committee was received courteously, and the president and vice-president made statements. The committee thereupon withdrew and vetoed these statements."

Now, ladies and gentlemen, when you live with young people like that— well, I don't know; I guess it keeps your sense of humor from being completely atrophied.

Critical? Yes, but again, critical in a good way; critical of old formulas that somehow don't seem to fit; critical of working compromises that don't work; and always critical in a constructive fashion—except, of course, when they are after the Board of Trustees.

And someone else says, "But aren't these young people shot through and through with radicalism? Aren't they Pinks? Aren't the American college and university campuses hotbeds of communism?" Now, ladies and gentlemen, if anyone asks you that question, just say, "No, they are not." For I know.

In any crowd of 10,000 young men or women, there will be a lunatic fringe of exhibitionists. In any faculty of 1,000 there will be a similar lunatic fringe of exhibitionists. But as far as this too often repeated statement is concerned—that our campuses are communistically inclined—it simply is not true. At least it is not true in the Mississippi Valley which I know reasonably well.

A year ago this time, when the two major parties were discussing the approaching national conventions, our young people thought it would be right and proper to settle the problem by having a mock election, a "straw" vote covering all the full-time students in our undergraduate colleges. I admit to having been a little worried about that vote, for I knew that if the newspapers found too many radical ballots cast, certain friends of the University would read about it and would call me up. And so I hoped that there wouldn't be too many communistic tickets in the ballot box.

But I was not at all prepared for the result. When the ballot boxes had been gathered together in the office and opened, one of the boys came in and said, "Mr. Snyder, do you know whom we have elected?"

"No, but I would rather like to know."

"Well," he said, "this is the result: Dewey, 1700; Willkie, 1300; Vandenberg, 750; Taft, 600; Roosevelt, 480; Hull, 325; Norman Thomas, 65; and not one for the Communist candidate." My figures may be wrong in detail; the general effect is not.

Radical? Why, of course, youth ought to be radical, ladies and gentlemen. Youth ought to be inquiring. Youth ought to be critical. If it were not, it would not be American and it would not be youth. But it is radical in a good way, and not in a subversive or un-American way.

Well, those are some of the qualities of these young people that stand out most prominently in my mind. I know these boys and girls and I believe in them. Their faults, when they have them, are those of their parents; their good qualities—and they have many of them—are those of their parents. There are a few slouches here and there, but most of them are straight-shooters; and if there is a row down the alley, I want the American college man and woman on my side.

And now, what are we trying to do for them? To prepare them for facing the emergency which this world presents today. When I say "we," I think I can speak not for one campus, but for many, many campuses. What are we trying to do with these young Americans whom you send to us? We are trying to give them a start toward an education. What does that mean? Well, it is a stupid question, perhaps. It is a little like asking what you expect to find in an American home. There are some things you can take for granted. You know when you go into an American home that you will find adequate plumbing and heating and lighting, and furniture and books and pictures, and some way of listening to music. All those things you take for granted. Most of those things the tax assessor could list and write figures opposite.

But you know that in the American home there is much that cannot be listed in that way. There are many intangibles; hope and ambition and love and suffering and memory, and all the other qualities which change a house into a home.

The same thing is true of an education, ladies and gentlemen. You may take it for granted that the American boy or girl who has the high-school or college opportunity comes out from that experience with at least the beginnings of the ability to communicate ideas by the written or the spoken word. You may assume that he knows at least the elements of mathematics, that he understands a little of what the scientist is trying to do today, that he has been brought in contact with the code of decent and civilized living. All that I think you may assume.

You may assume, also, that we are trying to weave into the picture other qualities, less tangible, perhaps, less easy to catalogue, but to my way of thinking just as important as these skills that I have been describing. You may assume that we who are trying to educate your boys and girls wish to give them, first of all, an opportunity for self-development and for self-discipline, primarily intellectual, but by no means wholly intellectual. We do not think that the educational process is a process of mental growth alone. We think it is social as well as intellectual. We remember what Cardinal Newman once said, that if he had to choose between a university which taught everything known to man, but did it by correspondence, and the university which taught nothing at all, but made men live together for four years, he would choose the second as giving the better education.

Perhaps that is an extreme statement. Nevertheless, America's definition of higher education today is a definition which factors together the intellectual, the social, the aesthetic, and the physical elements that make life worth while.

We believe, too, that one of the important by-products of an education which young America is entitled to is a sort of humility, intellectual and social. That is perhaps another way of saying toleration: an understanding of the other fellow's point of view. If our American colleges did nothing but make men and women live together and rub the corners off one another, they would be doing a great deal, and the toleration for another's point of view which you find on the American campus is a most encouraging thing!

We think, too, that such a by-product as higher standards of value is one of the important parts of an American education. We do not think for a moment that the faculty can impose upon young men and women new standards of value different from those which they have brought with them from home; but we do think that that faculty can and should expose young men and women to the best in art, in letters, in music, in religion, in conduct, so that when the young people go back home, their standards, perhaps inadvertently, and all unknown to them, will be a little higher than they were before.

And we think, ladies and gentlemen, that one of the great, not by-products, but end-products of an education is, and always should be, the ability to work hard at a job, whether you like it or not, and to find happiness under the discipline which society inevitably imposes upon a man or woman.

The word "discipline" is not in great favor with some schools of educational philosophers. The required course is not in favor with these young Americans whom you send to our campuses. But I like to remind the protestors now and then that in the book of life there are relatively few electives and a great many requirements, and if the university does not prepare its young men and women while they are still in the friendly atmosphere of the campus to meet with some courage and honesty and happiness the conditions which they will find awaiting them—if it doesn't do that, it has failed in its major task.

I do not mean when I say the chief end of an education is to teach a boy or girl to work hard at a job that there are not many other valuable things, and that intellectual development is to be slighted. Of course not. But I do think if I had to choose one thing for my own children to get out of their educational experience, it would be that old-fashioned ability to roll up one's sleeves and go to work and finish the job, even though it may not be the most pleasant task in the world.

A few years ago in the summer time I was spending two happy months in an English fishing village where I met a man who, without realizing what he was doing, gave me an educational philosophy, or one might almost say a philosophy of life, which I am going to pass on to you before I leave. The village was Cromer, in Norfolk, where that great bulge of land forces tself out into the North Sea. It is a dangerous part of the coast, and so here are in Cromer three lifesaving stations: one up on the cliff, the ocket apparatus," as they call it; and out at the end of the steel pier, 't well into the North Sea, there was a magnificent new power lifeboat ould go anywhere at any time; and in the old boathouse under the nused for fourteen years but ready for an emergency, was the old ig boat." Every morning at eight o'clock the coxswain of that boat, Blogg by name, seventy-three or four years old when I knew him, ne boathouse doors, ran the white ensign to the peak of the staff, spent the day waiting for the emergency that might arise. For as o me, "If anything goes wrong and the big boat is away, I will have the signal and get the crew down here, and we will have to go out o the job ourselves."

the end of my two or three months in Cromer, I went around to see ary Blogg, for I had spent a good many hours listening to his talk; and aid, "Captain Blogg, I wish you would stand up by the stern of your oat there and let me take your picture."

"No," he said, "I am not man enough to have my picture taken beside that boat. But if you will put sixpence in the box there, I will give you a real picture of her that you can take home with you." I went over to the box, a little miniature lifeboat with a slot in the center of the deck where the collection could be left for supporting that branch of the British service, and I dropped one sixpence, and then another. Then I saw in front of me a wooden plaque on which were printed the names of all the vessels which that little boat had aided, and the numbers of men and women rescued at each launch, as they called it. And I said, "Captain Blogg, have you been with the boat during all those experiences?"

"Yes," was the answer, "I was one of six who brought her here by water from London where she was built." Then, with a shade of wistfulness in his voice: "The other five are all asleep out there."

There seemed no reply, no comment for me to make at that point; so I kept silent. And then in a moment, from the old veteran in tones of command, "Add up the numbers on that board."

After a moment with a pencil and a bit of paper I said, "Three hundred and fifty-five."

"You are right," said he, "three hundred and fifty-five men and women brought safe ashore in that little cockle shell from death out there." And after another pause: "Divide three hundred and fifty-five by five," said the old veteran.

"Seventy-one," said I.

"You are right again." And then rising from his chair and pulling his cap from his head, he spoke what I think to be the most moving words I have ever heard from human lips when he said, "When the last day comes, and the sea gives up its dead, each of my five shipmates will have seventy-one witnesses to swear that he did his duty like a man."

If the colleges of America should do no more than teach young people the importance of "doing your duty like a man," they would be worth all they have cost in money and human energy. And that, in my judgment, is what we are really trying to do for the young people you send to us each autumn.

Oral report

In every business and profession there are innumerable times when specific and detailed information must be discovered, organized, and presented for use as a basis for deliberation or action. Such reports of information may concern the financial condition of the company, marketing and distribution surveys, personnel investigations, any other situation pertinent to efficient operations in business. In each instance, the purpose is simply to present the results of investigation and study. No attempt is made to persuade or influence action or belief, although the report itself may serve as the basis for action or change of belief.

Reports are usually presented in one of the following ways: it may be written, and sometimes published, for distribution; it may be presented orally in conference; or it may be presented as a public speech. We are interested primarily in the last two of these methods.

While it is never necessary for any kind of speech presentation to be dull and laborious, the oral report does not require the usual attention to materials of interest. The audience has, as a rule, requested the speaker to gather the information and is therefore ready to hear the facts. Humor, illustrations, and other methods of holding attention should be eliminated or used with discrimination. However, all of the speaker's skill in delivery must be employed. Even though an audience is eager to hear the report, they may be bored to oblivion or confused because the speaker shows no animation, uses a monotonous voice, or reveals a lack of sincerity and interest in his job.

The report should be as complete as is possible within the allotted space of time. For this reason it is sometimes essential to show or represent whole topics by the use of some visual aid, such as a chart, diagram, picture, or map. In fact, there is no clearer method of explaining the rise or fall of sales, for instance, than by the use of a chart that shows in one glance the progress, week by week, throughout a year or several years. In addition to making the subject much more easy to discuss, visual aids are valuable in holding the attention of the audience. If one may see as well as hear, the speaker's chances of holding attention are doubled.

Suggested Titles for Oral Reports

1. The 1942–1943 University Budget
2. Survey of the Campus Traffic Problem
3. Financial Statement of B Company
4. Present and Future Effect of Draft Law on University Enrollment
5. A Study of Positions Open to Commerce Students
6. A Study of Positions Open to Agriculture Students
7. Report on Status of Fraternities
8. A Hospitalization Plan
9. Study of Available Tank Cars for Shipment of Oil
10. Cost of Lend-Lease Policy to the Present Time
11. Report on Military Morale
12. Report of a Play Reading Committee
13. Report of Food Bill for a Co-operative House
14. University Scholarships
15. Market Survey
16. Inflationary Trends

Sample Oral Report

The following oral report was delivered by Col. John H. Jouett, President of the Aeronautical Chamber of Commerce of America, to the Conference Meeting on Transportation and Defense, at the 29th Annual Meeting of the Chamber of Commerce of the United States, April, 1941.

The Air [4]

It is fitting that a report on the progress of the national defense be rendered at business and industry's biggest annual foregathering of the year—the annual meeting, in the National Capital, of the United States Chamber of Commerce. It is fitting because it is business and industry, directed by

---

[4] Reprinted by special permission of the Chamber of Commerce of the United States of America.

the Government, that are carrying on the giant program of production for defense. I have been honored with the assignment of reporting the accomplishments of the aircraft manufacturing industry in connection with the armament program. In recent months I have made periodic reports on the defense achievements of the industry I represent. The industry deems these reports the just due of the American people. We feel that, in a democracy such as ours, the facts, during a national emergency, should be made public, insofar as consonant with military considerations. The truth should be told—whether the news is good or bad. So today I shall report on the latest developments in the vast program of building military airplanes. I have also been asked to discuss commercial aviation, present and future. I will take up that subject in a few minutes. First, let me repeat a few questions regarding warplanes and their constructions, questions being asked daily by America's millions—and answer them. In this way, I will bring you the aircraft manufacturing industry's latest report on defense progress.

First, just what is the job that the aircraft industry has been given? The industry has been asked to build about 44,000 military airplanes, broken down as follows: For the Army, about 16,500; for the Navy, about 8,500; for the British, including Canada, about 16,000, and 3,600 bombers under the so-called Knudsen Plan. The immensity of the job can be realized when I tell you that in 1939, the industry did $225,000,000 worth of business; in 1940 our people increased dollar volume output to $544,000,000, at the same time carrying on a tremendous plant expansion, and that this year we hope to turn out $1,500,000,000 worth of airplanes.

Second, when did our people get this job? The great bulk of the orders were not placed until the Fall of 1940, although President Roosevelt, in his notable defense message to Congress after the fall of France, on May 16, 1940, said the United States should have 50,000 airplanes. The unfortunate delay in actually placing orders for planes, which ensued upon Mr. Roosevelt's message, resulted in a lag in actual output of planes, a lag which now has been overcome by the tireless efforts of the aircraft industry. The program was too huge for any industry to handle without vastly expanded production facilities, and without placement of orders, such expansion was impossible. Our people were by no means idle while wondering whether and when orders would be placed. They went ahead and built as many privately-financed plants as they could.

Third, what was the condition of the industry when it got the job? Was the industry ready for it? Great expansion strides already had been made and, aided by British and French orders placed following Munich, the industry had embarked on an expansion program that, at that time, was considered tremendous. Between the outbreak of the European War in September, 1939, and July, 1940, at which time Federal financial aid in expansion was offered, the industry spent $52,000,000 for new plants and equipment, only $11,000,000 worth of which will be needed after this emergency.

In another way, the industry was ready—more than ready. Following World War I, when an inordinately rapid liquidation of war orders had reduced the industry to the brink of disaster, our people, in principle, made the Government this proposition, in an effort to keep aviation alive: Give us orders for military aircraft, and we will use profits to develop better warplanes for the United States. This cooperation by the Government, aided by export trade, has assured this country the best warplanes in the world. Not the most, because the orders placed were small—but the best. So, when the present emergency developed, we were in a position to build the most efficient and most durable warplanes in the world.

And our people are still, *today,* returning profits into research and development. Of 38 aircraft companies building for defense, all major companies except four, which have not reported yet during a survey currently being made, in the seven-year period covering 1934–1940, inclusive, spent $63,250,000 on development, or 79 per cent of total profits. They also spent $76,800,000 on plant expansion and equipment during the same period, or 97 per cent of total profits. Combined development and expansion costs were $140,050,000, or 76 per cent more than total profits.

Fourth, why does it take so long to build warplanes today? Warplanes are called upon today to perform functions undreamed of during World War I. They must be larger, carry greater loads, fly farther and faster, perform more difficult maneuvers with attendant immeasurably increased stresses. The modern warplane must embody all these capabilities in order to hold its own against the new warplanes that the enemy is always working on. It takes time and precise workmanship to build in these capabilities. Perhaps these facts, given offhand, might serve to illustrate:

There are 50,000 separate inspections on an aircraft engine; 30,000 man hours of labor go into a medium bomber; 450,000 rivets go into a heavy bomber; in one medium bomber 30,000 parts, not including bolts, nuts and rivets, are worked into 650 minor sub-assemblies, and these in turn into 32 major sub-assemblies, before they are put into the plane; modern air liners must have about 50 instruments built in, compared to 15 ten years ago. In addition, the lessons taught almost daily by the war must be assimilated and their substance translated into performance by the aircraft we are building. The tempo of this war is breathtaking; each side is constantly heightening the fire power at its planes, increasing the strength of armor plate, and incorporating new offensive and defensive features in its warplanes. These advances we must meet and surpass as we learn of them. This calls for re-designing. Re-designing takes time.

Fifth, what progress has the aircraft industry made on its tremendous assignment? Here are some revealing data never heretofore entirely disclosed: On July 1, 1940, the industry was operating 17,216,410 sq. ft. of floor space. Just eight months later, on March 1, 1941, the industry had expanded to 31,383,967 sq. ft.—an 82 per cent increase! On July 1, 1940, we had 120,106 employees. Eight months later we had 226,172 employees—an 88 per cent increase! And our people had to train virtually all its new employees in the unique and admittedly different art of building airplanes.

Sixth, is the industry working to capacity today, and did it work to capacity last year? The survey I referred to in connection with development also shows that the aircraft industry is today working to absolute capacity, insofar as acquisition of necessary materials allows. Twenty-four hour daily operation, in most cases six days a week, is the rule, the survey shows, with the seventh day devoted to vital maintenance of machinery, necessary plant clean-up, and evening up production. You must realize, when you hear criticism of any defense industry for not producing 24 hours a day, seven days a week, that the failure to do so is due to maintenance of vital machines and equipment, and to slowness in receipt of materials.

As regards last year: In 1939, our people made a survey which showed that 5,500 warplanes could be built in 1940 with existing facilities, if orders were received. The year passed, and nearly 6,000 warplanes were built. The industry surpassed its own estimate of all-out production.

Seventh, what has production of warplanes been, to date? Since the phase of the national emergency began—in other words, since July, 1940, our people have built nearly 7,000 military planes. The production curve has been accelerating steadily—700 in November, 800 in December, 1,000 in January, 1,200 in March. We are very near the British and German monthly production rates, which are estimated at about 1,500 a month each.

Eighth, how many planes has the aircraft industry built for Britain? In the 20 months since the outbreak of the war, nearly 3,500 American-built military planes, ordered from our people by the British, have been exported —no mean air force in itself.

Ninth, what are the prospects in the next few months and next year? Production will increase as rapidly as new plant facilities come into operation—and no more rapidly. As one of our people so aptly puts it: "You can put a hen to hatch a setting of eggs, and divide the setting among any number of hens, and put other hens to hatching part-time, but it is still going to take three weeks to hatch those eggs, because that is the time an egg requires to hatch." The March production of 1,200 planes should double by the summer of 1942. Each month in the interim will see sharply increased numbers of planes rolling off production lines. This year alone, estimates show, 18,000 planes will be turned out and next year, under present programs, 30,000. Even now, half our output, coupled with the British output, exceeds Axis plane production, according to best obtainable estimates.

The planes we are building and will build equal or surpass the best being built, or to be built, elsewhere. We hear much about new German types about to enter the war arena. We know that the Germans have a new twin-engined fighter, the Focke Wulf FW-189, powered with 2750 h.p., and carrying eight guns, including cannon. We know the Germans are to bring into service the new Heinkel HE-113, a fast fighter. Another new German fighter is the Focke Wulf FW 158, a single-engined craft with pusher propeller. Four new bombers are slated for service, including two four-motored ships, a new Heinkel and the Focke Wulf Kurier. But our people are engaged on new models, too. They are military secrets, of course, but I can tell you that there are at least 16. I can say that interceptors to combat night bombing—one form of attack which Britain has been unable to repel up till now— are being developed in the United States. Rest assured that our planes will not be excelled. We must build the best. An inferior warplane is worse than no plane at all.

Programs are in the mill today looking to placement of orders for additional thousands of planes for our air services and Britain, and for other governments eligible for aid under terms of the Lend-Lease Law. Scope of these programs has not been made public, but, I am told by Government sources, requirements under consideration will bring the total of planes on order from the present 44,000 up to 80,000! The aircraft manufacturing industry, which has made amazing progress against great odds in the last year, is ready to tackle any new assignment handed it. However, in the best interests of the defense program, I would like to offer these suggestions in connection with the new program: First, let every possible source of suitable subcontracting be utilized before launching another time-consuming plant expansion program; second, let any expansion of orders be in proportion to the available supplies of material and personnel.

In connection with subcontracting, a recent survey showed that there are today 28,000 industrial establishments holding *no* defense orders. Put some of these firms to work fabricating parts which our people can use in building airplanes, and we can save the precious time that would be wasted in waiting for new factories to be completed. One plane today may do the democracies more good than 100 planes a year from now.

That's the aircraft situation as of today. We are, with all jurisdiction, I think, satisfied with it. Not complacent, however. World events hourly demonstrated the gravity of the moment. A long succession of U. S. and British officials have told us that they are well pleased with our progress, both in number of planes built, and in their quality. American-built warplanes have, despite assertions to the contrary, participated on every front since the war began, are today performing meritoriously on every front— over England, in Africa, over the Mediterranean, in Greece, over the English Channel and the Atlantic. Production is mushrooming daily. America, within a short time, will see American warcraft rolling through factory doors. swarming through the skies in astonishing numbers. On behalf of the aircraft industry—I guarantee it!

Now, what's happening to commercial aviation today? What's going to happen to it, and to aviation in general, after the war? Those are questions that you, as businessmen and industrial leaders, are entitled to have answered and that we, who have grown up with aviation, cannot escape pondering. Let's take the present first.

The air lines have been unable to obtain all new equipment needed, because planes and engines are needed more by the military. Nevertheless, they were able, in 1940, to fly 108,800,000 miles, an increase of about 2½ million miles over 1939. They hope to obtain enough new equipment to permit maintenance of this volume of operation in 1941. Equipment allocation for 1942 has not been decided yet by the Government. But the Government realizes the vital importance of the air lines as a national defense adjunct, and is expected to provide for them.

How about private flying? An all-time U. S. record was set in 1940. Pilots of 16,500 private planes flew 220,000,000 miles during the year.

How about development of the air liner of the future? Several companies are working on bigger, faster, safer air giants to enable U. S. lines to meet the needs of the future and to meet international competition. The importance of this development is rather generally realized, although some opposition, claiming that the work interferes with military production, still exists. But, if this work does not continue, international competition will throttle our air lines and our industry. This in turn inevitably will be reflected in output of inferior military airplanes, and decline of the United States as a world air power. In times like these, this might easily be tantamount to national suicide.

How about the future, when the war ends? It is almost foolhardy to speculate, but there are certain indicated trends. In the first place, regardless of the war's outcome, all governments which survive certainly will maintain large air forces to protect their populations from aggression, just like they maintain police and fire departments for protection, regardless of general economic conditions.

In the private flying field, hundreds of thousands of pilots trained during the emergency will want to continue flying. To many, flying will be the only means of making a living. If a progressive airport program is carried out, we may expect to see a tremendously increased use of the private plane for everyday business and pleasure.

The air lines will be expanded. Air mail pickup and feeder lines will reach into every corner of the country unreachable by the trunk lines. Already there is great demand for this type of service. Applications from more than 1,000 localities for air mail pickup are on file with the Government.

Aviation has a particularly bright future in the international field. Were it not for the war, today there would doubtless be merchant fleets of the air operating over every ocean under half a dozen flags. Certainly we will have this development immediately after the war, with luxurious air liners of the future—liners our people are developing today—shuttling thousands of persons quickly, safely and comfortably from country to country. I believe that this field promises much, because it will make the people of the world closer neighbors, for betterment of the international relationships which are so sadly rent today.

Brightest future prospect for aviation, I believe, lies in Latin America. The lands to our South, due to topography and other causes, have not, in general, a comprehensive transportation network. Aviation will permit the establishment of an efficient transportation system and the consequent development of now dormant natural resources.

In connection with South America, I want to call your attention to a dangerous situation existing today, unknown to most people. You have heard vaguely of alleged Axis economic penetration of South America through control of air lines. Not enough Americans, however, realize the extent or stark reality of German and Italian incursions into South America. Listen to these facts: Out of 42 air lines in South America, Germany and Italy control nine. These operate in Brazil, Argentina, Chile, Peru, Ecuador, Uruguay and Bolivia. They move freely over routes aggregating 21,762 miles—better than 22 per cent of the total air line route miles flown in South America. On thousands of these miles they duplicate the services of older, more efficiently-operated air lines, and obviously serve no useful purpose—useful, that is, to anyone but Hitler and Mussolini, whose doctrines of totalitarian government they spread sedulously, using such devices as free transportation and feting of government officials; free distribution of world news, well-tinctured with Axis philosophy, to newspapers which cannot afford wire services, and provision of air line equipment to local air lines at cut prices, with five years to pay in depreciated marks or in barter. Meanwhile, German and Italian pilots are familiarizing themselves with terrain and flight conditions, valuable experience should the Axis Powers attempt military invasion of South America.

Belittlers of the significance of these activities might consider this incident: Just a month ago, a plane of the Italian Trans-Atlantic line, LATI, took off on several over-water flights, returning to its base at Natal, Brazil, each time. The crew claimed that the purpose of the flights, one lasting eight hours, was merely to test the engines. Was it a coincidence that, after this eight-hour flight—four hours out over the Atlantic and four hours back— that two heavily laden Italian freighters, knowing the coast was clear, made a dash from Brazilian ports, headed for Europe!

Recall the German technique of first softening up its intended victim through economic aggression and fifth-column activity, add the foregoing recital of fact, and see if you haven't a sum boding ill for the future of the Americas, as well as the future of aviation in South America?

Fire must be fought with fire! The Axis influence in South America obviously can be uprooted in one way only: Fire must be fought with fire!

Our future is inextricably tied to the future of the other countries of this Western Hemisphere. Culturally, economically and sentimentally we must cooperate to the fullest. No better means than rapid transportation and communication exist to accomplish such cooperation. And such cooperation must start now—by Government aid and by individual effort—and with commercial aviation of the Americas playing a dominant part.

Persuasive Types

Question of policy

As has been pointed out in an earlier chapter, the question of policy speech may be of two types, the policy-determining conference and the policy-confirming speech. Questions of policy are usually determined by discussion between two or more people. A problem exists, the causes are discovered, and a solution is determined that will either remove the causes or counteract them.

After policies are determined either by discussion or some other means, the problem of gaining acceptance or endorsement of the policy usually arises. Such a speech situation implies the necessity of speaking persuasively and making a final appeal for action. Although this may be done in conference, if only one person has the authority to act, the more common practice is to speak publicly to a group that has the power to vote for or against the proposed change. This type of speech is properly called a policy-confirming speech.

The policy-confirming speech follows in general the same steps recommended for a policy-determining discussion with the exception that an appeal for action is made. The history and definition of the problem must be clearly outlined, the cause or causes of the problem must be revealed, and the determined solution must be shown to have advantages that offset the disadvantages of the present policy. The speaker must make effective use of persuasion and suggestion, recognizing that, although a logical and reasoned process is necessary to determine a policy, people are moved to action more quickly by emotional appeal.

SUGGESTED TITLES FOR POLICY-DETERMINING SPEECHES

1. Free Parking Tickets Should Be Distributed to Our Out-of-town Customers.
2. Our Company Should Establish an Employee Health Program.
3. Our Direct Mail Advertising Should Be Done in Our Own Offices.
4. A Directory of Prospects Should Be Compiled for Our Salesmen.
5. Our Surplus Stock Should Be Decreased.
6. We Should Decrease Our Newspaper Advertising and Increase Our Radio Advertising.
7. Salesmen Should Be Made Responsible for the Collection of Overdue Accounts in Their Territories.
8. A Market Survey Should Be Made in the City of Freeport.
9. Our Organization Should Establish a Scholarship at Morgan College.
10. The City Council Should Endorse a Program of Rent Stabilization.
11. Only Grade A Milk Should Be Sold Within the City Limits.
12. A Committee Should Be Appointed to Investigate the Vice Problems in This City.
13. An Assessment Should Be Made for the Re-surfacing of Manitou Boulevard.
14. Students of Marlin College Should Be Required to Attend Convocation Programs.
15. A Fee of Twenty-five Dollars Should Be Established for Our Guest Speakers.

Sample Policy-Confirming Speech

The following policy-confirming speech was delivered by George Beam in a Business and Professional Speech class, University of Illinois, 1941.

LET'S ADVERTISE [5]

(The scene is the directors' room of a large, mid-western manufacturing company. Earlier on this same day, the company's advertising manager re-

---

[5] Reprinted by special permission of Mr. Beam.

ceived a notice stating that owing to the company's oversold condition resulting from defense orders, advertising was to be discontinued for an indefinite
period. The advertising manager has the floor. The board listens courteously.)

Mr. Chairman, Members of the Board:

Remember the old Chinese torture of the million drops?" The offender
was strapped immovably to a board and drops of water fell on his forehead
—in the same spot and at regular intervals. But if the victim moved ever
so slightly, or the drops of water halted for even a moment, the whole
method of punishment was totally ineffective.

This thought has been running through my head ever since I received
this notice from you this morning—this notice that temporarily eliminates
our advertising. Gentlemen, I beg you to reconsider. This is not the course
of action for us to take. Now, Mr. Jones, I know exactly what you are
going to say: "Government orders are absorbing our entire output; we can't
even supply our dealers; no end is in sight; so why should we advertise our
product?" A feeling like this is dangerous. This period actually presents
a danger to us. My thesis today is not only that we should continue advertising, but that we should even increase our advertising appropriation!
Startling? Let me explain.

At the recent regional conference of the National Industrial Advertising
Association in Chicago two facts were brought out very conclusively—two
facts that are dynamic in their implications. First, the post-emergency era
will see the most epic competitive struggle—get this gentlemen—the most
epic competitive struggle *for survival in United States history.* Second—
and remember, these were formulated by hard-headed business men like
ourselves—unseen forces harbor ambitions to use National Defense as a lever
for the subtle overturning of the established economic order—*the end of
private enterprise.*

Now let's examine these points, not emotionally or generally, but coldly,
from our own standpoint. We know first that this present emergency will
not last—I'm sure you will all agree with me on that point. It follows, then,
that this period of prosperity we are now enjoying will come to an end.
Third, we know that our old customers are being forced to find substitutes
for our products—substitutes that may, in many cases, prove entirely satisfactory. Gentlemen, if you agree with me on these points—and you must—
you will also agree with me when I say that we can win back our customers
much more easily *if we have never let them forget us;* if we have made them
remember us, not through *use* of our products, *but through our advertising.*
Remember Bruce Barton's quotation in his famous "Which Knew Not
Joseph" in which he tells us that advertising is a "day by day and an hour
by hour process. Every day and every hour the king dies, and there arises
a new king—which knows not Joseph." Gentlemen, don't let that happen
to us. Let's keep our drops of advertising water hammering at the same
spot—padding us for the epic competitive struggle to come!

Now let's consider the second point—the destruction of private enterprise.
We all know that there has been a growing tendency toward government
control during this emergency period. Edward Gardner, special reporter
for "Printer's Ink" in the April 11, 1941 issue says: "The consumer would

be taught to rely on Government information as a guide to buying. This is a broad doctrine. The axe is laid to the root of the tree. The manufacturer would retain the right to make goods, *but his right to sell them would be largely assumed by Government.*"

And Katherine Clayberger, associate editor of "Woman's Home Companion" says, in the same issue: "The education of the consumer is vital to the defense of the free enterprise system!"

Advertising, gentlemen, is the textbook for that consumer education. It alone can prevent this thing from befalling us. Let's make people remember us—not as the X company, located "somewhere in the midwest" and a maker of machine guns during the emergency; but as the Lamson Company, makers of fine domestic products!

We can actually gain business if we continue to advertise. Why? *Because many short-sighted manufacturers are going to discontinue their advertising, and they are going to lose their hold on their customers.* These people are just waiting to be told! This trend is illustrated in the "Printer's Ink" advertising index for May 9, 1941, which shows advertising to be just 80% of its May, 1940 level. Gentlemen, let's keep our hold on the market! Let's remind our old friends that we are still here, anxious to serve them as soon as Uncle Sam's needs are filled! Let's be sure that "new kings" arising will be conditioned to the same drop of advertising water that is being used so effectively on their parents!

Members of the Board—*Let's advertise!*

Promotional

The promotional speech is similar to the sales speech except that it does not make an appeal for immediate action. Promotional speeches are designed to arouse interest and desire in the hearers but not to consummate a sale. The speaker should make a careful analysis of the audience and adapt his material to that analysis by an astute appeal to fundamental wants, needs, and desires.

Suggested Titles for Promotional Speeches

1. Chemist—Synthetics in a World at War
2. Business Analyst—Profit from Loss
3. Advertising Representative—Customers through Advertising
4. Alumni Secretary—The Value of a Modern College Education
5. Red Cross Worker—Angels of Mercy

Sample Promotional Speech

The following promotional speech was delivered by Bruce Barton, President of Batten, Barton, Durstine and Osborn, at a meeting of the Public Relations Section of the National Electric Light Association, 1923.

WHICH KNEW NOT JOSEPH [6]

There are two stories—and neither of them is new—which I desire to tell you, because they have a direct application to everyone's business. The first concerns a member of my profession, an advertising man, who was in the employ of a circus. It was his function to precede the circus into various communities, distribute tickets to the editor, put up on the barn pictures of the bearded lady and the man-eating snakes, and finally to get in touch with the proprietor of some store and persuade him to purchase the space on either side of the elephant for his advertisement in the parade.

Coming one day to a crossroads town, our friend found that there was only one store. The proprietor did not receive him enthusiastically. "Why should I advertise?" he demanded. "I have been here for twenty years. There isn't a man, woman or child around these parts that doesn't know where I am and what I sell." The advertising man answered very promptly (because in our business if we hesitate we are lost), and he said to the proprietor, pointing across the street, "What is that building over there?" The proprietor answered, "That is the Methodist Episcopal Church." The advertising man said, "How long has that been there?" The proprietor said, "Oh, I don't know; seventy-five years probably." "And yet," exclaimed the advertising man, "they ring the church bell every Sunday morning."

My second story has also a religious flavor. It relates to a gentleman named Joseph, who is now deceased.

Those of you who were brought up on the Bible may have found there some account of his very remarkable business career.

The account of Joseph in the Old Testament is much more complete and to his credit. It tells how he left his country under difficulties, and, coming into a strange country, he rose, through his diligence, to become the principal person in the state, second only to the King. Now, gentlemen, the Biblical narrative brings us to that point—the point where Joseph had public relations with all the other ancient nations, while his private relations held all the best-paying jobs—it brings us up to the climax of his career and then it hands us an awful jolt. Without any words of preparation or explanation, it says bluntly:

"And Joseph died, and there arose a new king in Egypt, which knew not Joseph."

I submit, gentlemen, that this is one of the most staggering lines which has ever been written in a business biography. Here was a man so famous that everybody knew him and presto, a few people die, a few new ones are born, and nobody knows him. The tide of human life has moved on; the king who exalted the friends of Joseph is followed by a king who makes them slaves; all the advertising that the name "Joseph" had enjoyed in one generation is futile and of no avail, because that generation is gone.

Now, what has all that to do with you? Very much indeed. When we gathered in this room this afternoon, there were in this country, in bed, sick, several thousand old men. It perhaps is indelicate for me to refer to that fact, but it is a fact, and we are grown up and we have to face these things. On those old men you gentlemen collectively have spent a

---

[6] Reprinted by special permission of the author.

considerable amount of time and a considerable amount of money. It is to be supposed that you have made some impression upon them regarding your service and your purposes and your necessities. But in this interval, while we have been sitting here, those old men have died, and all your time and all your money and whatever you have built up in the way of good will in their minds—all your labor and investment have passed out with them.

In the same brief interval, there have been born in this country several thousand lusty boys and girls to whom you gentlemen mean no more than the Einstein theory. They do not know the difference between a Mazda lamp and a stick of Wrigley's chewing gum. Nobody has ever told them that Ivory Soap floats or that children cry for Castoria, or what sort of soap you ought to use if you want to have a skin that people would like to touch. The whole job of giving them the information they are going to need in order to form an intelligent public opinion and to exercise an intelligent influence in the community has to be started from the beginning and done over again.

So the first very simple thing that I would say to you (and it is so simple that it seems to me it ought to be said at every convention of this kind) is that this business of public relations is a very constant business, that the fact that you told your story yesterday should not lead you into the delusion of supposing that you have ever told it. There is probably no fact in the United States that is easier to impress upon people's minds than that Ivory Soaps floats, and yet the manufacturers of Ivory Soap think it is not inconsistent or wasteful to spend more than a million dollars a year in repeating that truth over and over again.

Cultivating good will is a day-by-day and hour-by-hour business, gentlemen. Every day and every hour the "king" dies and there arises a new "king" to whom you and all your works mean absolutely nothing.

Now, the second very simple thing which I might say to you is that in your dealings with the public, in what you write and say, you must be genuine.

When I came to New York a great many years ago I had a lot of trouble with banks. It was very hard to find any bank that would be willing to accept the very paltry weekly deposit that I wanted to make. Finally I discovered one which was not as closely guarded as the others, and I succeeded for a period of three years in being insulted by the teller every Saturday. At the end of three years, when I came to draw out my money, I had an audience with the vice-president who wanted personally to insult me. I said to myself, if I live and grow old in this town, some day I think I would like to take a crack at this situation.

And so the years passed (as they have a habit of doing), and I lived and grew old, and one day a bank official came in to us and said he would like to have us do some advertising for him. I said to this banker, "Now you go back to your office and shave off all the side whiskers that there are in your bank and you take all the high hats and carry them out into the back yard of the bank and put them in a pile and light a match to the pile and burn them up, because I am going to advertise to people that you're human, and it may be a shock to have them come in and find you as you are."

So he went back to his bank and I wrote an advertisement which said:

"There is a young man in this town who is looking for a friendly bank; a bank where the officers will remember his name, and where some interest will be shown when he comes in, etc."

It was very successful. It was too successful. It was so successful that we could not control it, and all over the country there broke out a perfect epidemic, a kind of measles, of "friendly banks." Bankers who had not smiled since infancy and who never had had or needed an electric fan in their offices suddenly sat up and said, "Why, we are friendly."

Well, our bank dropped out. The competition was too keen. But it culminated, I think, in a letter which I saw and which was mailed by the president of a really very important bank in a large city. I won't attempt to quote it verbatim, but it was to this effect:

"Dear Customer: As I sit here all alone in my office on Christmas Eve thinking of you and how much we love you, I really wish that you and every other customer could come in here personally so I could give you a good, sound kiss."

Well, that is a trifle exaggerated, but the fact is this—if you don't feel these things you can't make other people feel them. Emerson said, as you will remember, "What you are thunders so loud I cannot hear what you say." Unless there is back of this desire for better public relations a real conviction, a real genuine feeling that you are in business as a matter of service, not merely as a matter of advertising service—unless there is that, then it is very dangerous, indeed, to attempt to talk to the public. For as sure as you live the public will find you out.

The third very simple thing, and the last thing I suggest, is this: In dealing with the public the great thing is to deal with them simply, briefly, and in language that they can understand.

Two men delivered speeches about sixty years ago at Gettysburg. One man was the greatest orator of his day, and he spoke for two hours and a half, and probably nobody in the room can remember a single word that he said. The other man spoke for considerably less than five minutes, and every school child has at some time learned Lincoln's Gettysburg Address, and remembers it more or less all his life. Many prayers have been uttered in the world—many long, fine-sounding prayers—but the only prayer that any large majority of people have learned is the Lord's Prayer, and it is less than two hundred words long. The same thing is true of the Twenty-third Psalm, and there is hardly a Latin word in it. They are short, simple, easily understood words.

You electric light people have one difficulty. I was in Europe this spring, and I rode a great deal in taxicabs. In England I sat in a taxicab and watched the little clock go around in terms of shillings. Then I flew over to Amsterdam and watched it go around in terms of guilders. Then I went down to Brussels and it went around in terms of francs. Then I went to France and it went around in terms of francs of a different value.

I would sit there trying to divide fifteen into one hundred, multiply it by seven, and wonder just where I was getting off, and I have no doubt now that really I was transported in Europe at a very reasonable cost, but because those meters talked to me in terms that were unfamiliar I never stepped out of a taxicab without having a haunting suspicion that probably I had been "gypped."

In a degree you suffer like those taxicab men. You come to Mrs. Barton and you say, "Buy this washing machine and it will do your washing for just a few cents an hour." She says, "Isn't that wonderful!" She buys it, and at the end of the month she sits with your bill in her hand and she says, "We have run this five hours, and that probably will be so and so." Then she opens the bill and finds she has not run it five hours; that she has run it 41 kw. and 11 amp. and 32 volts, and that the amount is not so-and-so but is $2.67.

Well, that is a matter that I suppose you will eventually straighten out.

Asking an advertising man to talk about advertising at a convention like this is a good deal like asking a doctor to talk about health. I have listened to many such addresses and they are all about the same. The eminent physician says, "Drink plenty of water. Stay outdoors as much as you can. Eat good food. Don't worry. Get eight hours' sleep. And if you have anything the matter with you, call a doctor."

So I say to you that there is a certain technique about this matter of dealing with the public, and if you have anything seriously the matter with you—whether it be a big advertising problem or merely a bad letterhead (and some of you have wretched letterheads)—there probably is some advertising doctor in your town who has made a business of the thing, and it may be worth your while to call him in. But in the meantime, and in this very informal and necessarily general talk, I say to you, "Be genuine, be simple, be brief; talk to people in language that they can understand; and finally, and most of all, be persistent." You can't expect to advertise in flush times and live on the memory of it when you are hard up. You can't expect to advertise when you are in trouble, or about to be in trouble, and expect to get anywhere in that direction. It is a day-by-day and hour-by-hour business. If the money that has been thrown away by people who advertised spasmodically were all gathered together it would found and endow the most wonderful home in the world for aged advertising men and their widows. Don't throw any more of that money away. If advertising is worth doing at all, it is worth doing all the time. For every day, gentlemen, the "king" dies, and there arises a new "king" who knows not Joseph.

Inspirational

The purpose of the inspirational speech is to revive confidence or to generate enthusiasm. Often an organization finds that its members are losing interest in their work or are being discouraged by certain problems that have arisen. The morale of these people is at low tide. They need to be revitalized, given new hope, and fired with ambition. The speaker who undertakes this job must be highly skilled in the understanding of human nature and the techniques of persuasion.

There is a constant need for such speaking; salesmen often become discouraged; employees succumb to routine tasks; church members lose interest; and students forget the reasons for which they enrolled in their university; teachers, too, often slip into sluggish patterns of teaching. All of these people, and many more, need an occasional "jacking up." They need to be reminded forcefully of the purposes they now serve, of past accomplishments, and future possibilities.

The inspirational speech is largely persuasive in nature, and careful consideration must be given to the choice of material and to the construction of the speech. Starting out with a series of facts or questions aimed primarily at starting the thought processes is a good way of attracting immediate attention. From then on there must be continual use of the specific and the interesting in order to hold the attention first gained in the introduction.

It is often effective to use some sort of slogan as the keynote of the speech. Audiences need something they can remember and hang on to. A slogan used in a speech will be repeated over and over, so that even after the immediate effect of the speech is gone, the slogan will remain. One should avoid any definite appeal for action in the inspirational speech. Such an appeal might make the purpose too obvious and thus create a negative suggestion. It is more effective to allow the audience to draw their own conclusions as to their course of action from the choice of material you use.

The speech should abound in vivid language, examples, illustrations, contrasts, analogies, and strong appeals to fundamental wants and desires. If for one minute the attention of the audience lags, the success of the speech is seriously endangered. Remember you are speaking to an audience which has succumbed to self-abasement. They may be thrown deeper into the mire by an ineffective speaker. The speaker must first overcome this barrier of self-abasement and then rise beyond that to the heights of real stimulation.

Inspirational speech situations are not limited to the public platform or the sales meeting. A student is failing in one of his college courses. The professor calls him into the office ostensibly for a chat about his grade. Perhaps the student is devoting too much time to activities or perhaps he feels that he is outclassed by other members in the course. The helpful professor will find the cause, show why it must be overcome, present a solution, and inspire the student to greater effort by demonstrating the good effects which will result from hard study. Executives are often faced with the problem of stimulating their subordinates to greater achievement. A minister's whole job is one of inspiration and it should not be limited to an hour or two on Sunday morning.

In either the conference or public speech situation where inspirational speaking is demanded the speaker himself will be the most important element in effectiveness. He must reveal unusual confidence and enthusiasm. If any sign or cue is given that reveals that the speaker is not sure of his ground, the audience will immediately suspect him of being insincere. Enthusiasm, like yawning, is contagious. Regardless of the quality of the speech itself, the speaker remains the most persuasive element in producing inspiration.

SUGGESTED TITLES FOR INSPIRATIONAL SPEECHES

1. Service Is to Serve.
2. The Man in Salesmanship
3. After 40—What?
4. Optimism and Hop-to-it-ism
5. Sportsmanship
6. Who Owns Our City?
7. Invitation to Disaster
8. Citizenship and Ownership
9. A Business in a Democracy
10. An Unknown Soldier
11. Living Vigorously
12. Don't Die on Thirds.
13. Ready—For What?
14. How to Be Happy Though Wealthy
15. That Old Time Religion
16. Trade Your Shotgun for a Rifle.
17. Don't Hate your Friends.
18. Silk Purses
19. If You Should Die Tomorrow
20. An Education for Living

Sample Inspirational Speech

The following inspirational speech was delivered by Dr. Ernest Fremont Tittle, pastor of the First Methodist Church of Evanston, Illinois, to the 1924 graduating class of the School of Speech of Northwestern University.

LEARNING TO SPEAK [7]

One day, without any very definite outline in mind, Robert Burns sat down to write a poem and frankly confessed:

> "Which way the subject theme may gang
> Let time and chance determine;
> Perhaps it may turn out a sang—
> Or probably a sermon."

I wish—how I wish tonight—that I might produce a song. But, if I succeed in producing anything, it will probably be a sermon. When Coleridge asked Lamb, "Did you ever hear me preach, Charles?" Lamb replied, "I n-never heard you do anything else." The bearing of this famous retort upon the present instance is, I am afraid, only too obvious.

But be it a "sang," or be it a "sermon," the theme which I have chosen for this occasion is Learning to Speak. And I marvel at my own temerity. I can only hope that some of you will consider it pertinent. You need not suggest—I already know—that it is also impertinent!

Everybody ought to learn how to speak. First, because speaking clarifies thought. I am going to suggest farther on that clear thinking is the primary requisite for good speaking; but just now I should like to suggest that honest effort to express thought usually results in clarifying it.

When some one complains, "I know what I want to say but cannot say it," you may not confess your well-founded suspicion that he doesn't quite know what he wants to say; but you may, perhaps, tactfully suggest that if only he will try to say what he knows, he will even better know what he is trying to say.

Once you have got your thought expressed you have a clearer understanding of the thought that you have wanted to express. Everybody, therefore, ought to learn how to speak if for no other reason than for the purpose of clarifying his own thinking.

But is it not also true that "a word fitly spoken is like apples of gold in pictures of silver"? It gives pleasure. Listening to good English, like listening to good music, is one of the most satisfying enjoyments of life. The brilliant conversationalist is a social asset even though it must be said of him, as it was said of W. T. Stead, that "his idea of good conversation is to have another man to listen to him."

And is not the clever after-dinner speaker a public servant? There is, to be sure, a vast difference between post-prandial orators. Once upon a time a mayor of Chicago introduced Chauncey Depew by suggesting that he was like an automatic machine—"You put in a dinner and up comes a speech." When Mr. Depew gained his feet, he suggested that the difference between his after-dinner speaking and the chairman's was that his Honor, the Mayor, "puts in a speech and up comes your dinner." But you will, I think, agree with me that the accomplished after-dinner speaker is a public servant. If

---

[7] Reprinted by special permission of the author.

he adds but little—and he usually does—to the sum total of the world's knowledge, he adds considerably to the sheer enjoyment of life.

Moreover, the pleasure which may be given by a gifted speaker is by no means the only service which he is able to render. For, as Walter Savage Landor once remarked "On a winged word hath hung the destiny of nations." The speeches of Demosthenes in Athens, of Cicero in Rome, of Pitt and Burke and Gladstone in England, of Webster and Lincoln and Wilson in America, were not only utterances; they were events. They not only appealed to history. They made history. And this, at least to some extent, has been true of speeches made by far lesser men.

History used to be written as though it were merely a string of great men's biographies. This, as you remember, was the method of Plutarch. It was the method, also, of Carlyle, who once said of England that she boasted twenty-seven millions of people—mostly fools; and of the United States, "They have begotten with a rapidity beyond recorded example eighteen million of the greatest bores ever seen in this world before."

History for Carlyle was simply a succession of great men's biographies. He worshiped the hero and despised the crowd.

But the crowd, as we are beginning to realize, is not to be despised.

Think of the reformers before the Reformation: the unnumbered thousands who prepared the way for Luther; who helped to create the intellectual and moral environment of which Luther availed himself when he nailed his ninety-eight theses to the door of the old church in Wittenberg, and carved for himself a conspicuous place in the memory of mankind. Think of the unpictured, unpraised persons who fanned the fires of conviction which lighted the way for Abraham Lincoln to move into immortality as the emancipator of four million slaves. Think of the unfamous persons in every country in the world today who are forging the demand that war shall be placed in the same category with dueling, piracy, and human slavery.

It has been said that "The frail snowflake has sculptured continents." Is it not equally true that the spoken thought, not only of great men, but of millions of ordinary men, has molded the lives of nations and determined the course of civilization? How important, then, it is that everybody should learn how to speak. The voice of the ordinary man may not carry very far. All the more reason why, as far as it does carry, it should be made as clear and compelling as possible.

Everybody may learn how to speak.

By learning to speak, of course, I mean something different from learning to talk. Not long ago I heard an American Indian suggest that when the White man says to the Red man, "Why don't you talk more?" the Red man would like to reply to the White man, "Why don't you say more?" A vivacious representative of the gentler sex once asked Henry James whether he did not think that American women talk better than English women. "Yes," he replied, "they are more ready and much more brilliant. They rise to every suggestion. But," he added reflectively, and with rare tactfulness, "English women so often know what they are talking about." And has not Christopher Morley sententiously remarked that "The unluckiest insolvent in the world is the man whose expenditure of speech is too great for his income of ideas"?

By learning to speak one wishes to mean something more than learning to vocalize. The latter accomplishment is not beyond the reach of a parrot.

But everybody who is not an idiot may learn not only how to talk but how to speak. Ability to speak like ability to swim, or to drive a golf ball, or to play the piano, may be cultivated. You may never develop into a Wendell Phillips, or a Frances Willard, any more than you may develop into a Sybil Bauer, or a Bobbie Jones, or a Paderewski; but you need not go stuttering and stammering through life. As a biological descendant of Adam and Eve, you have a tongue and some teeth, and a modicum at least of intelligence. As a linguistic descendant of Shakespeare and Milton, you have nine parts of speech and a possible vocabulary of more than three hundred thousand words to choose from. If, therefore, you do not learn how to speak, it is your own fault. It is not because you cannot learn. It is merely because you will not go to the trouble of learning.

What then are some of the essential requirements for learning to speak as over against the mere ability to vocalize in a half-dozen languages? Let me mention, first, the ability to think. The man who has something to say can and will find some way to say it. If any man remains a "mute inglorious Milton," it is not because he cannot say what he thinks; it is rather because he has never thought anything worth saying.

If you cannot gather grapes from thorns, or figs from thistles, neither can you gather golden sentences from an empty mind. The reason why most of us do not say more is just because we have nothing more to say. We cannot speak in public, because we do not think in private.

A somewhat distinguished English preacher, who was naturally fluent, once declared that he could always go on saying something until he had something to say. But a far safer guide for most of us to follow is that deservedly famous stump speaker who advised, "Fill yourself with your subject, then knock out the bung and let nature caper."

Remy de Gourmont has remarked that "Works well thought out are invariably well written." Allowing for the inevitable exceptions, he has, I suspect, stated the rule—a rule which applies not only to effective writing but to effective speaking. Works well thought out are almost invariably well written; and ideas well thought out are almost invariably well spoken. A poor speech may be the result of a number of causes, including, perhaps, milk-fed chicken, vanilla ice cream, and French pastry; but it is even more likely to be the result of sloppy thinking. The ambitious speaker would do well to spend more time in clarifying his thought than in choosing his words.

Yet words, too, are important. There are colorful words that are as beautiful as red roses; and there are drab words that are as unlovely as an anaemic-looking woman. There are concrete words that keep people awake; and abstract words that put them to sleep. There are strong words that can punch like a prize-fighter; and weak words that are as insipid as a "mamma's boy." There are warm sympathetic words that grip men's hearts; and cold detached words that leave an audience unmoved. There are noble words that lift every listener, at least for a moment, to the sunlit heights of God; and base words that leave an audience in the atmosphere of the cabaret. And so, other things being equal, including abstemious eating and clear thinking, the most effective speech will be the speech that contains the greatest number of colorful, concrete, strong, sympathetic, and inspiring words. Provided. . . . . . What?

Very much of the effectiveness of public speaking depends upon the technic employed by the speaker.

An exasperated parishioner, who felt it incumbent upon him to protest against the feebleness of the clerical profession, remarked to the Reverend Sidney Smith, "If I had a son who was an idiot, I would make him a parson." To which the Reverend Sidney Smith replied, "Your father evidently was of a different opinion." Some protest, no doubt, needed to be made; but the gentleman who ventured to make it had not developed the right technic.

There are, as I have discovered, two very different ways of calling someone's attention to the fact that he has taken certain unwarranted liberties with the truth. If you employ the wrong way, the response is very likely to be, "You're another!" But if you employ the right way, the response may be, "Perhaps I have; and I shall endeavor hereafter to confine myself strictly to facts."

I was present some time ago at a meeting at which two speeches were made on the same theme. Both speakers, as it happened, took substantially the same position. But when the first speaker sat down, the audience was distinctly unfriendly; and when the second speaker sat down, the same audience vigorously applauded him. Both had said the same thing; but the first had said it in a way that merely irritated his audience, whereas the second had said it in a way that had convinced his audience. Many a speaker has met with opposition not so much because of what he said as because of the way in which he said it.

There is, of course, the exactly opposite danger that a man may say something that needs to be said, but say it so cautiously that no one will realize that he has said it. He will get it out, but he will not get it over; and if he fails to get it over, he has made an ineffective speech.

Not long ago, in the course of an address, I repeated the deservedly famous story of the merchant who hung out a sign reading, "I am a One Hundred Per Cent American: I hate Jews, Catholics, Negroes, and foreigners"; whereupon his competitor across the street hung out a sign reading, "I am a Two Hundred Per Cent American: I hate everybody." At the close of the meeting, an ardent member of the local Ku Klux Klan came forward and warmly congratulated me! I had gotten it out; but I had not, apparently, gotten it over.

One way to get something out without getting it over is to confine yourself to glittering generalities. Almost any audience will applaud glittering generalities, especially if they are couched in familiar rhetorical phrases.

Some one gets up and affirms, with the air of Christopher Columbus discovering America, that what this country needs is a good old-fashioned revival of religion. Shouts of Amen! from the Methodist corner. Decorous cries of Hear! Hear! from the Presbyterian corner. Smiles of approval from the Congregational corner. Slight intimations of approval from the Episcopalian corner. Even the out and out pagan in the audience feels an impulse to applaud! A good old-fashioned revival of religion sounds harmless enough. To the traditionalist it suggests the theology on which he was brought up. To the dogmatist it suggests the truth—as he sees it. To the emotionalist it suggests a perfectly wonderful opportunity to enjoy the luxury of inexpensive tears. To the pious profiteer and the orthodox exploiter, it suggests a type of religion which raises no embarrassing questions, makes no inconvenient demands, but leaves men undisturbed in the enjoyment of the fruits of other people's labor, and furnishes a divine sanction for the maintenance of the status quo. And so, as a sonorous platitude, almost any audience will endorse the statement that what this country needs is a good old-fashioned revival of religion.

But suppose the speaker feels under some obligation to descend from the pleasant heights of glittering generalities to the arduous lowlands of particular applications. Suppose he feels impelled to suggest that a good old-fashioned revival of religion would involve, as it did in the days of John the Baptist, an urgent, unflinching demand that the rough ways of industry shall be made smooth; and that the crooked ways of politics shall be made straight; and that every mountain and hill of unearned wealth shall be brought low; and that every valley of undeserved poverty shall be filled; and that all flesh shall be given equality of educational and economic opportunity; and that nothing less than this shall be termed the salvation of God. Having made a suggestion of this sort, would not the preacher discover a sudden drop of at least forty degrees in the temperature of the audience?

To be effective, a public speaker must develop a technic which will enable him to get out what needs to be said without needless and fruitless irritation, and at the same time to get it over.

But if much depends upon the technic of speaking, much more depends upon the life of the speaker. You cannot make silken purses out of sow's ears; nor can you get a big speech out of a little speaker. Schools of speech may give you a faultless technic. But what shall it profit a speaker if he acquire a faultless technic but fail to develop his mind and to enrich his soul?

When Senator Hayne had delivered, in the United States Senate, his famous speech defending the right of a sovereign state to withdraw from the Union, there were men of no little discernment who declared with heavy hearts that his argument was unanswerable. But, on the following day, Senator Hayne's unanswerable argument was brilliantly answered by Daniel Webster; and the Senate chamber had witnessed probably the most wonderful burst of pure oratory yet heard on the continent. Afterwards, Webster was asked how long he had been in the preparation of his great Reply. His answer was, "Twenty years." Said he, "When I stood up in the Senate Chamber and began to speak, a strange sensation came to me. All that I had ever thought, or read in literature, in history, in law, in politics, seemed to unroll before me in glowing panorama; and then it was easy, whenever I wanted a thunderbolt, to reach out and take it as it went smoking by."

Great speeches are not born in a day. It may require as long as twenty years to bring them forth. For they come out of the slowly nourished minds of men. They come out of the slowly maturing souls of men. They come very often out of suffering and heartache and loneliness and all but despair. They never come out of shallow minds and sordid secular souls.

How fearfully flat mere declamation falls. "Give me liberty or give me death," cries the school boy; and his declamation may be rhetorically impeccable. Yet somehow it is unconvincing. The words appear; but they are like wax figures in a museum. Only the flaming soul of a Patrick Henry could give them life.

I do not mean to suggest that it is beyond the power of a great actor to give convincing expression to words that another has written or spoken. I do mean to suggest that, in order to do so, the actor himself must, as a man, be great enough actually to experience the sentiment he is expressing.

Carlyle used to insist that "Sincerity is the first characteristic of all men in any way heroic. All the great men I have ever heard of," he declares, "have (sincerity) as the primary material of them."

Can you think of any permanently effective public speaker who was not deeply and even passionately sincere? I expect, of course, the mere rhetorician: the popular preachers, the political spell-binders, the matinee idols, and every other kind of vocalizing idol whose feet are of clay. They have, to be sure, their little vogue, their little coterie of worshipers. But if they go up like a rocket, they come down like a stick, leaving no permanent light in the sky. It is not of such, but only of men who, being dead, yet speak, that I am thinking when I ask: Can you recall any single permanently effective public speaker who was not deeply and even passionately sincere?

In preparation for the important speech which he was to deliver on the occasion of his nomination to the United States Senate, Mr. Lincoln read that famous classic to which I have already referred, Webster's "Rely to Hayne." It begins, as you may remember, in this fashion:

"Mr. President: When the mariner has been tossed for many days in thick weather, and on an unknown sea, he naturally avails himself of the first pause in the storm, the earliest glimpse of the sun, to take his latitude, and ascertain how far the elements have driven him from his course. Let us imitate this prudence, and before we float farther on the waves of this debate, refer to the point from which we departed, that we may at least be able to conjecture where we now are."

But the sonorous sentences of the silver-tongued orator of the East were not natural to the plain-speaking lawyer of the West; and when Lincoln sat down to compose his speech, he began:

"Mr. Chairman: If we could first know where we are and whither we are tending, we could better judge what to do, and how to do it."

And, having before him, as I cannot but believe, these two classical examples, Woodrow Wilson began his own last published article in this fashion:

"In these doubtful and anxious days, when all the world is at unrest, and, look which way you will, the road ahead seems darkened by shadows which portend dangers of many kinds, it is only common prudence that we should look about us and attempt to assess the causes of distress and the most likely means of removing them."

In this last introduction one finds neither the ponderous oratory of a Webster—quite natural to him; nor the home-spun speech of a Lincoln— equally natural to him; but just that peculiar combination of embroidered Latinity and Anglo-Saxon simplicity which was natural to Woodrow Wilson.

Webster, Lincoln, Wilson—three Americans whose speeches became historical events. And different as they were in many respects, they were alike in this respect that Webster, during his great days, and Lincoln and Wilson during all their days, were passionately sincere.

Whosoever would be permanently effective as a public speaker must be sincere. If a personal confession be allowed, I may say that no man, however brilliant or eloquent, can move me to anything save anger if I have reason to believe that what he is contradicts what he says.

Is it not also true that whosoever would move his audience must lose sight of himself?

An old schoolmate of Joseph Parker once came to him in great distress. Joseph Parker was, at that time, one of the greatest of living preachers. The schoolmate was an undistinguished country curate.

"Parker," he said, "what is the matter with me? I have got a brain that is just as good as yours is; but for some reason, I am not able to get anywhere with it."

"Well," said Joseph Parker, "let me see what you do. Stand at the other end of this room and deliver for me your last Sunday's sermon."

The undistinguished curate did so, and received this criticism: "My old friend, the trouble with you is that you are trying to get something off instead of trying to get something in."

In the year 1858, the eyes of the American people were fixed upon two men. These men were engaged in a series of debates. And they were debating the greatest question of the age. One of them was trying to be eloquent; the other was trying to be honest. One was endeavoring to get something off; the other was endeavoring to get something in. One was seeking to win an election; the other was seeking to win a cause.

When Judge Douglas finished speaking, men shouted themselves hoarse, and exclaimed, "What a wonderful speech!" When Mr. Lincoln sat down, they said to one another, "Old Abe is right."

Douglas won the election. Lincoln said in a letter to a friend: "I am glad I made the late race. It gave me an opportunity to be heard on the greatest question of the age such as I could have gotten in no other way; and now, though I sink out of sight and become forgotten, I think I have made some marks which will tell for the cause of Liberty after I am gone." But, Abraham Lincoln did not sink out of sight or become forgotten. The American people—a determined portion of them—were looking for just such a man. It now appears that God Almighty was looking for just such a man. And when He found him He highly exalted him, and gave him a name that is above every name in American history.

When Douglas died, he moaned, "I have failed." When the spirit of Abraham Lincoln returned to the God who gave it, Edwin M. Stanton remarked, "And now, he belongs to the ages."

How everlastingly true it is even of public speakers; whosoever would save his life shall lose it; but whosoever will lose his life in devotion to a great cause will save it.

QUESTIONS

1. How does the business and professional public speech differ from the business and professional conference speech?

2. Does the Edwin A. Boss speech on "How to Modernize and Manage a Hotel" have too many main ideas? Do you feel that it contains the proper type of detailed material? Explain.

3. Why is the goodwill speech of special value to the small businessman?

4. Are there more opportunities for presenting goodwill speeches today than there were twenty years ago? Why?

5. Why does the Paul G. Hoffman speech on "Prices of Things Which Farmers Buy" qualify as a goodwill speech?

6. Do you believe that Dr. Snyder's speech before the United States Chamber of Commerce created goodwill? Discuss.

7. What are the characteristics of the oral report?

8. Do you believe that Mr. Jouett's speech demonstrates the essential characteristics of an oral report? Explain.

9. Why is the policy-confirming speech usually a platform speech while the policy-determining speech is usually a conference speech?

10. What constructive comments can you offer on Mr. Beam's speech "Let's Advertise"?

11. Do you agree with the statement that promotional speeches are designed to arouse interest and desire in the hearer but not to consummate a sale? Explain.

12. Do you have a greater or lesser belief in the value of advertising after having read Mr. Barton's speech "Which Knew Not Joseph"? Explain.

13. What is the purpose of the inspirational speech? Name five situations in which this type of speech would be appropriate.

14. Does Dr. Tittle's speech on "Learning to Speak" increase your enthusiasm for the work involved in learning to speak? Explain.

EXERCISES

1. Select one of the titles on page 241 for the instructional speech and outline a speech suitable for an audience of high school seniors in your home town.

2. Select one of the titles on pages 241–242 for the explanatory speech and outline a speech suitable for your local chamber of commerce audience.

3. Outline the Edwin A. Boss speech on "How to Modernize and Manage a Hotel." Explain the merits and demerits of this speech as an instructional speech.

4. Select one of the titles on page 255 for the goodwill speech and outline a speech suitable for an audience of steel workers.

5. Outline either the Paul G. Hoffman speech or the Dr. Franklin B. Snyder speech. Explain the merits and demerits of the speech as a goodwill speech.

6. Select one of the titles on page 269 for the oral report speech and outline a report suitable for an audience of college seniors.

7. Outline the Col. John H. Jouett oral report. Is it an informative or an examination report?

8. Select one of the titles on page 276 for the policy-confirming speech and outline a speech suitable for an audience of your own selection. Write a brief analysis of your audience.

9. List the types of persuasive appeals found in the speech "Let's Advertise" by George Beam.

10. Select one of the titles on page 278 for the promotional speech or some other title suitable for this type of speech and outline a speech suitable for an audience of small business retailers.

11. List the types of persuasive appeals found in the speech "Which Knew Not Joseph" by Bruce Barton.

12. Outline five different speech situations that would call for the presentation of an inspirational speech.

13. Write out the reasons why one should learn to speak as gathered from Dr. Ernest Fremont Tittles's speech on "Learning to Speak."

14. Summarize the qualities of a good speaker as gathered from the same speech.

Index